The Sword of Rome

The Sword of Rome

A Biography of Marcus Claudius Marcellus

Jeremiah McCall

Pen & Sword
MILITARY

First published in Great Britain in 2012 by
Pen & Sword Books Ltd
47 Church Street
Barnsley
South Yorkshire
S70 2AS

Copyright © Jeremiah McCall 2012

ISBN 978-1-84884-379-0

Typeset in 11pt Ehrhardt by
Mac Style, Beverley, E. Yorkshire

Printed and bound by MPG

Pen & Sword Books Ltd incorporates the Imprints of Pen & Sword Aviation,
Pen & Sword Family History, Pen & Sword Maritime, Pen & Sword Military,
Pen & Sword Discovery, Wharncliffe Local History, Wharncliffe True Crime,
Wharncliffe Transport, Pen & Sword Select, Pen & Sword Military Classics,
Leo Cooper, The Praetorian Press, Remember When, Seaforth Publishing
and Frontline Publishing.

For a complete list of Pen & Sword titles please contact
PEN & SWORD BOOKS LIMITED
47 Church Street, Barnsley, South Yorkshire, S70 2AS, England
E-mail: enquiries@pen-and-sword.co.uk
Website: www.pen-and-sword.co.uk

Contents

For Olivia

Introduction

There were few names from the middle Republic that were better known to later generations of Romans than Marcus Claudius Marcellus. 'Sword of the Republic' he was labeled by one writer for his audacity in battle,[1] and he secured a reputation for valour with generations of Romans. Yet for all the consideration the Romans gave to their hero Marcellus, there exists no modern biography of him. Such a study is worthwhile, however, because Marcellus' military and political career gives modern readers an excellent vantage point from which to view the military and political struggles of the Romans in the late third century BC and the role of military successes in the aristocratic culture of the Roman Republic. For readers relatively new to the military and politics of the late third century Republic, Marcellus provides perhaps the best point of access; for those familiar with the period, Marcellus offers a different perspective. Indeed, his military honours were unmatched by any other aristocrat of the middle Republic.

He was of the generation that fought in the First and Second Punic Wars, the greatest of the struggles against Carthage to dominate the Mediterranean. As Plutarch, a later biographer, put it:

> They were the foremost Romans of his generation. In their youth they campaigned against the Carthaginians for the possession of Sicily: in their prime they fought against the Gauls for the defence of Italy itself, and as veterans they found themselves matched once more against the Carthaginians, this time under Hannibal. In this way they never enjoyed the relief from active service which old age brings to most men, but because of their noble birth and their prowess in war they were constantly summoned to take up new commands.[2]

Plutarch, like most Roman authors, tended to wax more than a bit poetically on the nobility and prowess of the old Romans, but he still had a point. Marcellus's career and reputation from early adulthood to his death in the saddle, were based on his military exploits. As a young soldier fighting in Sicily he won a reputation for skill in single combat. When first elected consul, one of the two chief military and political officials of the Republic, he earned the grand victory celebration known as a triumph for soundly defeating a Gallic tribe in battle. Rarer still, he slew the Gallic king Virdumarus in single combat on that day when the Gallic army crumbled and earned the *spolia opima*, an honour, according to Roman antiquarians, that had only been earned by two others: a semi-legendary consul two centuries earlier and Romulus himself, the even more legendary founder of Rome. When Hannibal of Carthage brought an army across the Alps and inflicted a series of disastrous defeats on Roman armies (218–216 BC), Marcellus preserved a ray of hope for the Republic by being the first to check Hannibal's string of victories in a skirmish outside the central Italian city of Nola. The war against Hannibal continued, and Marcellus soon won a special military command by the grant of the Roman people; by 214 BC, he had won the consulship again. Now his task was to return to the island of Sicily, where he began his military career, and subdue the powerful rebel city of Syracuse. After several years of campaigning, the Roman armies under his command occupied Syracuse and, at Marcellus' orders, plundered the city. The wealth was carried through the streets of Rome in his second triumph, and used to decorate the city and fund the construction of his victory temple to the gods Honos and Virtus. His exploits, and the fascination with the period when the Republic went from a regional power to controlling a sizable part of the western Mediterranean, made Marcellus a fascinating subject for Roman writers. He remains so today.

For Romans of the Republic who were interested in the history of the aristocrats who led them, Marcus Claudius Marcellus stood out. Simply put, he had one of the most distinguished military and political careers in the Republic, one that dwarfed those of most who came before or since. By the time he died in 208 BC, the victim of a Carthaginian ambush, he had won election five times to the consulship, a feat matched by a small handful and topped once during the four centuries the office existed in the Republic. He was a field commander for nine consecutive years during the struggle against Hannibal, surpassed in this record only by Publius Cornelius Scipio Africanus, who defeated the great Carthaginian general Hannibal himself on the plains of North Africa. Consequently, Marcellus' career and exploits became the stuff both of history and legend for later writers. The late Republican politician and orator, Cicero, contrasted Marcellus as a model of honour and moderation with the corrupt governor Verres. The grand historian of the Republic, Livy, emphasized his tenacity on the battlefield and his dogged pursuit of Hannibal when the Republic seemed on the verge of collapse. For Frontinus, that recorder of military stratagems in the early empire, Marcellus was a consummate strategist. Silius Italicus was inspired to capture Marcellus' exploits in verse. The Greco-Roman moralist Plutarch recorded Marcellus' deeds to illustrate to his audience the virtues of a simpler time. Nor are these the only examples; Marcellus' deeds were trumpeted by the Romans for the better part of 1,000 years.

None of this record of praise does anything to alleviate the problem of accurately representing Marcellus' life and career, the problem posed by the available evidence and its sources. It is a problem central to any historical analysis of the Roman Republic and its men and women, one which many approaching the history of the Republic may not fully appreciate, and one that must be exposed before looking too carefully at the records for Marcellus.

Modern readers interested in current events and recent history, modern figures and movements, are aware that, if anything, there are too many records, too many documents, too much information available. In addition to the mountain of print resources, there is a digital Everest of blogs, forums, and tweets; YouTube videos; Facebook profiles; WikiLeaks; and so on. A staggering number of records exist for all but the most private, intimate, or casual events and their causes. Someone wins the lottery, and the event and the winner's reactions are captured on local news, blogged about, twittered about, perhaps even disseminated through a home video on YouTube. A politician commits an indiscretion, and hundreds of takes on the situation spread across the globe, fuelled by the internet. Resistance and revolution erupt in countries like Iran, Egypt, and Libya, and we can access a constant stream of information not only from 24–hour news feeds, but from the activists themselves on social media sites and even websites custom crafted for spreading movements. Celebrity foibles, crimes, political and military decisions, religious crusades, the records and patterns of private citizens, if it happened in anything but the most private or banal of arenas – and sometimes even then – broadly speaking, the records exist for it. While the countless number of human actions and interactions on any given day insure there are many more undocumented events than documented, even in the modern world, the point is still well made: students of the modern world have access to more evidence than they can possibly use.

The Roman Republic, in contrast, though one of the better documented periods in ancient history, left a paltry few records. This is the case for even the best documented figures in the ancient world, and even more so for only adequately documented figures like Marcellus. Consider the problem. He lived between approximately 268 BC and 208 BC, during a period generally called the middle Republic. (Readers should note that from here on, unless otherwise indicated, all dates are BC.) We are reasonably certain of his death but know nothing about his birth. We do not know directly how he felt and what he thought about anything, why he entered the sphere of politics, how he viewed himself. We know he had a son of the same name, but do not even know the name of his wife. The evidence available for this period and its sources are simply too thin. There are essentially no primary sources, no eyewitness accounts for anything that Marcellus did or said. Indeed, with very few exceptions, there are no surviving eyewitness versions of anything that happened in Rome during most of the

Republic – the end of the Republic in the first century being the notable exception. This does not mean, however, that Marcellus and his contemporaries wrote no letters, speeches, proclamations, perhaps even diaries; far from it. It's simply the case that whatever was written by those who were there in the middle Republic is mostly lost.

Those studying the period and the person, therefore, need to rely on the accounts of secondary sources, later Roman writers who described, analyzed, and interpreted the actions of Marcellus and his contemporaries. Here too historians run into trouble. The Romans themselves did not even write history – in the sense of evidence-based, narrative interpretations of their people's past – until after Marcellus had died; the first to do so was the Roman senator Fabius Pictor, who began writing a history of Rome – in Greek, as it happened – around 200. Fortunately for this study, Fabius was a senator during the Second Punic War (218–201), a conflict in which Marcellus played a critical role. He would have been at senatorial meetings with Marcellus, and witnessed the man in speech and action. Sadly, Fabius' history is lost to us. It exists only in the form of a few passages quoted here and there by later Romans. It is not clear, then, how much he wrote or did not write about Marcellus – indeed it is not clear whether Fabius' history went past 217.[3] The same can be said for the second known historian of Rome, Marcus Porcius Cato. Cato the Elder, as he became known, served as a young military tribune under Marcellus at Syracuse[4] and went on to have a highly distinguished career in politics of his own. He wrote the *Origines* ('Origins'), a history of Rome. His account is also lost and his surviving manuscript on the management of a plantation, though precious for what it does tell historians, offers nothing directly about Marcellus. This pattern continues into the second century. A growing handful of Roman historians practiced their craft, so far as we know all of them senators, and nothing but fragments of their works survive. Perhaps these sources provided detailed, credible information about Marcellus and served to bolster the accounts of later writers. There is simply no way to know, however, and any strong claim based on such a speculation is a house built on sand.

The earliest surviving source to provide any sort of detailed information about Marcellus, then, is Polybius.[5] He was a politician and military commander in the Achaean League, a federation of Greek city states that ran afoul of the Romans in the 160s. Polybius was one of 1,000 hostages taken by the Romans to Italy to guarantee the Greeks' good behaviour. Polybius, unlike most of the other hostages, had the good fortune to become a mentor to a young Roman aristocrat from a distinguished family, Publius Cornelius Scipio Aemilianus. As a result of this relationship, Polybius was able to travel in important political and military circles, observing in great detail the workings of the Republic and its people. He crafted what he had learned over the years into a history of the Romans in the third and second century. His stated goal was to explain to Greek readers everywhere – and Greek was the common language of the educated throughout the Mediterranean east of Italy – why and how the Romans had come to dominate the Mediterranean so swiftly. On the bright side, Polybius was in a position to have spoken to people who witnessed the great war against Hannibal, and indeed he claimed to have done so – though at least forty, if not fifty or sixty, years had passed since that struggle. When it came to Marcellus, however, Polybius seems to have made some effort to dim that Roman's achievements, particularly when those achievements threatened to make Marcellus appear more distinguished than members of the Cornelius Scipio family, Polybius' patrons. The context within which Polybius wrote his history illustrates that for the ancients, history was an important means of justifying and explaining the present and could be all the more slanted because of that.

The next surviving accounts of Marcellus come in the various references found in Cicero's writings. Marcus Tullius Cicero (c. 106–43) was a Roman politician and orator at the very end of the Republic. Though never the most powerful of aristocrats, he had a full career and was wholly invested in the struggles that eventually ended in the collapse of the Republic and the creation of a monarchy, the Empire. Perhaps even more than the historians, however, Cicero seemingly always wrote to persuade his audience into some course of action; his references to Marcellus, accordingly, are tailored to fit his rhetorical purposes. The most straightforward example of this comes from Cicero's speeches prosecuting the Roman governor Verres in 70. Verres was the governor of Sicily, a province in which Marcellus had spent several years during the Second Punic War. Cicero charged that Verres had milked the populace of Sicily and generally behaved tyrannically. When Cicero refers to Marcellus, who had sacked the rebellious Sicilian city of Syracuse and effectively placed the eastern half of the island under direct Roman control, he uses him, somewhat surprisingly, as a model of restraint and honour in a time of war, in order to emphasize Verres' alleged excesses and deceits in a time of peace. Years later, in a work on reading the signs of the gods, Cicero calls Marcellus the 'best of the augurs', those priests charged with determining the signs.[6] In general, Cicero seems to have believed, or wanted at least, Marcellus to represent a military man who was nevertheless respectful of the traditional institutions and values of the Romans, something that Cicero often found lacking in his contemporaries like Pompey, Caesar, and Antonius. So one must read Cicero's remarks about Marcellus with care, trying to filter out Cicero's first-century read of a third-century Roman.

As is so often the case when studying anything in the early and middle Republic, the main narrative account for Marcellus, both in terms of length and completeness, comes from Livy. It is particularly important, then, to gain some sense of who this writer was, for so much of our evidence about Marcellus is filtered through him.[7] Titus Livius was a Roman of letters and books born around the year of Julius Caesar's first consulship (59) and a child when the civil war between Caesar and his enemies in the senate broke out. During Livy's youth Caesar was murdered (44), leaving his adopted son Octavian and his trusted lieutenant Marcus Antonius vying for control of the failing Republic. Under these men many Roman citizens were arbitrarily declared to be public enemies and slaughtered, including Cicero, and a series of new civil wars broke out. When Octavian crushed Antonius at the battle of Actium (31) and became the last warlord standing, Livy was about twenty-five. It will suffice to say that Livy came of age during the disintegration of the Republic, a time of civil war, and life-or-death domestic political wrangling for many Romans. Small wonder, then, that Livy began his monumental history of Rome, *Ab Urbe Condita* ('From the Founding of the City'), with this clear declaration of purpose:

> I invite the reader's attention to the much more serious consideration of the kind of lives our ancestors lived, of who were the men, and what the means both in politics and war by which Rome's power was first acquired and subsequently expanded. I would then have him trace the process of our moral decline, to watch, first, the sinking of the foundations of morality as the old teaching was allowed to lapse, then the rapidly increasing disintegration, then the final collapse of the whole edifice, and the dark dawning of our modern day when we can neither endure our vices nor face the remedies needed to cure them. The study of history is the best medicine for a sick mind. In history you have a record of the infinite variety of human experience plainly set out for all to see. In that record you can find for yourself and your country both examples and warnings; fine things to take as models, base things, rotten through and through, to avoid.[8]

Livy wrote what was, for him, fundamentally an epic moral tale, and he did it on an epic scale. The *Ab Urbe Condita* begins with the legendary landing of the Trojan Aeneas in Italy and the subsequent – perhaps slightly less legendary – founding of Rome by Romulus and Remus. From there it recounted the Monarchy and the whole of the Republic – more than seven centuries by Livy's reckoning. The overall tenor of the epic history is established in Livy's preface:

> I hope my passion for Rome's past has not impaired my judgment; for I do honestly believe that no country has ever been greater or purer than ours or richer in good citizens and noble deeds. No country has been free for so many generations from the vices of avarice and luxury; nowhere have thrift and plain living been held in such esteem for so long. Indeed, poverty, with us, went hand in hand with contentment. Lately, however, wealth has made us greedy, and self-indulgence has brought us, through every form of sensual excess, to be, if I may so put it, in love with death both individual and collective.[9]

Accordingly, Marcellus, like the rest of the characters in *Ab Urbe Condita*, would be described in ways that exemplify moral and immoral behaviours. Certainly, Livy was educated, intelligent, and skilled at his task and we should not expect to find crude statements of praise and censure at everything Marcellus did or said. In the end, however, there is little escaping the sense that for Livy Marcellus was a paradigm as often as he was a human.

What were Livy's sources for his grand work? In the books that include references to Marcellus, Livy relied heavily upon the earlier Roman historians, Quintus Fabius Pictor from the late third century, Polybius and Lucius Calpurnius Piso from the later second century, and the first century historians Gaius Licinius Macer and Valerius Antias.[10] With the exception of Polybius, all of these historians were Roman; none of their works survive in any significant fashion. Of them all, only Fabius Pictor had actually seen, and presumably spoken with, Marcellus. While Pictor could have used his memory and conversations with contemporaries, and Polybius asserted that he talked to eyewitnesses to encompass events at Rome between c. 220 and his own day, what other sources did these and other historians have for the period of Marcellus' life?

Presumably an important source of information was the public records the Roman priests kept, the *Annales Maximi*. So far as we know, however, the annals provided only brief records of facts that had religious significance. These could include – though this is speculation at best – the chief officials of the year; the celebrations of religious festivals; special or strange events; and omens like plagues, celestial abnormalities, and unusual victories and defeats. These records probably did not, historians think, provide substantial enough details to fill out a history, but could provide a framework for a history. An additional source of structure for Livy came from the *Fasti*, the record of office holders and of those who had earned the military honours of a triumph or ovation.

Then there were the histories kept by the great aristocratic families of the Republic to preserve the deeds of their famous ancestors. Clearly, these were not unbiased accounts, a point fully recognized by Roman writers such as Cicero, who notes:

> Speeches in praise of the dead are indeed extant; for families kept them as a sort of honour and a record, in order to preserve the memory of the achievements of the family and document its nobility. Of course, the history of Rome has been falsified by these speeches; for there is much in them which never happened – invented triumphs, additional consulships, false claims to patrician status, and so on.[11]

A generation later, Livy complains similarly of the difficulties brought on by spurious family records:

The record has been falsified, I believe, by funeral eulogies and fictitious inscriptions on portrait busts, when families try to appropriate to themselves the tradition of exploits and titles of office by means of inventions calculated to deceive. This has led to confusion both in individual achievements and in public records of events.[12]

In a time when there were few authoritative documents to counter dubious claims, a family historian might insert extra distinctions and honours. If done judiciously, these would be difficult to detect. There were practical limits to what fabrications might be achieved, of course, since the outlandish claim of one family history might be checked by the accounts of others. It is not clear at all, however, that Livy and the Roman historians on whom he based his account exercised that level of source criticism.

Where Livy's work can be the most troublesome is in his discussion of military affairs. Marcellus was a military man, but Livy clearly never was – he attempted to capture the details and emotions of battlefields, never having experienced a battle first hand. Where his account is derived from sources containing accurate military information, his accuracy in these matters is presumably greater. However, this is clearly not always the case. There are some notable examples where Livy clearly drew directly from Polybius and made – accidental? – slips in the translation that create simply ridiculous military situations. The best known comes from his description of a battle between Roman legions and a Macedonian phalanx. Polybius says, 'Since the enemy was close at hand, the men of the phalanx were ordered to lower their pikes (into position) and charge,' meaning that the pikes were lowered into a suitable position for attack. Livy translates the passage as something like, '[the commander] ordered the Macedonian phalanx to lay down its pikes, the length of which was hindering the troops, and to fight with swords.' The primary slip is the translation of Polybius' 'lower pikes' to 'lay down pikes'. From there, however, Livy seems to have felt the need to explain the situation and adds the phrase about the length of the spears proving unmanageable to the phalanx. In doing so, Livy fundamentally mangles for readers the core characteristic of the phalanx as a unit that depended on its long spears to function at full effectiveness.[13]

After Livy came a number of biographers, poets, and chroniclers from the Roman Empire, the period that began late in the first century BC. Writing centuries after Marcellus lived, they offer the possibility of independent historical accounts of the general. Plutarch's writings are the most substantial of these sources. Plutarch was from Chaeronea, a town in mainland Greece, and when he lived, during the first and early second century AD, Greece was completely part of the Roman Empire. Plutarch's great literary task was to write parallel biographies matching famous Greeks and Romans that seemed in some way similar in their careers. Marcellus' biography was paired with that of

Pelopidas, the fourth century Greek commander who helped his city-state of Thebes achieve a measure of political power at the time. Plutarch, in some ways similarly to Livy, uses his characters to exemplify virtues and vices. His chronology of events can be confusing and his details fuzzy. Nevertheless, he does provide information about Marcellus. He also at times clearly used sources that provided different versions of the evidence for Marcellus, which allows us to corroborate and challenge the evidence in Livy and Polybius' versions.[14]

At this point it would be quite reasonable for a reader to wonder how anything substantive can be said about Marcellus at all. The answer quite simply, is that only by following the rules of historical method can anything worthwhile be said about Marcellus. The first of these is that one must always consider the sources of evidence and be aware of the potential of those sources to distort, lie outright, or simply misinterpret the causes and effects of the past. The second is that whenever possible, the evidence in one source should be checked against that in others to test its validity. Livy might moralize as might Plutarch; Polybius might skimp on praise; where all three agree, however, it generally can be considered a solid point of evidence. Even when there is corroboration of evidence between sources, however, it is critical to test the evidence by its ability to be woven into a plausible explanation of the past. This is, if anything, even more critical when, as is so often the case, there is only one source of evidence. It is important to remember that, despite the remoteness of the past and the difficulties the sources pose, all things are not equal, some are not plausible, others not possible. Evidence must not only be critiqued and corroborated, therefore; it must be worked into consistent and plausible models of cause and effect. Otherwise, there is no point to the endeavor of studying the past critically.

Using these historical tools to dig into the available evidence, a picture of Marcellus far more complicated than that simply of the heroic general can be unearthed. What makes Marcellus particularly interesting is that he exemplifies the double-edged sword a reputation for courage and success in military ventures was in the Republic. In a society that prized military virtues so highly, it may be surprising that Marcellus met with considerable political opposition in his spectacular career. Here is a partial list, which will be explored in greater detail throughout this book. When he was in the field in 216, some senators complained that he had been sent away by his enemies to prevent his running for the consulship of 215. He had just been elected consul in 215, the first time two plebeians had ever been elected to the office, when an augur heard a clap of thunder. In the ensuing debate the decision came about that the gods were displeased, and Marcellus stepped down. When Marcellus returned to Rome from Sicily, fresh from his victory over the city of Syracuse, he found an embassy of Syracusans there, protesting to the senate his excessive cruelty. Sponsored by his rivals, the Syracusans presented their case to the senate, and Marcellus had to deliver a speech formally defending his actions. Marcellus overcame all these political obstacles and yet still he was put on trial by a tribune in 208 for losing a battle against Hannibal. In fact, an excellent case can be made that Marcellus met with some of these obstructions in part because he was so successful – the senate as an institution had a way of limiting the success of individual aristocrats so that they would not become too powerful and eclipse their colleagues. Even in the depths of the war against Hannibal, aristocratic competition for prestige, influence, and power carried on largely unhindered. Yet through all the positioning and posturing, maneuvering and checking, Marcellus managed to earn a series of unparalleled honours that ensured his reputation would last millennia longer than the Republic itself.

Maps

List of Maps

Diagrams

List of Diagrams

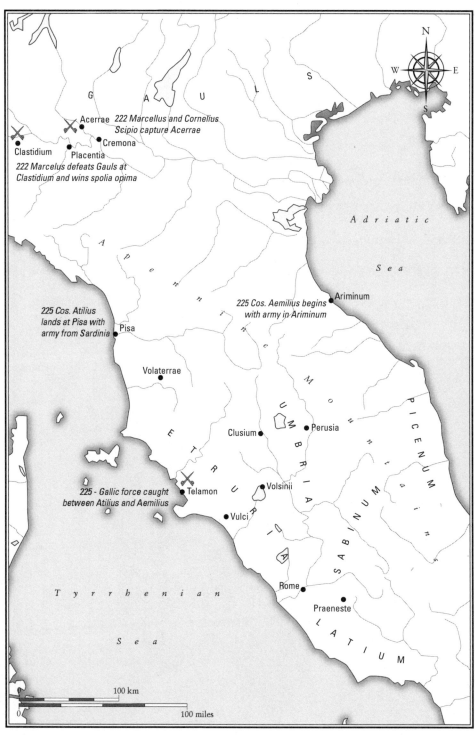

Gallic Campaign, 225–222 BC.

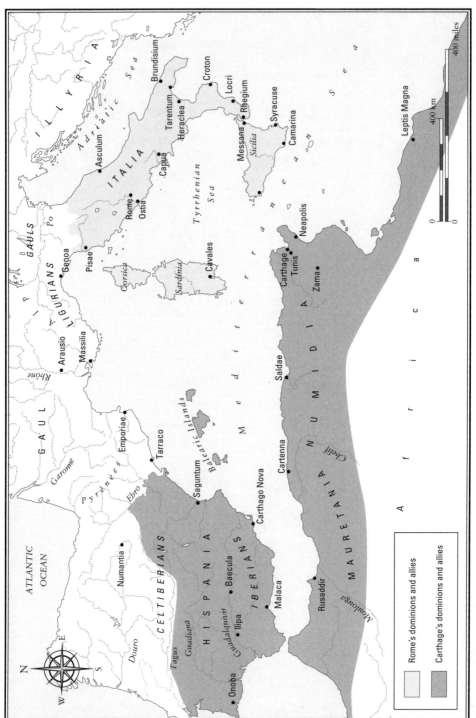

Roman and Carthaginian Territory in 218 BC.

	Rome's dominions and allies
	Carthage's dominions and allies

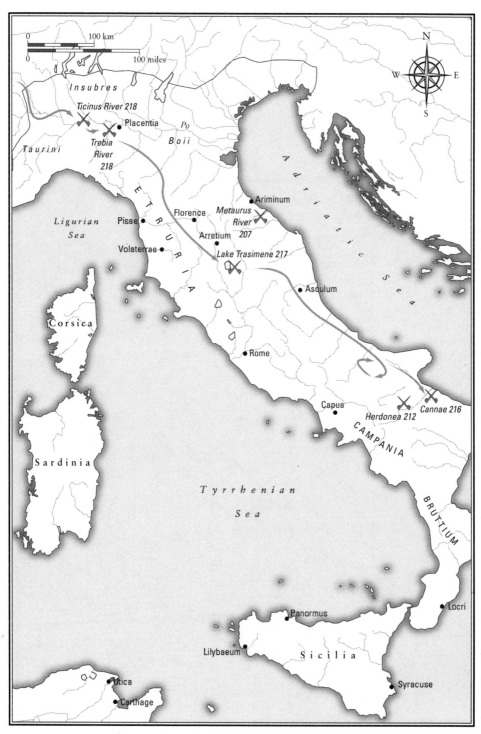

Hannibal's Route to Cannae.

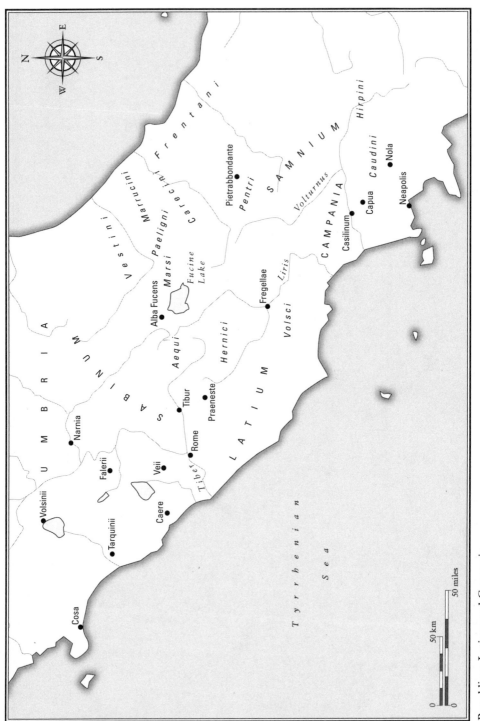

Republican Latium and Campania.

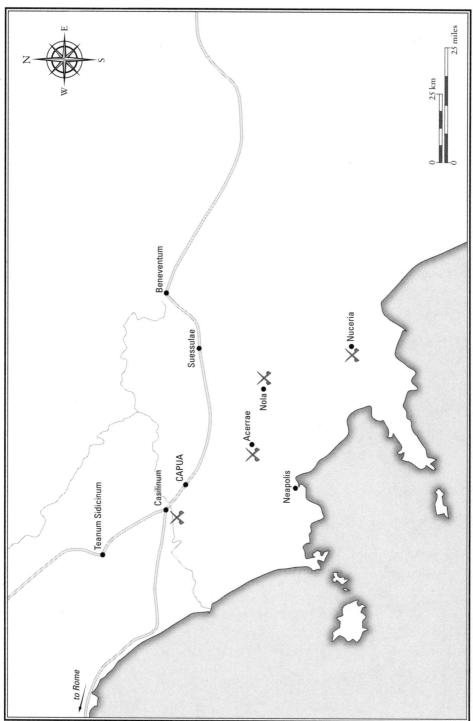

Campania, 216–215 BC.

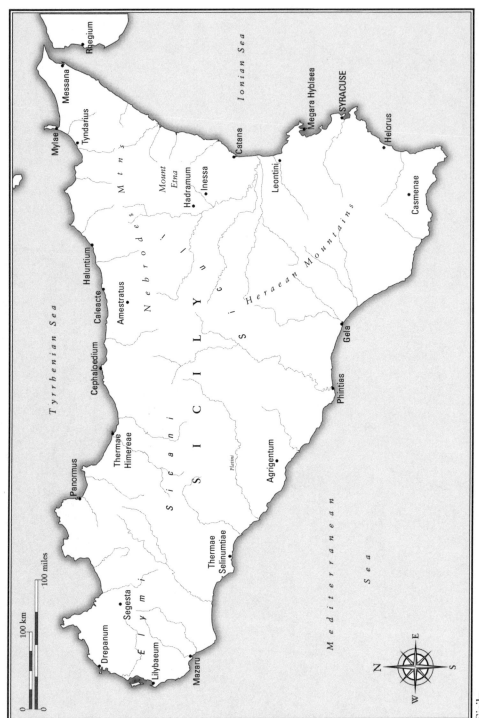

Sicily.

Syracuse.

South Italy, 210–208 BC.

Chapter 1

The Early Career

Though many Romans from the social and economic elite of the middle Republic happily chose to avoid a life in politics, Marcellus was not one of them. Born sometime around the year 268 BC, the 485th year since the founding of Rome, as the ancient Roman historians preferred to date things, he came from the Claudii Marcelli (the plural in Latin of Claudius Marcellus). This minor family had been part of the Roman political class meaning that it had members who had held political office in the Republic for less than a century. The first Marcus Claudius Marcellus in the historical record was the consul of 351. He had the distinction of being appointed dictator some time later, a position normally assigned when the state was in a military emergency. A religious objection, however, caused him to be removed quickly from office – these sorts of things happened not infrequently in the Republic. It was not until 287 that the next Marcellus held the consulship. There may have been members of the family who held lower offices in the years in between, but if so, the historical records – which are, admittedly, very sparse – do not mention them. So, when the Marcellus who is the subject of this biography was elected to his first political office it was an important distinction for his family.

Marcellus himself, however, had begun to carve out a reputation of his own decades before holding office. He had begun his military service during the time of the long Roman struggle with Carthage later called the First Punic War (264–241). During that conflict, according to Plutarch:

> Marcellus was efficient and practiced in every kind of fighting, but in single combat he surpassed himself, never declining a challenge, and always killing his challengers. In Sicily he saved his brother Otacilius from peril of his life, covering him with his shield and killing those who were setting upon him. Wherefore, although he was still a youth, he received garlands and prizes from his commanders.[1]

Marcellus had earned a reputation in these years of war as a skilled duelist, fighting in single combats during the course of battles against the enemy. The tradition of single combat, duels on the battlefield resulting from formal challenges, was far more common during the Republic than might be imagined. It was an important way for a young aspiring aristocrat to establish a name for himself and a reputation for *virtus*, that quality of martial manliness that served as currency among the ruling elite. Marcellus, however, exceeded the traditional standards, fighting not one single combat but many. In this he was among the very few; only two other Romans were recognized by the ancients for having fought in numerous single combats: the aristocrats Lucius Siccius Dentatus (mid-fifth century) and Marcus Servilius Geminus Pulex (late third to mid-second century).[2]

While skill with spear, sword, and shield was highly valued in Roman society, it would not normally by itself allow Marcellus to stake a claim among the political elite of the Republic by entering the ranks of the senate. That required election to office. Unlike modern governments where politicians can campaign for and be elected directly to the legislature, a Roman did not win election to the senate directly. Instead, a Roman earned the right to be a senator, essentially a lifetime position, as a consequence of winning election to a magistracy. By winning election to the aedileship, or perhaps an earlier unattested office, Marcellus could expect to be enrolled in the senate when the next vacancy appeared. In doing so, he joined the ranks of the Roman aristocracy that governed the Republic. Though the definition is not without its problems, those Romans who held political office and their families can usefully be termed the aristocracy. They were the political elite among the Romans and members of the social elite.

Marcellus, like most of his peers in the senatorial aristocracy, competed intensely for offices and honours, and any understanding of Marcellus requires an understanding of Roman aristocratic culture and the competitive system of politics and elections.[3] For the modern reader, a useful analogy for understanding Roman politics in the Republic is a game, so long as it is understood that the participants in no way saw it as trivial. Simply put, like most games, Roman politics was a competition organized and limited by rules, with winners and losers. The players were the aristocrats. For these players the goal was to exercise power and influence in the Republic, which for practical purposes meant in the senate. Power and influence in the senate, in turn, were inextricably linked to election to offices and the honours that came with those offices. It is no coincidence that the word *honos* in Latin can mean both 'political office' and 'honour', for the latter came with the former for the Roman aristocrat. By the late third century, tradition and custom had ranked these offices into something of a *cursus honorum*, a ladder of offices that the most successful politicians would hold. Though one might begin the *cursus* as a quaestor serving as the financial secretary for a commander in the field, this was not a firm requirement. The first-rank offices that were generally required were the aedileship and the tribuneship. There were four aediles elected annually who served as general city maintenance officials, and sponsored public festivals and games.[4] Of the same rough rank but offering a different route into the senate were the tribunes of the plebeians; these ten magistrates were responsible for protecting the rights of the plebeians, i.e. commoners, ostensibly by vetoing oppressive legislation and protecting wronged debtors. Since these offices, like almost all those in the Republic, could only be held for one year, this meant fourteen Romans, in the third century, could fill all these offices yearly. Doing so would ultimately, though not always immediately, give each a seat in the senate if they had not previously been awarded one.

From then on, however, the opportunities for higher offices grew more limited. For half of the third century, there was one praetorship, the praetor serving primarily as the judge in Roman lawsuits. Perhaps by the 240s, a second praetor was created. By Marcellus' time – perhaps 227 – the number of praetors increased to four, the two newest praetors serving as military governors for the provinces of Sardinia and Sicily, acquired in the first war against Carthage (264–241).[5] The total number of praetors did not increase again until the 190s, when the demands of governing the newly acquired province of Spain required the addition of two more praetors. Whether in the period of two praetors or four, the supply of offices available to ambitious aristocrats decreased dramatically from the first rungs of offices to the praetorship and, in doing so, drove up demand considerably.

The crowning achievement in a successful political career was the consulship. Though the office of censor, which two Romans were elected to hold for about eighteen months once every five years, was rarer, the consulship brought with it the greatest opportunities to earn the currency of aristiocrats: distinction, dignity, and influence, and, above all, a reputation for *virtus*, the Roman ideal of manly military courage. These magistrates had full *imperium*, a term that is difficult to translate concisely but which expresses both the right to have one's commands obeyed immediately and the rightful power to levy and command armies in the field. As wielders of *imperium*, the consuls were the chief executives for the year. They customarily chaired debates in the senate, selecting the topics for debate and the order in which senators would be allowed to respond. They also commanded the armies in the field, which provided the best opportunities for an aristocrat to earn the greatest honours through military victories.

Certainly, though, the consuls were not in a position to ignore the will of the senate. One need only imagine the reception a consul that had abused the senate would receive when his year of office had ended and he returned to the ranks of that same senate. The practice of remaining a senator for life, punctuated by some one-year tenures in office, was hardly conducive to a true separation of government branches. Still, one consulship, for those few aristocrats who could win it, was generally the capstone of a political career – exceedingly few held the office more than once. Since there were only two consulships every year, competition for that office was that much more fierce than for the lower ranks of praetor, aedile, and tribune.

Special mention should be made of the proconsuls and, less common, propraetors. When the senate wished to extend the term of elected officials, usually because they were in the middle of a campaign, it could grant them the ranks of proconsul or propraetor. Normally, when such an extension occurred, a consul became a proconsul and a praetor a propraetor. These appointments carried the military authority of consuls and praetor, respectively, without the civil powers. They tended to expire after one year but could be renewed by the senate as it saw fit. Because these appointments usually brought military authority with them, they provided important opportunities for Roman aristocrats to increase their prestige. Since appointment to one of these posts almost always required election first to the consulship or praetorship, these fell outside the normal arena of competition for elected office.

The assemblies of Roman citizens voted to elect officials every year.[6] The plebeian officials – the ten tribunes and the plebeian aediles – were elected by the tribal assembly. This assembly consisted of all eligible voters, the full Roman citizens who showed up to vote, grouped into the assigned voting blocs the Romans called tribes. The curule (as opposed to plebeian) aedile, praetors, consuls, and censors, on the other hand, were elected by the centuriate assembly. In the late third century, this voting body consisted of considerably more than 300 voting centuries ranked according to wealth. Whatever the majority in a century voted became the vote of the whole century; no matter how many individual voters in a century, each century cast a single vote in the assembly. This is vaguely similar to a modern bicameral legislature, although instead of two total votes, one from the upper house and one from the lower, there were several hundred. The Romans organized the centuriate assembly so that the wealthier citizens, though a minority of the population, had more centuries representing them. Consequently, the wealthier theoretically had a disproportionate amount of influence in elections so long as they voted for the same candidate. Whether in practice the system amounted to rule by the wealthy or functioned in a more egalitarian way, however, continues to be a matter of debate.[7]

Beyond the benefits elected office might bring an aristocrat during his year in power, it also conferred ranking in the senate. When there were up to 300 voices that might be heard on an issue brought before the senate and not enough time for all to be heard, the order in which senators had the right to give their opinion was particularly important. The consulars, those who had held the consulship, had the right to speak first. First of all among the consulars was the *princeps senatus*, or 'first man of the senate', chosen for his distinguished record and age by one of the censors. Then those who had held the praetorship spoke, and so on. It is far from clear whether the priority in speaking associated with each rank was set in stone and the extent to which the presiding magistrate, usually a consul, could play favourites and circumvent the normal order of speaking. Still there is sufficient evidence demonstrating that rank in the senate was highly dependent on the offices one had held. [8]

Such a system in which the members of the political class competed fiercely for the honours of high office was fraught with potential problems. First, from the competitors' point of view, came the problem of sharing the political wealth – how could newcomers and men of lower status within the elite effectively compete with sons of established aristocratic families who benefitted from the fame and prestige of their ancestors? Then there were the problems inherent in maintaining such a competitive system. Too much focus on competition and the essential administrative and military needs of the Republic could not be fulfilled. Or, equally undesirable, too much competition could lead to infighting that might tear the Republic apart. These are problems that continue to plague modern republics whose officials have made politics a career rather than a temporary service. Modern career politicians tied to political parties are often criticized – at times justly so – for devoting more energy to defeating their opponents than to addressing the pressing needs of their societies.

Despite the potential dangers and instability inherent in such a highly competitive political system, the Republic survived and even thrived for centuries. This is a result, returning for the moment to our metaphor of politics as a game, of the ruling class developing a number of rules that placed limits on how aristocrats could compete for offices and honours. These rules governed by-and-large the intensity of competition. First was the annuality of office. With the exception of the censors, who served several months longer, the elected officials of the Republic served one-year terms, and this limited their ability to over-capitalize on the power of any given office. Second was the collegiality of offices. With the exception of the dictator, a supreme political and military commander chosen to lead the Republic in times of emergency, there were at least two of every official every year, each with the power to veto his colleagues. This practice served to check the power of any individual official. Other rules were matters of custom and subject to lapsing, reviving, and bending through negotiation. Generally speaking, for example, one had to hold lower offices before holding the consulship – though this was not formalized in law until after Marcellus' day.[9] Generally speaking, one did not usually hold offices in consecutive years, having to wait for two years between offices – though this was certainly not a practice followed during the war against Hannibal. Collectively, these practices distributed offices among a wider number of aristocrats rather than limiting them to the few most successful competitors. There were other rules of play that focused on obstructing individuals from gaining honours, but these will be considered in due course as they were used against Marcellus.

This was the system in which Marcellus played his role. A bit of historical detective work and some arithmetic, however, suggests his initial entry into politics was delayed. To begin, a rough date for Marcellus' first known elected office needs to be established. Plutarch provides a passing reference to Marcellus as a curule aedile, the most junior office he can be said to have held. More specifically, Plutarch notes that during Marcellus' aedileship, he accused his colleague Capitolinus of making inappropriate advances toward his son, also named M. Claudius Marcellus. At that time, again according to Plutarch, the younger Marcellus was 'in the flower of youthful beauty', which would mean somewhere between 13 and 16 years old.[10] Combined with several more pieces of evidence, a rough date for Marcellus' aedileship can be calculated with reasonable certainty. First, the younger Marcellus held the consulship in 196 during a period when the average age for plebeian consuls was around 40 and perhaps several years older.[11] The younger Marcellus had, so far as we know, a regular and highly successful career, climbing steadily up the *cursus honorum* and eventually reaching the censorship.[12] The regularity of the younger Marcellus' career suggests he was probably of the average age when he was plebeian consul, say 45 to be conservative. This would make his birth year 241 and the year of his father's aedileship, when the son was 13 to 16, somewhere between 228 and 225.

This means that Marcellus, who was over 60 years old when he died in 208 and thus born no later than 268, was at least 40 when he held the aedileship. This figure gives cause for pause. The average age of Romans holding the curule aedileship in that period was a bit over 30.[13] One could reasonably expect that Marcellus, coming from a family of consular rank should have been able to win election to the aedileship at the typical age for Roman aristocrats. Instead, he was a decade or more behind his contemporaries. Not surprisingly, this initial delay bubbled through the rest of his career. When Marcellus won election to the consulship in 222 he was at least 46 years old, when the normal age of plebeian consuls was 36 to 39.[14] In other words, Marcellus began his rapid political ascent late in life. Why would this have been so? Certainly, he was willing to serve in high offices; after all, the man won election to the consulship five times in the span of fourteen years. Unfortunately, any attempt to answer this question requires considerable speculation. His career from the consulship forward was marked by his ability to capitalize on opportunities for glory and honour, even when those opportunities – in his opponent's eyes – contradicted if not broke the rules of aristocratic competition. Perhaps this tendency to stretch the limits and inspire opposition manifested itself at an earlier age when Marcellus' political career was less secure. Perhaps Marcellus rubbed one or more powerful aristocrats the wrong way, slowing his political career in the process. This certainly is possible, but the absence of clear evidence demands caution.

What can safely be said is that Marcellus' father, either dead or politically insignificant, was in no position to help his son's career. Normally, a young Roman aristocrat's father would have played an important role in fostering the youth's political career. A politically established father provided connections with the upper class that made up an influential part of the centuriate assembly.

Through his father's sponsorship a young man could become known to his elders, certainly important at election time. A father's good reputation might also serve as insurance of proper behaviour on the part of his son when he reached office. Long before a young Roman aristocrat entered the senate and learned its traditions, customs, and values, he learned about Roman political life and values from watching and listening to his father. The good reputation of the father would reflect favourably upon the son.

If any Claudius Marcellus held office between 287 and ca. 226, however, the sources are silent on the matter. So it is certain that Marcellus' father did not hold the consulship, and he may not have won election to any political office at all. Perhaps he died at a young age. Whatever the case, the absence of his father from the political scene certainly would have disadvantaged Marcellus. Perhaps this was enough to delay his entry into the aedileship, especially since the Claudii Marcelli themselves were relatively new to politics and as many as sixty years had passed since one had held high office.

Perhaps, too, the newness of the family and this large hole in Marcellus' political pedigree helps explain what followed. When Marcellus entered the consulship seven to ten years later than the average, he clearly seized several uncommon opportunities that laid the foundation of a reputation lasting well after the Republic collapsed. The scene for this ascent was set in 225, three years before Marcellus' first consulship. Later writers particularly noted the Roman panic that year when news came that the Insubrian Gauls and their allies had declared war. There certainly had been enough precedents to strike fear into Roman hearts. Though it is misleading to speak of Gauls as a collective since the label refers to a variety of Celtic tribes stretching from north Italy through France and into Britain, the Romans often did just that, and the relationship between the Romans and the Gauls had been shaky under the best of circumstances. Nearly two centuries earlier, in 390, the Gallic Senones had sacked the city of Rome itself, burning it to the ground, an event branded into the Roman psyche, judging from the references to the event made by writers centuries later. Then in a far more recent event that the very oldest Romans of Marcellus' day would well remember, Gallic tribes in north Italy had capitalized on the invasion of southern Italy by King Pyrrhus of Epirus in the 270s and invaded Roman territory. From the Roman perspective the Gauls were an imminent danger, simply waiting for an opportune time to eradicate the Republic.[15]

There were, however, other legitimate perspectives. Sometime in the decade before 225, probably 232, the tribune Gaius Flaminius passed a proposal to parcel out the region of Picenum, once held by the Gauls, to Roman citizens.[16] This act in Polybius' judgment sparked a renewed war with these Gallic tribes after almost half a century of peace.[17] His reasoning holds up well; the confiscation and settlement of lands that had once been under the control of the

Gauls were ominous signs that the Roman presence in north Italy was there to stay; the ultimate victims of Roman expansion here were to be the Gauls. That the critical fertile farmlands of the expansive valley of the River Po were likely to be next on the Roman list after Picenum could not have settled Gallic fears any. The course of Roman expansion in Italy in the previous century provided a clear enough portent to any who cared to look; the Etruscans, the Latins, and the Samnites had all been major regional powers; all had been eclipsed by the Romans. The Greeks of the south had been humbled and even the Carthaginians defeated in their first war with the Romans. Modern historians have, rightly, spent a great deal of energy trying to determine whether the Romans intended to carve an empire from these peoples or simply acquired it through a series of defensive wars and entangling diplomatic commitments. For the Insubres and the Boii, however, such a question, if it ever even occurred to them, was beside the point: the Romans would keep coming so long as nothing stopped them.

So, spurred by the latest Roman encroachment, this time in the form of farmers ploughing under the meadows of Picenum, the Insubrians and Boii chose to make war on the Romans. Nor did they mean it to be a minor threat. They hired the services of the Gaesatae, a Gallic people known to fight for pay.[18] A great force was mustered and headed south into the Roman heartland. According to Polybius, this was the largest Gallic invasion force ever, consisting of 50,000 infantry and 20,000 cavalry and chariots – numbers that are certainly extremely large though within the realm of possibility.[19] The invaders marched south across the River Po, the unofficial boundary between Roman and Gallic lands, and into Etruria, laying waste to the countryside as they marched.[20] These were lands the Romans had dominated for far more than a century; they were facing a large-scale invasion on their veritable doorstep.

News of this invasion must have reached Rome after the consuls of the year had received their military assignments. One of the consuls, Gaius Atilius, had already been dispatched to Sardinia with legions – no doubt to continue pacifying the island the Romans had seized from Carthage at the end of the First Punic War more than a decade before (238/7). This helps explain the heightened concerns at Rome – a massive invasion force on the move and one of their consular armies was not even in Italy. The senate crafted an initial defensive strategy. A missive called Atilius back from the island. Meanwhile, the other consul, Lucius Aemilius took a force to Ariminum, a city in northern Umbria on the Adriatic coast. Finally, one of the praetors of the year, officials who were still judges as much as they were military commanders at this point in Roman history, was sent to Etruria.[21] Presumably the plan was for the praetor, as the junior commander, to hold in Etruria pending the return of the Consul Atilius to the west coast. Aemilius, then, would head east either to flank the Gallic army or defend the eastern side of the peninsula.

When the Gauls reached Clusium in central Etruria they had passed the praetor's position. He subsequently led his forces to cut off the Gaul's return route. The Gallic army turned to do battle with the Roman force and defeated it soundly, killing thousands and trapping the remnants on a hilltop.[22] Laden with spoils from their adventures, the Gallic king, Aneroestes, ordered the host to return home for the season. Meanwhile, Aemilius had marched his forces from Ariminum into Etruria. He received word of the dire straits the praetor's army was in and managed to relieve the hilltop survivors, adding them to his own forces. Aemilius at this time decided to avoid a pitched battle, preferring to wait and observe the Gallic army as it moved north. With the arrival of Atilius' legions imminent, time could only improve the Roman position. [23]

As the Romans' good fortune had it, Atilius soon landed his army at Pisa and began the march south along the coastal plain of Etruria toward Rome. Essentially, this meant that the Gallic army was trapped between the forces of Atilius and Aemilius, though neither the consuls nor the Gauls seemed immediately aware of this. Soon, though, Atilius' vanguard soldiers captured some Gallic foragers near the River Telamon in Etruria – midway between Rome and Pisa – and reported the position of both the Gallic army and Aemilius' force.[24] Atilius must have been amazed by his luck or, perhaps, by the gift the gods had handed to him. Here was a chance to trap the entire enemy force between two Roman armies, a commander's dream. According to Polybius, Atilius ordered his tribunes 'to put the legions in fighting order' and marched to intercept the Gallic forces.[25]

Polybius' casual reference to 'fighting order' underscores the fact that ancient writers, when they were not ignorant themselves, tended to assume their readers were familiar with the realities of ancient infantry battle. This leaves the modern reader at a disadvantage, since ancient battlegrounds were far different from modern ones and the details have not always been represented accurately. Since the functioning of the late third century Roman army is central to a full account of Marcellus, it will be well worth the time to explore the characteristics of that army and of ancient infantry battle in the third century Mediterranean world.[26]

Any account of the Roman army in the middle Republic must begin with Polybius, who took time in his history to describe the soldiers, their equipment, and organization.[27] The largest unit in the Roman army of the middle Republic was a legion. Though the actual strength could vary with the recruits available and the conditions in the field, on paper each legion consisted of approximately 4,200 soldiers, 5,000 during emergencies. Each legion had four categories of infantry. These categories were determined by the age of citizens, their wealth, and – because citizens provided their own weapons and equipment at this stage in the Republic – their panoply. The youngest soldiers, those closest to the minimum recruit age of seventeen, were the *velites*. As the light infantry of the legion, they were also the lightest equipped, armed with javelins and a sword,

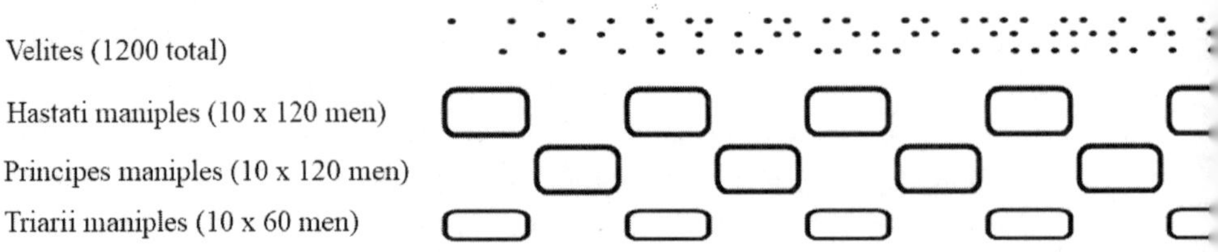

Velites (1200 total)

Hastati maniples (10 x 120 men)

Principes maniples (10 x 120 men)

Triarii maniples (10 x 60 men)

Diagram 1: Standard components of a Roman legion.

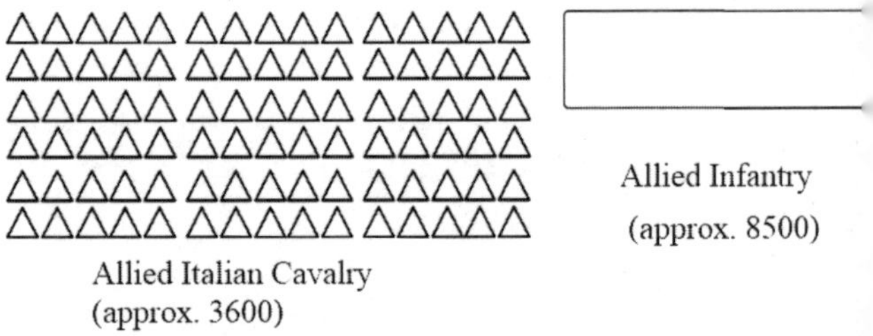

Allied Infantry
(approx. 8500)

Allied Italian Cavalry
(approx. 3600)

Diagram 2: Typical Roman army with Roman and allied forces.

Equites (cavalry)
(10 turma x 30 troopers)

4 Roman Legions
(approx. 17,000)

Allied Infantry
(approx. 8500)

Roman Cavalry
(approx. 1200)

and protected by a round shield, but little or no body armour. In the framework of ancient warfare, light infantry tended to serve as missile troops. They harassed enemy armies within reach of a javelin and screened the movements and deployment of their own comrades in the heavy infantry. The *velites* also were commonly used in combination with cavalry as skirmishers and more mobile squads employed to occupy advantageous or critical positions quickly.

The main infantry line was manned by the *hastati*, *principes*, and *triarii*. All were heavy infantry soldiers, armed and equipped to fight in close quarters against enemy combatants. The *hastati* were younger than the *principes*, the men in their prime, while the *triarii* consisted of older soldiers closer to the maximum service age of forty-five. The core of these soldiers' panoply was the *scutum*, an oblong or rectangular shield some 4 feet high and 2.5 feet wide. According to Polybius, who certainly was in a position to know, the shield consisted of a convex core of wood covered with canvas and hide, perhaps ¾ of an inch thick overall, with a central iron boss and grip. Since the average Roman male was well under 6 feet tall, the shield effectively covered the entire body of the soldier and could also assist in driving back an enemy. For body armour the heavy infantry wore a square bronze plate perhaps 9 inches to a side that protected the centre of the chest. Wealthier soldiers supplied their own mail coats. Finally, all these soldiers wore a helmet with a crest. For weapons, all three classes of soldier had a *gladius*, the short, sharp Roman sword useful both for stabbing and slashing, and the *hastati* and *principes* also had *pila*, heavy javelins. The *triarii*, by contrast, bore long, sturdy thrusting spears rather than *pila*. This fit with their primary role as a reserve line used to provide a defensive spear wall should the *hastati* and *principes* be driven back in battle. In a given legion of 4,200 there were, on paper at least, some 1,200 *velites*, 1,200 *hastati*, 1,200 *principes*, and 600 *triarii*. These troops were subdivided into maniples, smaller tactical units that could maneuver and deploy far more flexibly than the larger legion of which they were a part. Each maniple consisted of perhaps 120 soldiers plus *velites*, who were divided among the maniples.

In addition, each Roman army was, so far as we know, accompanied by an allied contingent of soldiers. The allied infantry were armed and equipped like their Roman counterparts and in Marcellus' day at least equaled the number of citizen infantry in any standard army. With the exception of the *extraordinarii*, the hand-picked elite infantry from the allies, the bulk were divided into two forces labeled the left and right wing.[28]

The cavalry forces of a Roman army consisted of citizen and allied cavalry. On paper, each legion had a citizen contingent of 300 cavalry and an allied contingent of somewhere between 600 and 900. The cavalry were subdivided into *turma* of thirty riders to allow for tactical flexibility. Throughout the Republic they were armed with spears and swords and protected by shields. At some point, perhaps early in the Second Punic War, they abandoned their light shields and adopted the heavier protection of Greek-style shields and mail cuirasses.[29]

So much for the basics of equipment and organization. A critical question remains: what was a Roman battle actually like for the combatants? Warfare for the Romans, and indeed most Mediterranean and European peoples of the period, was fundamentally similar in that clashes between large formations of heavy infantry were the basis of most battles. Soldiers arranged in more-or-less close order – roughly shoulder-to-shoulder or up to several feet apart – stood close enough to their enemies to fight with melee weapons. Combat in these circumstances was intensely physical, personal, and brutal. One had to stand close enough to one's enemy to strike with spear and sword. In practice, this meant a distance of several feet – a grim prospect indeed, and strikingly different from contemporary war, where it is possible for combatants to be separated by thousands of miles.

For the Greek world from the seventh to the fifth centuries, heavy infantry combat revolved around the phalanx, a solid formation of infantry armed with spear and shield. The phalanx was a tactically inflexible unit compared to other formations. It relied on presenting the enemy a murderous wall of shields and spears to win the day, not complicated deployments and flanking maneuvers. Battles between phalanges tended to be relatively swift and one-sided. The men in the opposing phalanges charged one another, each side seeking to break the morale of the other at the very onset. On many occasions, the charge itself was sufficient to decide the battle. The soldiers on one side proved unwilling to receive the enemy charge and fled at – sometimes even before – the first clash of shields and spears. When the initial charge did not decide the matter, the heavy infantry settled into a match of stabbing and shoving, each side attempting to disrupt the other side's formations. When one side broke, the battle was over, the defeated fleeing and the victors often pursuing the defeated for a time, engaging in the type of indiscriminate slaughter that served as an object lesson in the ancient world. Phalanx battles were generally characterized by their lack of grand maneuvers and tactical flexibility.

By the fifth century, however, and in the Hellenistic period where the successors of Alexander the Great plied their martial trade, cavalry, light infantry, and missile troops became more important components of the army. Consequently, the tactical options available to commanders increased. The core of the armies, however, remained the massed-infantry phalanx – though the shield had shrunk considerably and the spear extended from six to eight feet into a pike that could in some circumstances be over twenty feet long.

The Roman army did use the phalanx at an early stage in its development, but transitioned to the manipular army, which was well-established by the middle Republic. Though the idea of a typical battle is highly misleading, the Roman armies do seem to have had a somewhat standard approach to battle with the manipular army. Certainly, Polybius had a penchant for mentioning in his battle descriptions that the Roman army was deployed in the 'usual order'. Based on his accounts[30] the general order went as follows. The army would deploy with the heavy infantry maniples forming the centre of the Roman battle line, presumably *hastati* in front, *principes* next, then *triarii*. The allied infantry, organized into left and right wings, occupied the appropriate space to the left and right of the citizen infantry. The light-armed *velites* took position in front of the battle line, and the cavalry, often separated into citizen and allied contingents, occupied the left and right flanks of the battle line. Initially, it was the task of the *velites* to begin the battle by casting their javelins at the enemy forces, seeking to wound and demoralize them before the main struggle. Once their missiles were exhausted or the closing of the enemy heavy infantry forced them back, the *velites* retired, presumably through the gaps in the maniples, and the main infantry lines engaged.

Though the exact operation of the manipular legion in battle is far from clear, the maniples clearly provided a tactical flexibility missing from the phalanx. Typically, the maniples deployed in a quincunx formation. In short, each maniple in the first line was separated from the maniples on either side by a gap slightly more than a maniple's width. The second line was offset accordingly so that each maniple in it was aligned with the gaps in the first line, and the third line mirrored the first, as in the diagram below.

Hastati maniples
Principes maniples
Triarii maniples

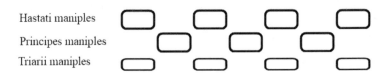

Diagram 3: Infantry maniples in a quincunx formation.

Theoretically, this arrangement allowed the second line maniples to move forward and relieve the first line, which retreated through the gaps. The third line was occupied by the *triarii* who ordinarily did not enter battle unless things had gone very poorly for the *hastati* and *principes*; in this case the *triarii* formed a defensive spear wall and bought time for the others to rally and reform.

When the heavy infantry clashed, the most important battle was not on the field but in the mind. Morale, the psychological will to fight, determined success or failure on the battlefield. Modern historians of ancient battle who recognize this reality pay their respects to Colonel Ardant du Picq, a French officer in the latter half of the nineteenth century who wrote a study on the power of morale in ancient combat.[31] He asserted that ancient battles were not to be understood as simple brawls where formations disintegrated upon contact with the enemy and combatants became hopelessly intermingled in an archipelago of single combats. Such an understanding violates both the available evidence and the soldierly common sense that du Picq brought to his subject. Rather, only the front ranks of each infantry formation fought in actual hand-to-hand combat. Meanwhile, the rear ranks felt extraordinary amounts of stress as they waited for their turn in battle, watching the struggles just a few yards in front of them, but having no outlet for their stress. It was in the rear, not the front, that ancient armies were most often defeated. If the pressure of watching and waiting became too great, if the fear of death and defeat overwhelmed, the soldiers in the rear ranks would give way first – those in the front simply had no place to go with the ranks behind keeping them in place. Once the soldiers in the rear began to run, the formation lost its cohesion: individuals fled for their own safety, the front lost the moral support of comrades behind it, and the unit collapsed.

Ironically, though individuals' overwhelming fears of injury and death caused them to break ranks and seek safety, it was the very breaking of ranks that exposed them to the greatest danger. So long as an infantry formation stayed intact, any individual's risk of death or wounding was much less. When a formation dissolved and individuals turned in flight, however, they lost the safety of their comrades' protection and exposed their backs to the enemy and to slaughter. There was a reason why, when a Roman felt the desire to publicly display his scars in order to reaffirm his *virtus* to the crowd, he made sure to point out that none were on his back. Being wounded in the back only occurred when one had fled the battlefield; fleeing the battlefield meant deserting one's comrades and leaving them as easier prey for the enemy.

The key to victory on the battlefield, then, was to ensure that one's own soldiers could withstand the pressures of battle – the shouts, the scraping and clanging of metal on metal, the grunts and screams of those fighting and dying. When enough soldiers were sufficiently distracted and frightened so that the compulsion to flee overwhelmed any obligations to stay in their positions in the group, the effectiveness of the combat unit was lost. Unless rallied, the individuals in the unit would seek their own safety by retreating or, if sufficiently demoralized, fleeing the battlefield. The victors, meanwhile, had the opportunity to slay as many of their fleeing opponents as possible – here cavalry helped charge down the defeated.

Applying this understanding of the Roman army to the strategic situation in Etruria in 225, the trapping of the Gallic army between two Roman armies meant that the Gallic force had to split to meet both foes, or fight with its backs vulnerable to one. Either proposition would be demoralizing for the Gauls and encouraging for Romans. Building on this advantage, Atilius opted to add an additional vector of attack; seeing a nearby hill that the Gallic forces would eventually pass, he rode with his cavalry to occupy the hill and threaten the Gallic flank. The Gallic forces eventually arrived and, apparently unaware that Atilius' cavalry on the hill belonged to a different army than the one they knew was pursuing them, sent mixed forces of cavalry and light infantry to contest the hill with the Romans. Soon learning of their tactical dilemma, however, the Gauls formed two battle lines, one facing forward toward Atilius' legions, the other rear toward Aemilius.[32]

Aemilius, for his part, learned that the Gallic army was penned in, observed the struggle along the hillside flanking the Gauls, and sent his own cavalry forces to aid Atilius. According to Polybius, so many cavalry were engaged that both armies observed the battle on the hill for quite some time. Indeed, if all the citizen and Italian cavalry from both armies were engaged, thousands of horses and riders were swarming about the hill, surely a spectacle. As the struggle to take the hill continued, the infantry forces engaged. According to Polybius, the Insubres and Boii wore only their trousers and light cloaks as protection, in addition to carrying shields, smaller than those of the Romans. The Gaesatae, however, opted to fight naked though still with their shields, trusting that their physical superiority to average Romans, in addition to the bravery of the decision itself, would demoralize their foes.

Though the tactical situation certainly favoured the Romans, who had the Gauls hemmed in on both sides, the battle was far from a foregone conclusion. The battle began, as was often the case in the Roman world, with the *velites* casting their javelins into the mass of the Gallic infantry. Wounded by the javelins, the naked Gaeseatae lost their stomach for battle and panicked. They broke and either fled back into the lines of their comrades, causing disruption wherever they went, or flung themselves futilely upon the orderly Roman formations. Despite the chaotic break of the Gaeseatae, the lines of Insubres and Boii stood firm and met the Roman maniples in hand-to-hand combat. Polybius assessed the strengths and weaknesses of both sides:

[The Gallic infantry] met the enemy and kept up a stubborn hand-to-hand combat. For, though being almost cut to pieces, they held their ground, equal to their foes in courage, and inferior only, as a force and individually, in their arms. The Roman shields, it should be added, were far more serviceable for defence and their swords for attack, the Gallic sword being only good for a cut and not for a thrust.[33]

During the infantry melee the Roman cavalry had finally seized the hilltop, though the consul Atilius died in the engagement. Now ideally positioned to punish the flanks of the Gallic infantry, the Roman cavalry charged down the hill and attacked. It is important to note that when Roman cavalry charged, the goal was not to collide with the enemy. Even if a horse could be impelled to collide with a solid wall of men, such a maneuver would only destroy an extremely valuable warhorse, and incapacitate or kill an elite rider, at the cost of a few inflicted casualties – hardly a reasonable trade off from the Roman perspective. Rather, the goal was either to frighten the enemy to give way or to work into the open spaces between soldiers and disrupt the formations. The flanks of infantry formations were especially vulnerable to such attacks since shields and weapons normally faced forward. In this case, the pressure on three sides by Roman forces, and the disruption caused by the cavalry, in addition to the additional casualties inflicted as a result of the disruption, proved decisive. The infantry formations collapsed, and tens of thousands of were slaughtered by the Romans.[34] According to Polybius, most of the Gauls were cut down in the field – 40,000 by his estimate – while another 10,000 were captured. These prisoners became part of the spectacle that was Aemilius' triumph, a formal procession held in the city to celebrate the crushing victory.[35] Their invasion blunted and their military might disintegrated, the Insubres and Boii fell prey to Roman invasions for the next two years. In 224, the consuls subdued the Boii and forced them to surrender.[36] In 223, the consuls defeated an Insubrian army in its own territory, a decisive blow that pushed the Insubrians to sue for peace.[37]

So, the Insubrians sent emissaries to Rome, and it is at this point that Marcellus appears in the accounts. According to Polybius, the Insubrians were authorized to accept any conditions the Romans cared to impose in return for peace. The consuls of the year, Marcellus and Gnaeus Cornelius Scipio, however, insisted that the Insubrian emissaries should be dismissed and the war continued.[38] Plutarch includes additional details: in his version the senate was generally open to reaching a peace agreement but Marcellus in particular – he does not mention Scipio in this context – tried to move the popular assembly to continue the war.[39] Plutarch's account, however, is confused. He suggests that peace was made despite Marcellus' efforts and that it was the instigation of the mercenary Gaesatae that continued the war into another year. It makes little sense that the Insubrians would so desperately seek peace, a point on which Polybius and Plutarch agree, and then immediately renew the war after receiving peace – all at the instigation of their hired warriors. So it seems that

Polybius' version, in which both consuls agitated for war, is to be preferred for its lucidity.

There are two points worth keeping in mind when considering the testimony of Polybius and Plutarch. First, Marcellus and Scipio were neither the first nor the last consuls to push for war when peace was in reach. The consulship was a rare prize in an aristocratic career. Since there were only two consuls elected every year, most Romans who entered the senate would never hold that office. Those who did manage to win the office so coveted among the most powerful and prestigious aristocrats would very likely never be consul again. This meant they had to make the most of their one year in office, and there was no surer path to glory than to prosecute a war successfully. A year of peace generally meant a year of relative insignificance for a consul.[40] Not that such years were common; it is a good guess that the Romans only had a handful of years free from war in the Republic.

Second, while Plutarch may have been correct that there were senators who favoured peace, he can hardly have been correct to suggest that the senate collectively felt that way. The Insubrians had started this war, laid waste to the country of Roman allies, and slain thousands of Roman soldiers. Certainly some, if not many senators, would have been more than willing to see the Insubrians destroyed as a fighting power once and for all, and, equally as important, their territory pacified after the fears raised by the invasion of 225. Thus, while it is reasonable to believe Scipio and Marcellus pushed for continued war, it is hardly necessary to suppose that Marcellus needed to take the unorthodox tactic of agitating the popular assembly instead of persuading the senate. In the end, the war did continue, and that was assuredly the result of at least some senatorial support. Rebuffed, the Insubrians again obtained the services of Gaesatae mercenaries and prepared for an inevitable Roman invasion.

When the spring arrived and the campaigning season began, the consuls led their forces across the Po and laid siege to Acerrae.[41] Appreciating their choice of targets requires some consideration of Insubrian territory. The Po is a lengthy river running essentially west to east across northern Italy with its mouth roughly equidistant between modern day Venice and Ravenna. In the Roman world the large and fertile Po valley was the heartland of the Gallic peoples south of the Alps. The territory of the Insubrians began roughly at the confluence of the River Addua and River Po, which is approximately in the middle of the Po's course, and extended north and west into the foothills of the Alps. The main settlement of the Insubrians, Mediolanum (modern Milan), was approximately seventy-five miles from the confluence. To reach this settlement, indeed to penetrate to any extent into the interior of Insubrian lands, required first passing the settlement of Acerrae. The very fact that the consuls needed to besiege it and could not storm it outright suggests the settlement was large and reasonably well defended. In short, to invade Insubrian territory and not take Acerrae meant leaving an enemy settlement positioned across Roman communication and supply lines as the armies progressed into the Insubrian interior.

In an effort to lift the siege of Acerrae, a detachment of 10,000 soldiers from the Insubrian and Gaesatae forces separated from the main body, crossed the Po, and besieged the settlement of Clastidium belonging to the Anares, a Roman ally.[42] Thus began the operation that was to be the cornerstone of Marcellus' reputation for centuries. Marcellus left Scipio in charge of the siege operation at Acerrae and headed to relieve Clastidium with a force of cavalry and light infantry. The numbers involved are not completely clear. Polybius simply says that Marcellus took 'the cavalry and a small body of infantry.'[43] If 'the cavalry' refers to all of the Roman cavalry with the army, this would have totalled anywhere from 3,600 to 4,800 Roman and Italian cavalry – the arithmetic is four legions with 300 citizen cavalry and 600 to 900 allied cavalry per legion. Plutarch is more specific, saying that Marcellus took two thirds of the cavalry and 600 light infantry.[44] This would put the force of cavalry somewhere between 2,400 and 3,200. While accepting the word of Plutarch over Polybius on military affairs can be risky, Plutarch's figures are the more likely in this case since Scipio would almost certainly have wanted to keep at least some cavalry with him to serve as scouts and foragers, not to mention to fend off any potential enemy cavalry attempting to disrupt the siege at Acerrae.

Marcellus had sound strategic reasons for heading to Clastidium with a small mobile force. When he arrived at Clastidium, however, the larger enemy force besieging the city may well have been more than he bargained for. To bolster the morale of his small forces, invoke the power of the gods, prepare memorials to his hoped-for victory, or some combination of these reasons, Marcellus made two vows to the gods that day prior to engaging the enemy. First, he dedicated a temple to Honos and Virtus, deified character traits that can be roughly translated as Honour and Manly/Martial Valour.[45] It was a not uncommon tradition among Roman generals to vow temples to the gods in return for receiving a military victory. These temples served as lasting public monuments to an individual aristocrat's victory and, it was believed, further cemented the bonds between the Romans and their gods. In Marcellus' case, this was a particularly important opportunity to burnish his reputation and increase his glory in the eyes of the Roman people. For all he knew, the battle at Clastidium might be the only time he was in sole command that year. Nevertheless, it was a striking choice of gods to honour, for, as he certainly well knew, Honos already had a temple dedicated just over ten years before by the distinguished noble, Fabius Maximus.

As it happened the god Honos had strong ties to the Roman cavalry, the men of the socio-economic elite who provided their military service to the Republic on horseback. Cavalry service was the most elite form of service and the cavalry symbolized at Rome the qualities of nobility and bravery, powerful associations for a Roman aristocrat. The connection between Honos and the cavalry was reasonably clear to all. [46] Every year the members of the *equites equo public*, the 1,800 most distinguished members of the cavalry class who received a stipend at the public's expense for purchasing and maintaining a warhorse, undertook a parade celebrating the prestige of the cavalry. The temple to Honos was an important stop for this parade, the *transvectio equitum*. Furthermore, the sacred day of celebration for Honos was 17 July, two days after the *transvectio*. When the temple was built in 233 by Fabius Maximus Verrucosus, the most distinguished living representative of the Fabii clan, it was almost assuredly done to emphasize the connection of the Fabii to the cavalry. It was Fabius Maximus' great grandfather, Fabius Maximus Rullianus, who some seventy years earlier as censor had elevated the prestige of the *transvectio equitum* from a more minor religious ceremony to a larger scale, spirit-building military review. Rullianus may also have been responsible for ruling that cavalry troopers who received the honourific state-subsidized horse needed to remain physically fit for duty and could not simply count on their family's high status for a horse. In these ways Rullianus enhanced the prestige of the cavalry as a warrior class and connected their prestige to the Fabii, a link that Fabius Maximus reinforced when he defeated the Ligurians of north Italy and used the loot to build a temple to Honos.[47]

Marcellus was certainly aware of these connections and equally well aware that, in a culture where religion and politics were so closely linked, his dedication of even half a temple to Honos was a challenge to Fabius' claims, an encroachment. Whether he had time to consider the implications of challenging such a powerful aristocrat fully, however, is not clear. After all, the dedication was apparently made right before the battle at Clastidium. The most likely explanation is that Marcellus' forces were in a tight spot. They were a small cavalry force facing a much larger enemy force. The evidence for this battle suggests Marcellus was nothing if not attentive to the morale of his soldiers. What better way to inflate the morale of his cavalry troopers than to dedicate a temple to the gods that most represented the qualities associated with the cavalry, Honos and Virtus? Regardless of the justification in the moment of battle, however, Marcellus had stepped on the toes of a rival, one from an ancient Roman family, and one who had already held two consulships at that.

The politics of the temple to Honos and Virtus would occupy Marcellus intermittently for the rest of his life, but it was his second vow of the day that would win him a reputation that would last as long as Roman civilization did. According to Plutarch, just before Marcellus closed with the enemy, he pledged a gift to Jupiter Feretrius, the finest enemy armour from that day's spoils. That Marcellus made a dedication of this kind is wholly consistent with the reputation he had earned in his earlier years as a skilled practitioner of single combat. This was not a skill shared equally by Romans, certainly not by generals. What better way to add a unique element of glory to his battle than to dedicate enemy armour to the gods and look for an opportunity to be the one to claim that armour personally? Furthermore, beyond the personal prestige such a claim might earn him, it certainly could only help the morale of his forces to see their general was so sure of victory that he was focused on the spoils that the Romans would win that day. Attention to these details of morale was an important component to Marcellus' success as a commander.

What happened next is not entirely clear insofar as Plutarch relates the event in some detail, while Polybius, an earlier and generally sounder source on military affairs, is silent – as for Livy, the book of his history that covers this year was lost centuries if not millennia ago. In Plutarch's version, Marcellus and his cavalry approached the Gallic army, whose own cavalry were arrayed in the front. Before the forces closed, he dedicated the best suit of enemy armour despoiled that day to Jupiter Feretrius. Then the Gallic king Virdumarus, riding at the front of his cavalry, caught sight of Marcellus. He challenged Marcellus to a duel. Marcellus gamely agreed, and as the two riders charged close, he speared the Gallic leader off his horse and dispatched him on the ground. He then loudly declared that this was the armour he had promised to Jupiter and that victory should be granted to the Romans.[48]

Though Plutarch gives the only detailed description, Marcellus' duel and victory is quite well attested by other Roman sources.[49] Polybius is wholly silent, however, on the duel between the enemy commanders, by far the most extraordinary part of the entire battle. Yet Polybius, it should be noted, had a marked tendency to pass over Marcellus' achievements. The historical record is firmly against Polybius; Marcellus did clash with and kill the Gallic king in single combat. The main outlines of the battle after the duel are clear, though presented in a cursory fashion by the sources. Marcellus with only his small force of cavalry defeated a substantially larger Gallic force and broke the siege. On this point our main sources, Polybius and Plutarch are agreed. Plutarch rightly added the note that such a victory of so few cavalry over a much larger combined force of infantry and cavalry was uncommonly rare.[50]

When we separate the strands of this battle, several important components help explain the Roman victory against the odds. The first is the attention Marcellus paid to raising the morale of his soldiers. Marcellus' vow of a victory temple to the gods was not the only example. According to Plutarch, right before Marcellus led the charge, his horse in a fit of independence wheeled and headed toward the rear. Worried that his soldiers might see this as a bad sign from the gods, Marcellus wheeled his horse back around and 'at the same time he went through the movements of praying to the sun, as if it was for this purpose that he had wheeled his horse, for the Romans always turn in this way when they offer worship to the gods.'[51] The prayers and the victory temple showed the troops that Marcellus had gone beyond the call of duty to secure the good will of the gods and was so certain of victory that he had dedicated a temple to some of them.

These were important symbolic gestures that could make a great deal of difference for soldiers about to risk death.

Marcellus did more than simply talk about victory. He went out of his way to lead by example and show his courage through single combat. The skill set of a soldier in a formation, particularly a close-order formation such as the heavy infantry maniples of the third century Roman legions, was a different thing from the skill set of the warrior who could win unaided in a struggle to the death. The victor raised the morale of his comrades in the ranks while the slain cast the shadow of a doubt in the minds of those comrades who survived him. It does not take any naiveté to agree with the ancient authors on this point: single combats, because of their impact on morale, could play a critical role in the success of a battle.

What happened in the duel at Clastidium, however, was more than any ordinary contest of the kind for which Marcellus had earned an early reputation. No, there he had killed the king and commander of the Gallic force in a highly visible display before the battle had started in earnest. The shock of seeing their king slain in single combat and despoiled by the enemy commander helps to explain how the Roman cavalry alone were able to defeat the Gallic forces. As we saw earlier, morale was the lynchpin to ancient battle. So long as soldiers maintained their formations and received the benefits of their comrades' protection, casualties were generally minimized. Once the individuals came to feel – through wounds, noises, confusion, and fear – that their chances of survival would be better without the group, formations began to disintegrate, units lost their ability to fight, and the battle was lost. Begin the battle with the horror of seeing one's king struck down, and it would take very little sensitivity to symbolism for an ancient soldier to feel unease if not outright foreboding about the battle to come.

Certainly, Polybius' description of the battle, terse though it is, highlights the critical role of morale in this battle and hints at the skill with which Marcellus commanded the Roman cavalry. The Gallic infantry were arrayed in battle formation outside the city. While the exact details of Gallic infantry formations of the late third century are mostly unrecoverable, they appear to have had a distinction between heavy infantry – in which the soldiers fought in close order – and light infantry – dispersed units of soldiers.[52] It is not clear the extent to which Gallic heavy infantry forces were articulated into smaller units for maneuver, but it seems highly likely they lacked the sophisticated articulation of the Roman manipular army with its four types of infantry units. Based on Polybius' description of the Gauls at the Telamon three years earlier, it is reasonable to assume that most wore only their clothing for armour, in addition to a shield, though perhaps some chose, as others had before, to fight completely naked, the better to intimidate the Romans.[53] The primary weapon of the Gallic heavy infantry seems to have been their sword, an edged blade that, as Polybius assessed when describing the battle of the Telamon, was effective for slashing but unsuitable for stabbing.[54]

Polybius suggests that the Gallic infantry stood their ground initially, but that the Roman cavalry attacked from the flanks and the rear. Where was the Gallic cavalry to protect the infantry's flanks? While Plutarch explicitly refers to Gallic cavalry at the start of the battle, Polybius does not. The brevity of his overall description of the battle, however, suggests he did not wish to dwell on the matter. His silence does not rule out the presence of cavalry, which we would expect of most any Gallic field army, and certainly a detachment sent to raid into enemy territory. So while it is possible that the Gallic cavalry force was extremely small to begin with, no more than a bodyguard for Virdumarus, it is more likely that the force was larger. If the Gauls, as Plutarch says, had a legitimate cavalry force, they presumably were driven from the field after Virdumarus died, allowing the Roman cavalry to attack the main Gallic force unhindered. This would not have been the only time a cavalry force routed and left the infantry to their fate: most recently, the Roman cavalry had driven off the Gallic cavalry at the Telamon before charging the exposed Gallic infantry.[55]

After the Gallic cavalry fled, the main attack on the infantry began. Again, Polybius notes the Gauls held firm initially when the Romans 'boldly charged them with their cavalry alone.'[56] It would be an over-confident if not incompetent general who ordered his cavalry into an all-out charge against the front of a well-ordered heavy infantry formation. Occasionally, though, such charges could be successful if the infantry was already in a state of disorder. Perhaps Marcellus hoped to capitalize on the momentum gained by slaying the enemy king and driving off their cavalry by scattering the Gallic infantry with a charge. In this case, however, it is difficult to explain how the cavalry successfully charged the front of the infantry when it was in an orderly state, and indeed the infantry continued to be in an orderly state after the charge. Certainly, Marcellus was well aware that cavalry had little hope of success in a frontal assault against infantry ready to receive the charge. Perhaps he was testing the mettle of the Gallic infantry by making a feint at the front line. Once the feint proved unsuccessful, however, the Roman cavalry engaged in the standard tactics for defeating enemy infantry; attacks on the flanks and rear.

However it came to pass, it was not until the cavalry attacked the flanks and rear that they, in Polybius' words, literally 'rendered' the Gallic combatants 'useless in battle.'[57] In other words, the attacks did not destroy the Gauls themselves, only their ability to fight. With their king already dead and his corpse despoiled, the Gauls would have been particularly vulnerable to the kind of fear that shattered armies. Those panic-stricken soldiers who were not cut down in the rout threw themselves in the river, and the current carried them off. Marcellus had taken advantage of the speed and flexibility of the Roman cavalry to do what it did best; attack the more vulnerable flanks and rear of enemy formations.

After the victory at Clastidium, the accounts of Polybius and Plutarch diverge somewhat again. That Roman forces soon took Acerrae and, subsequently, moved on to storm the Insubrian stronghold of Mediolanum is agreed to by both sources. Polybius, however, suggests that Scipio alone marched on Mediolanum. When he arrived, the Gauls kept safe behind the walls of the settlement. Scipio opted to return to Acerrae, but while marching his army was attacked in the rear and a number of Roman soldiers died. Scipio rallied his troops and won the day.[58] Plutarch, on the other hand suggests that Marcellus returned with his detachment to find Scipio besieging Mediolanum and the two consuls took the city together. Polybius, however, had already shown a willingness to understate Marcellus' achievements in the campaign of 222; he may have done so in this case as well. His close connection to the Cornelii Scipiones, whose ancestor was Marcellus' consular colleague in 222, may have prompted him to prefer evidence and a narrative that gave some credit to the consul Scipio that year, while still preserving a reasonably accurate narrative of the campaign.

In the end, though, however much of a role Scipio did play in ending the Gallic war, Marcellus wholly eclipsed his colleague, as the only one of the pair to earn extraordinary recognition for the achievement. When a Roman commander achieved a particularly grand military victory, the Roman assembly might award him a triumph. The triumph was a military parade in which the commander and his troops processed through the streets of Rome together with the spoils and captured soldiers of the enemy while the Roman populace watched and cheered. It was a sacred ceremony designed to highlight Roman military might and humiliate Roman enemies at the same time.[59] Marcellus was awarded a triumph for victory over the Gauls and for his slaying of Virdumarus; there was no such honour for Scipio.

Not content with this rare and grand military honour, however, Marcellus claimed that because the enemy he had slain and despoiled in single combat was the king and commander of the enemy army, his armour qualified as the rarest of all battle spoils, the so-called *spolia opima*. As a reward, Marcellus claimed the right to dedicate the spoils to Jupiter Feretrius, depositing them in the god's temple on the Capitoline Hill. That this claim was affirmed is shown in the official entry on the lists of triumphs, at least as they were restored by Augustus at the very end of the first century BC. Furthermore, Marcellus incorporated the spectacle of dedicating the spoils into the triumph he earned for his victory at Clastidium.

This deed was critical to Marcellus' reputation in life and in legend after his death.[60] In all of Roman history, only three figures were identified as commanders who had killed enemy leaders in battle and won these legendary spoils. The first was Romulus himself, the founder of Rome and the stuff of legend. The second was Aulus Cornelius Cossus, a fifth century commander, and hardly easier to substantiate than Romulus. Marcellus was for all practical purposes the only firmly historical example of a commander who had won these spoils, and it is likely that he was the historical inventor of the *spolia opima* as a special honour, a tradition that became firmly rooted in the psyche of the Roman political class. Whatever the impact of his deed on contemporary Romans, it evoked commentary in history, poetry, and epic for centuries to come. Indeed, within twenty years of the victory, the playwright Naevius crafted a play, *Clastidium*. It exists only in a few fragments today but was held at Rome and celebrated the grand achievements of the consul that day – it may have been the first example of a play at Rome celebrating the deeds of a contemporary Roman figure.[61] One of Marcellus' descendants, also named Marcus Claudius Marcellus, over 150 years later sought to capitalize on his family's grandeur by commemorating the dedication of the spoils on a coin series minted at Rome. The great epic poet of Rome, Virgil, even rendered the deed in verse when he composed the *Aeneid* at the beginning of the Empire.[62]

Given the great emphasis Virgil and other writers in the age of Augustus placed upon the tradition of Marcellus as the third and final recipient of the *spolia opima*, however, it is all too easy to assume anachronistically that the magnitude of his achievement was equally recognized and accepted in 222. This is highly unlikely. Not only did the others who had reputedly claimed these spoils live centuries before Marcellus, the historical records for these earlier victories were suspect at best, if any even existed beyond the tales handed down over the centuries. It is worth considering the possibility that very few Romans were even aware such an honour existed. In this light, when Marcellus claimed the right to be compared to the likes of Romulus and Cossus, he had either revived this tradition of the *spolia opima* or invented it as a special honour that had the patina of antiquity. Either way, the tradition that only three Romans ever won the *spolia opima* – the last Marcellus – became firmly rooted in the stories of the Roman political class. Marcellus seems to have had a penchant for reviving traditions such as the *spolia opima* at times and in ways that allowed him to earn rewards above and beyond those normally accessible to a Roman general, even beyond the rare distinction of a triumph. For, even if few had heard of the honour previously, Marcellus made sure his celebration clarified for all what the victory meant and how it advertised his valour.

Plutarch's claim that Marcellus' triumph was 'seldom equaled in its splendor and wealth and spoils and captives of gigantic size'[63] can be safely rejected as a common tendency by later writers to over-aggrandize the victory celebrations of Romans from the middle Republic. The spoils from the relatively poor Mediolanum can hardly have matched the riches displayed in later triumphs over Syracuse, Carthage, Macedonia, Pontus, Asia Minor, and Egypt, just to name a few places Romans would conquer. As for the size of the captives, the Romans had been fighting Gauls for centuries and would continue to do so for almost two centuries more; they were well-accustomed to their greater stature. Surely, though, Plutarch is correct in noting that Marcellus' triumph stood out from all others because it incorporated the dedication of the *spolia opima*:

> The most agreeable and the rarest spectacle of all was afforded when Marcellus himself carried to the god the armour of the barbarian king. He had cut the trunk of a slender oak, straight and tall, and fashioned it into the shape of a trophy; on this he bound and fastened the spoils, arranging and adjusting each piece in due order. When the procession began to move, he took the trophy himself and mounted the chariot, and thus a trophy-bearing figure more conspicuous and beautiful than any in his day passed in triumph through the city. The army followed, arrayed in the most beautiful armour, singing odes composed for the occasion, together with paeans of victory in praise of the god and their general. Thus advancing and entering the temple of Jupiter Feretrius, he set up and consecrated his offering.[64]

The triumph was a grand and rare honour, but the *spolia opima* essentially unique. Marcellus was making a claim to honours that simply could not be matched by his peers in the aristocracy; indeed, never again was the *spolia opima* claimed in the Republic.[65] In a group characterized by intense competitions for glory and the honours and offices that came with glory, this was a bold move by a member of a family that, while not insignificant, certainly did not rank among the most distinguished aristocratic clans. That he did so while his colleague received no distinction made the move that much bolder. This was the nature of political competition in the middle Republic. Those contending for the highest offices and honours at Rome tended to view politics as something of a zero-sum game, where many could be important but only a few could be truly outstanding.

Perhaps there were aristocrats that were not avidly concerned with expanding their prestige and influence, but Marcellus was certainly not one of those. The triumph and the claim to the *spolia opima* already put Marcellus in a unique position of honour among his contemporaries. It also helped Marcellus associate himself firmly with the cavalry and its traditions of honour in battle. As noted already, though, this claim had already been staked by Fabius. Why would Marcellus dedicate a victory temple to a god that already had a temple established by a very powerful and prestigious former consul from one of the oldest and most distinguished patrician families at Rome? Fabius' temple to Honos had been dedicated only eleven years before Clastidium, when Marcellus was in his mid-thirties; he can hardly have been unaware. No firm answer can be given, but it is difficult not to conclude that in dedicating a temple to Honos, Marcellus purposefully attempted to enhance his own reputation as a cavalry commander and warrior at the expense of Fabius. Certainly, the other unique element of his victory had been emphasized to his own benefit. It would be strange, therefore, to think that Marcellus naively chose these particular gods with their particularly advantageous symbolism.

Fabius need not, perhaps, have taken this dedication as an overtly hostile move by Marcellus, but it is hardly likely that he was pleased by the encroachment. At the least, it likely seemed brash to Fabius that a late-to-the-game consul from a less distinguished family would attempt to win honour from an association cultivated by one of the oldest families of the Republic. And while it cannot be decisively proven that Fabius pushed back, there is good reason, as we will see later, to suspect that he countered Marcellus by blocking his efforts to build the temple and possibly in other ways too.

There was a time when modern historians of Rome imposed structure and meaning on the fragmentary evidence for the middle Republic by using a model of factional politics. According to this model, relatively stable and long-term political blocs formed around politicians from the most powerful families. These faction leaders could, in various accounts, secure elections for their supporters, dictate the political stances of their subordinates, and control Roman politics in various ways. The key to identifying these blocs, proponents of the factional model asserted, was to look for patterns in office holding, especially trends where members of two families held the same offices in the same years. Marriages and other shreds of evidence about political allegiances were taken as evidence of deeper ties between families. While this interpretation of Roman politics was simplistic to a certain extent – there is little evidence, for example, that Roman aristocrats tended to form long-term, lasting alliances, and certainly not parties – it appealed because it offered the hope of constructing a clearer and deeper understanding of political behaviour from scanty evidence.[66]

The factional model of politics, however, led to a number of tendentious assumptions. Not least of these was the assertion once commonly made that Marcellus was a political client of Fabius Maximus. This meant Marcellus followed the lead of his patron and largely subordinated his political interests to those of Fabius. What the dedication of the temple to Honos and Virtus and the associated claims to ties with the cavalry make clear is that not only is that particular understanding of Marcellus' behaviour and politics in the period in general simplistic, so is any understanding that places politicians in simple camps without sufficient evidence. The relationship between Marcellus and Fabius, as it was for most politicians, was complicated. It is worth noting again: it is simply incredible that Marcellus was unaware that his dedication impinged upon a traditional prerogative of the Fabii, and it is equally incredible that Fabius accepted such an encroachment without fighting back: the arena of political competition was far too important to these aristocrats for such behaviour. But Marcellus must have felt it was worth the risk. It was his time to shine. How could he know that Rome would soon be locked in a life-and-death struggle against the Carthaginians and he and Fabius would be called upon to share positions of power?

Chapter 2

Hannibal and Campania

The First and Second Punic Wars, so-called from the Roman name for the Phoenician-descended Carthaginians, were decisive episodes in the growth of the Roman empire. By the time Rome had come to dominate central and southern Italy, the city-state of Carthage had created a maritime empire centred on its home city, in what is now Tunisia, and extending to Sicily and Sardinia. The island of Sicily occupied a critical strategic position in conflicts between the Romans and Carthaginians, the western tip of the island perhaps 150 miles away from the port of Carthage and the eastern tip within sight of the Italian peninsula. Controlling key ports on the island meant controlling travel and trade in the central Mediterranean – something desired both by Carthage and by the Greek polises scattered across the Mediterranean. This made Sicily a prized target for the naval and commercial empire of the Carthaginians and a site of settlement for Greeks in the eighth through sixth centuries. Major conflicts broke out between Carthage and the island polises beginning in the sixth century. The Greek polises of Sicily had some significant success in blunting Carthaginian advances in Sicily for centuries. By the late fourth century, however, the power of Carthage had waxed and that of the Sicilian polises waned to the point where Carthage had established firm control over the west and south of the island.[1] On the south-east side of the island, the city of Syracuse, founded by the Greek polis of Corinth in the eighth century, dominated.

Eventually, the Romans, who steadily expanded control over southern Italy in the fourth and third centuries, came to have an interest in eastern Sicily, and the first war between Rome and Carthage, from 264 to 241, was fought largely over control of the island. This war marked the first significant time, so far as we know, that Roman armies had operated outside Italy, and they did so ostensibly at the invitation of the Mamertines. This group of Italian mercenaries had brutally occupied the Sicilian city of Messana and controlled it for the past twenty years. Now they found themselves hard pressed in a war with King Hiero and the forces of Syracuse. The Mamertines sought aid from both of the greatest powers of the region, Carthage and Rome. Conflicts of interest soon erupted and the two powers had maneuvered into a great war.[2] The majority of the war took place in and off the waters of Sicily as the Romans fought the Syracusans, the

Carthaginians, and a variety of Greek city states on the island. King Hiero of Syracuse, an astute diplomat, quickly shifted from his initial alliance with the Carthaginians to the Romans when faced with the prospect of battling two consular armies. From then on, the Romans directed their energies against the Carthaginian forces. Though the Romans did launch a brief campaign against Carthage itself, landing an invasion force in Tunisia, they were ultimately unsuccessful in this effort, and the war shifted back to Sicily for another fifteen years or so. Finally, after more than twenty years of conflict, the Carthaginian land forces in Sicily, commanded by Hannibal's father, Hamilcar Barca, were ultimately forced to surrender when the Carthaginian fleet was destroyed at the naval battle off the Aegates islands and Hamilcar's supply lines were severed. Among the other terms of this surrender, Carthage was forced to remove all its forces from Sicily, yield the island, and pay a considerable sum of reparations to the Romans.[3] Eventually, perhaps by 227, it became regular practice for a Roman praetor to govern western and northern Sicily; eastern Sicily was essentially under the administration of Hiero of Syracuse, who had become a trusted ally of the Romans. In addition to the strategic importance of the island, Sicily also seems to have provided Romans with grain from its fields, so important for feeding the Roman army and the growing population of the city.[4]

The First Punic war had not settled matters between the Romans and Carthaginians. Carthage had lost control of Sicily, Sardinia, and Corsica to the Romans but subsequently acquired an empire in the Iberian Peninsula. Hamilcar, the father of Hannibal and the commander who conducted the final surrender in Sicily, spearheaded the Carthaginian efforts in Spain. When he died in 226, control of Carthaginian operations in Spain passed to his son-in-law, Hasdrubal. Finally, in 221, Hannibal took the reins of command. Later Romans for whom Hannibal was the ultimate terror – an excellent bogeyman to frighten recalcitrant children – had no doubt that the Carthaginian had dreamed of avenging his humiliated father since childhood. Livy states that the boy swore an oath to his father to do so as soon as he was able.[5] Whether this was true – and it certainly seems possible that the father hoped his son would avenge his defeat – it is only reasonable to suppose Hannibal hoped to exact some measure of vengeance from Rome.[6]

The technicalities that started the war are a bit complicated and not completely understood. Suffice to say, when Hasdrubal had succeeded Hamilcar, the Romans sent envoys to make a treaty with the Carthaginian. This designated the River Ebro as the northernmost limit to Carthaginian expansion in Spain. It may well have been understood that the Romans would, in turn, not attempt to influence Spain south of that border. If this was the understanding, however, it is difficult to reconcile with the fact that the Republic had already forged an alliance with the city of Saguntum, south of the Ebro, several years prior to 226. Regardless of who had the more easily justified view of the conflict, Hannibal took advantage of an opportunity to provoke the Romans by besieging the city of Saguntum. The Saguntines, in turn, sent messengers to their Roman allies asking for aid against the Carthaginian army. When the request for assistance reached the city, the senate apparently debated the matter for some time. Small wonder; any effort to stop Hannibal's attack might well lead to another war, one that would be costly and require the Romans to send soldiers to Spain, farther away than they ever had before. Rather than jump immediately into a major war, the senate decided to deliver an ultimatum to Carthage first.[7]

Hannibal, however, seemed to have been planning an invasion of Italy already, for he finished besieging Saguntum, sent emissaries to the Gauls, and began his long trek from Spain to Italy, apparently without any news that an ultimatum had been delivered to Carthage. This should cause no surprise, however, considering how slowly messages traveled in the age of sail, horse, and foot. His army marched along the coast of Spain and France, eventually reaching the River Rhone by September of 218. In the meantime, the Romans prepared to send an army to Spain, only to find, much to their surprise, that Hannibal was no longer there. The consul Publius Scipio had harboured his army at the mouth of the Rhone at the same time Hannibal's force was farther up the same river. Roman cavalry engaged the Carthaginian cavalry successfully, but Hannibal was able to move on. At this point, Publius Scipio opted to send his brother and military legate Gnaeus ahead to Spain with the legions, while he returned to northern Italy to prepare a defence against Hannibal.[8]

What was Hannibal's plan? His strategy has been analyzed by historians as best as can be, considering he left no writings and no eyewitness accounts of his actions. Certainly, he would have anticipated the Roman invasion of Spain should war break out. He could have opted to prepare to meet the Romans in Spain. As some historians have noted, however, the Romans had proven capable of sustaining and replacing staggering military losses in their first war against Carthage over Sicily. No doubt, Hannibal was fully aware of this. Based on what he did do, it seems his goal was different: to shatter the core of Roman political and military power. That core was the Roman alliance system.[9]

The Roman alliance system was strong and flexible, based upon a series of bilateral treaties between Rome and other Italian states. Once a state became part of the Roman alliance, its sole treaty was with Rome, keeping Rome at the centre of the whole system. One of the fundamental treaty relationships was that which granted Latin status to an ally. After the difficult struggle known as the Latin War, the Romans imposed a settlement in 338 on the defeated Latin states. Essentially, these states were given various degrees of citizenship with or without the right to vote. This meant, among other things, that each state was obligated to provide Rome with soldiers and to follow Rome's lead in foreign policy. Members of these states with so-called 'Latin Rights' could also intermarry and trade with Romans and had the right to move to the city of

Rome itself and exercise full citizen voting rights. Throughout the Republic, Latin rights were given to various states, most often to those that were culturally Latin, including colonies of Roman and Latin citizens that were founded during the Republic.[10]

The second form of treaty relationship existed between Rome and its allies, the *socii*. The exact terms of treaties between Rome and each *socius* must have varied. The general terms are believed to be based upon those established in the *Foedus Cassianum*, a treaty crafted in 495 and quoted by the first century historian Dionysius of Halicarnassus:

> Let there be peace among the Romans and all the Latin cities as long as the heavens and the earth shall remain where they are. Let them neither make war upon one another themselves nor bring in foreign enemies nor grant a safe passage to those who shall make war upon either. Let them assist one another when warred upon, with all their forces, and let each have an equal share of the spoils and booty taken in their common wars. Let suits relating to private contracts be determined within ten days, and in the nation where the contract was made. And let it not be permitted to add anything to, or take anything away from these treaties except by consent both of the Romans and of all the Latins.[11]

The core, then, was a military alliance complete with the provision that spoils of war be shared among Roman and allied soldiers.[12] Over the century before Hannibal's invasion, this alliance had proved strong enough to secure Roman control over Italy, then allow Rome to wage war successfully against Carthage. This was the alliance system that Hannibal seems to have targeted.

By the end of 218, Hannibal began his legendary trek across the Alps and into Italy. The march was costly; by the end, his large army was reduced to half its size, perhaps 20,000 African and Spanish infantry, and 6,000 cavalry. Marching south, Hannibal encountered the legionary forces in north Italy now commanded by Publius Scipio, who had made his way there quickly from the Rhone. At the Ticinus, a river which branches north from the western end of the River Po, Roman and Carthaginian forces had their first battle, limited almost entirely to cavalry. Hannibal deployed his heavier cavalry in the centre of his formation with the swifter Numidian light cavalry on the flanks.[13]

Scipio, on the other hand, deployed Gallic cavalry in his font line, with the Romano-Italian cavalry in support. He also followed the common Roman tactic of deploying light infantry along with the cavalry. Unaided, light infantry would generally fare poorly against cavalry. Unlike close-order heavy infantry soldiers, who held the psychological advantage against cavalry so long as they stood their ground, light infantry tended to fight in an open order. While this open formation allowed light infantry to dodge missile weapons – arrows, sling bullets, javelins, etc. – more easily, it also made them quite vulnerable to cavalry. It took an unusually determined individual to stand and receive charging. However, light infantry provided an excellent complement to cavalry, particularly against enemy cavalry. In this role, the light infantry served as a quick-moving defensive line that anchored the charges and wheels of their mounted comrades, providing protection. They could also form around downed troopers and provide support in other ways. If the Roman cavalry pinned its opponents into a stationary battle, something the Roman cavalry had a penchant for, the light infantry could go on the offensive, working their way into the battle, dodging between the horses, and causing harm to the enemy.[14]

When the two forces engaged, the Carthaginian horses swiftly drove the Roman light infantry back, forcing them to retreat through the gaps between the cavalry squads. Then the cavalry forces engaged front-to-front. For a time, the Roman forces held their own, but the Numidian cavalry on the wings ultimately flanked the Romans and launched a devastating attack on the Roman rear line. The Romans fled from the battle and Scipio shifted his army into a defensive posture, camped in a strong position on high ground.[15] Hannibal clearly did not wish to assault the Roman position. At the same time, the Carthaginian army was able to roam the countryside freely, while the Roman forces were dug in. Hannibal used this freedom to his advantage, marching to Clastidium and persuading the Italian commander there to surrender the Roman grain depot.[16] Provisions like these were both critical and in short supply for Hannibal's army throughout its stay in Italy, so the acquisition of the Clastidium granaries was a significant victory.

Prior to this battle, the Senate had received word that Hannibal was in Italy. The consul Sempronius Longus was recalled from Sicily where he had been preparing to invade Africa. By the time Sempronius reached Rome, reports had reached the city of the defeat at the Ticinus, and the consul was sent to reinforce Scipio's army. When he arrived, he found Scipio's army still safely ensconced in its defensive fortifications on high ground and Hannibal's camp several miles distant. Once the two Roman armies combined, an expeditionary force of light infantry and cavalry patrolled the countryside, looking to hamper Carthaginian movements. One day, perhaps 4 December, the Roman forces engaged in a significant skirmish, checking the Gallic and Numidian cavalry forces. Carthaginian reinforcements arrived to tip the balance. Sempronius opted to commit all of his light infantry and cavalry to the engagement. Hannibal refused to escalate further, or at least did not do so, and the Roman forces got the better of their opponents that day.[17]

The next day, Hannibal's Numidian cavalry lured the Romans out of their camp before they had eaten their breakfasts. Sempronius, buoyed by his success the day before, ordered his cavalry to take the lead and the rest of the army to follow. In their pursuit of the Numidians and the main Carthaginian army, they crossed the River Trebia, the waters high from heavy rains and, since it was in the winter, no doubt quite cold. Cold and wet, hungry and exhausted, the Romans engaged Hannibal's forces. Hannibal's cavalry drove the Roman cavalry off and his infantry attacked the exposed Roman flanks. When a Carthaginian reserve force emerged from its hiding place in a shallow stream bed and attacked the Roman rear, the Roman infantry crumbled and routed.[18] Ten thousand legionaries made their way to safety. The fate of the rest of the army, which potentially numbered between 30,000 and 40,000 soldiers, is unclear.[19]

The next year (217), the senate determined to face Hannibal in the field again and sent the consuls, Gaius Flaminius and Marcus Servilius Geminus, with full consular legions to engage Hannibal. The battle of Lake Trasimene was the result, where the Roman infantry were surprised and trapped on the lakeside, forced to choose between a death by iron or water. Reeling from two major defeats in half a year, the Romans named Fabius Maximus Verrucosus dictator. Fabius adopted a strategy of attrition, shadowing Hannibal's army and hampering its movements, while avoiding pitched battles. These tactics gave the Romans time to regroup in 217.[20]

It is in the context of the elections for 216, held presumably in the autumn of 217, that Marcellus' name surfaces in Livy. After noting the consuls Marcus Terentius Varro and Lucius Aemilius Paullus and the praetors charged with judging suits between citizens and foreigners, Livy reports that two additional praetors were elected, Lucius Postumius Albinus and Marcellus. The former was assigned a military command in Gaul, while Marcellus was charged with command in Sicily – later in Livy's account it appears this included command of a fleet. Livy went on to note that Marcellus, along with most of the other candidates, was elected in absentia.[21] In other words, Marcellus was not present at Rome as a candidate for election. This raises a number of questions that, unfortunately, cannot be answered with any certainty.

First of all, where exactly was Marcellus during the elections? The most reasonable implication of noting that a candidate was elected in absentia is that he was away on official business, which at that point would likely have meant a military command. But if Marcellus held any magistracy in 217, there is certainly no mention of it in any source. It is more likely that he was on some business as a member of the senate, perhaps even as a propraetor or some such rank, though what exactly that business might have been remains hidden, and there is no evidence to support such a position. Second, why was Sicily a land and naval province? The strategic importance of Sicily at the time is unquestionable, but, so far as our sources suggest, the only theatres of war were Italy and Spain. Perhaps the Roman senate wanted to be ready to attack Africa, as it did in the first war, should it appear advantageous, but it is difficult to imagine that the senate anticipated expanding Roman military operations in this way after the losses at Trebia and Trasimene. More likely, senators reasoned that the Carthaginians might invade Sicily and wanted to bolster the Roman province. Finally, did Marcellus actually submit his name for election to the praetorship or was he elected without announcing any desire for the office on his part? Unfortunately, there is no way to know and both options are plausible.

What is clear, however, from the elections for 216 is that it cannot be assumed, however reasonable it seems, that the Romans elected their consuls even during times of war solely because of their perceived military experience and success. While Lucius Aemilius Paullus had been consul in 219 and earned a triumph against the Illyrians on the Balkan side of the Adriatic, similar things could be said about other men of consular rank, including Marcellus. Marcus Terentius Varro, however, had no such distinction, coming from a new family to politics and having only a praetorship before this office. When the ranks of potential candidates included men such as Fabius Maximus and Marcellus, there were far more illustrious choices than Paulus and Varro if voters were motivated solely by the military records of their candidates.

The elections for 216 may have brought hope for a change in the trend of defeats. As it happened, there was still worse to come for the Roman armies – the disastrous defeat at Cannae. Hannibal's infantry in that battle numbered perhaps 40,000 – he had supplemented his forces with Gallic allies. The exact size of the Roman army was debated even in the ancient world. Polybius explicitly states the Romans had eight legions of 5,000 citizen soldiers each at Cannae and that these troops combined with the allied infantry brought the Roman force up to 80,000 infantry. Livy, on the other hand, notes two conflicting traditions, the one recorded by Polybius and a rival account that said the total number of Roman and allied infantry amounted to somewhere between 50,000 and 55,000. Both Polybius and Livy agree that there were about 10,000 Spanish, Gallic, and Numidian cavalry in Hannibal's army; the Roman cavalry forces were presumably somewhere between 4,000 and 8,000, depending on how many legions one supposes the Romans fielded and whether each had the normal sized cavalry contingent.[22]

On the day of battle, the citizen cavalry deployed on the right wing next to the river, the Italian allied cavalry deployed on the left wing, and the Roman infantry occupied the centre. The consul deployed the maniples of the Roman legions, according to Polybius, so that they were much deeper than wide and closer to each other than normal. While this could theoretically give higher morale and greater penetrating power to the columns, the practical result that day was that the infantry had far less room to maneuver and engage in their typical function of rotating maniples in and out of combat. In front of the entire force, Varro positioned the *velites*.[23]

The Spanish and Gallic cavalry deployed opposite the citizen cavalry, while the Numidian cavalry faced the Italian allies. Because the Spanish and Gallic contingents numbered significantly more than 4,000, they outnumbered the citizen troopers on the right flank by at least 2:1 and perhaps by considerably more. The key to the cavalry battle at Cannae was the restricted space in which the Roman cavalry on the right wing operated. On their left stood the heavy infantry, packed in an unusually close and deep formation. On their right was the river, and they deployed close to it. Their primary task was to guard the flank of their army rather than to assault the enemy flank. Hannibal's significantly larger cavalry force also probably forced the cavalry along the river to focus on defence. The right wing was important enough for the consul Aemilius to command it.[24]

As it happened, Hannibal's Spanish and Gallic cavalry drove the Roman horsemen back, cutting them down as they went. Once the cavalry along the river were decimated, Hannibal's troopers rode past the right flank of the Roman infantry, wheeled across their rear, and attacked the Italian allied cavalry, already engaged with the Numidians. The allied cavalry units scattered under the dual attack. Finally, the Spanish and Gallic horses turned his forces once more and assaulted the rear ranks of the Roman infantry. While these cavalry engagements occurred, the Roman infantry drove back the centre of the Carthaginian line, only to find itself enveloped by the wings of the Carthaginian infantry. Attacked on the flanks by infantry, the rear by cavalry, and compressed into a tighter space than normal anyway, the demoralized Roman infantry were hemmed in, then slaughtered.[25] It was a disastrous defeat. The commander Varro survived, but the consul Aemilius Paullus died leading the Roman cavalry on the right flank. The exact number of Romans slain that day is unclear, but a good guess is somewhere in the range of 40,000 – a horrific figure even by modern standards.[26] The damage to the political classes was perhaps even more severe when it came to the percentage of casualties. According to Livy, those among the dead included both the quaestors attached to the consuls, Lucius Atilius and Lucius Furius Bibulcus, twenty-nine military tribunes, several ex-consuls, ex-praetors, and ex-aediles (amongst them Gnaeus Servilius Geminus and Marcus Minucius, who was Master of the Horse the previous year and, some years before that, consul), and in addition to these, eighty men who had either been senators or filled offices qualifying them for election to the senate and who had volunteered for service with the legions.[27] This amounted to roughly a third of those who were or would have been senators within the next few years slain in one day.

Meanwhile, Marcellus was in command of the fleet at Ostia, the main port of Rome, and played a critical role managing the crisis that faced the Republic for the remnant of the campaign season. When news reached him about Cannae, Marcellus sent 1,500 soldiers from his command to help garrison Rome. Meanwhile, the senate hurriedly deliberated on the proper course of action under such dire circumstances. On the coast, the remnants of the Roman army that had fought at Cannae slowly gathered at the Apulian town of Canusium, approximately ten miles inland from Cannae.[28]

The senate instructed Marcellus to join the army at Canusium and relieve the consul Varro so that the latter could return to Rome and report. Accordingly, Marcellus sent ahead a legion south-east to Teanum Sidicinum in Campania. This town was located along the Appian Way, one of the most important Roman roads running from Campania into Samnium and then into central Apulia. Then he made the necessary arrangements to transfer command of the fleet to Publius Furius. In a few days, the transfer was complete and Marcellus hurried with a force to Canusium, perhaps collecting the legion at Teanum along the way.[29]

Meanwhile, fresh from their victory at Cannae, Hannibal and his troops first marched to Samnium, establishing a base at Compsa in the southern part of the region and less than 20 miles from where the Appian Way passed. He left his lieutenant Mago there with a portion of the army and instructions to bring the towns of the region over to the Carthaginian cause. Then Hannibal moved to Campania. This fertile coastal plain lay directly to the south-east of Latium and was a critical agricultural centre dominated by the powerful city of Capua. Capua remained loyal to Rome until the defeat at Cannae; soon after this the Capuan senate decided to ally itself with Hannibal.[30] Allying with Capua was a critical step for Hannibal to secure the loyalty of Campania, and its defection weakened Rome. Hannibal still needed, apparently, an acceptable port in western Italy through which he could receive supplies and soldiers from Spain, Sicily, and Carthage itself. Accordingly, Hannibal moved with his army to the Campanian port of Neapolis, near Capua, in the hopes of winning over the city.[31] The leaders of the city refused to ally with Hannibal, however, and rather than bog his army down in a siege of the formidably defended city, Hannibal shifted his sights to the important inland city of Nola. Nola was one of the main urban centers in Campania, less significant than Capua and Neapolis, but critical to any strategy for controlling the region. The city was well fortified and approximately twenty miles from Capua, roughly in the center of Campania, perhaps offering slightly better access to Neapolis. There seems to have been considerable conflict within the city concerning the approaching Hannibal. The leaders of Nola wished to remain loyal to Rome, according to Livy, while the general populace wished to side with Hannibal.[32]

As Hannibal began operations in Campania, we find Marcellus stationed with his army at Casilinum, a town several miles north of Capua. This fortified settlement guarded the northern reaches of the Appian Way and the Latin Way, the two roads that ran straight from Campania to Rome itself.[33] Marcellus must have positioned his forces there to hold the route to Rome once he determined that Hannibal had moved westwards from Cannae, first to Samnium, then Campania. The Nolan senate sent messages to Marcellus at Casilinum airing their concerns that the city walls would be betrayed to Hannibal in an act of treachery and asking him to come to Nola and reinforce the Roman loyalists.[34] Nola, as Marcellus must surely have calculated, was too important to lose to

Hannibal, since it was one of the main Campanian settlements, a fortified town at that, and one within striking distance of the road to Samnium.

Marcellus responded that he would come to the city's defence. A direct march to Nola from Casilinum, however, was barred by the now hostile Capua, which had a strong cavalry force that could pose considerable difficulties for a Roman army on the march. Instead of the more direct route, Marcellus circumvented Capua by marching east/north-east along the River Volturnus to Caiatia. Then he crossed the river, and passed south-east, keeping Mount Tifata as a buffer between his army and Capua. The army continued this way into the hill country north of Suessula and, finally, arrived at Nola.[35] When the Roman army approached, however, Hannibal withdrew west to the vicinity of Neapolis to try his hand again at negotiating with the Neapolitans.

A quick study of a map of Campania suggests that Hannibal was essentially maneuvering in a very small territory around Marcellus – the two armies were likely never more than twenty miles apart at any moment and closer than that most of the time. His goal was to gain an advantage in the remaining key settlements of Campania: Neapolis, Nola, and Nuceria. He may well have concluded that a pitched battle over Nola was an unnecessary expense at the moment when other important targets existed. Neapolis continued to hold firm against Hannibal, however, and his army soon moved on to Nuceria. Bounded on the south by hills, Nuceria was the southernmost major settlement of Campania. Hannibal did not succeed in winning the loyalty of Nuceria and ultimately destroyed the settlement through what must have been a quick siege.[36]

Marcellus, on the other hand, remained at Nola. Perhaps he reasoned that attempting to follow Hannibal around would simply allow the latter to control the pace and timing of another battle. He may also have been busy strengthening the resolve of the Nolan senate and rooting out those inclined to surrender the city to Hannibal. With the disaster at Cannae, the shifting allegiances of so many key southern cities, and Campania wavering with the defection of Capua, Marcellus must have judged that securing Nola was critical to maintaining Roman influence in Campania, particularly since Neapolis, another critical location, persisted in rebuffing Hannibal. It seems incredible to think he would not have received word about Nuceria, but whether he was unwilling or unable to come to the town's aid is a mystery.

Livy and Plutarch suggest that at this point a distinguished young Campanian cavalryman, Lucius Bantius, was one of the focal points for disaffected Nolans wishing to join Hannibal. This Bantius had earned a reputation among the allied cavalry as an outstanding rider and combatant. The disaster at Cannae, however, moved Bantius to question the Roman cause. He had apparently fought with great distinction at Cannae, slaying a number of opponents. The weight of the enemy's numbers eventually overwhelmed him, and he was left for dead on the battlefield.[37] Found among the slain by the victorious Carthaginians, the young cavalry trooper was brought to Hannibal, who had his injuries nursed then sent him home to Nola with gifts.[38] Upon arriving at Nola, Bantius was among the leaders who advocated joining Hannibal. Though historians must be cautious when such an anecdote crops up in the ancient sources, this particular episode is not farfetched. A pillar of Hannibal's Italian strategy was to dissolve the bonds of the Roman alliance system by gaining the support of the Italian peoples. If Hannibal came across a young man like Bantius who was not only a member of the Italian municipal elite – all allied cavalry were – but from an important city in Campania, he would assuredly have recognized the potential to form an advantageous relationship with the man.

While at Nola, Marcellus learned of Bantius' political leanings through personal observation or report and opted to address the situation directly. He summoned Bantius to a meeting and discussed his concerns. Livy and Plutarch both offer direct quotations of the words Marcellus offered Bantius; at best these might reflect the gist of the conversation. Marcellus praised Bantius for his service at Cannae and rewarded him with a large sum of silver coins and a warhorse.[39] Livy adds that Marcellus encouraged Bantius to serve with him personally in the future. The results of these and any other encouragements were that Bantius came to support wholeheartedly the Roman cause. It is hazardous at best to try to unearth the character of Marcellus from an event of this sort, but it certainly is plausible that one who had carved out a reputation for audacity and valour in cavalry battles would have found Bantius to be a kindred spirit of sorts.

With Nuceria destroyed, Hannibal decided the time was right to make an attempt on Nola.[40] He returned to the vicinity of the town and camped near the Roman army, itself camped outside the city walls. According to Livy, though each army's foragers and light infantry scouts engaged in sporadic skirmishes, neither commander would commit to a pitched battle. Hannibal, for his part, had apparently been negotiating covertly at night with disaffected Nolans for the surrender of the city.[41] For the moment, waiting in the hope of gaining the city through treachery was the more sound strategy, particularly now that the alliance with Capua – not to mention most of southern Italy – must have helped alleviate Hannibal's daily supply problems somewhat. Hannibal had turned waiting patiently for his enemies to make mistakes into an art form, and it would have made little sense to commit to battle precipitously.

Marcellus, for his part, probably had little strategic reason to initiate a battle with Hannibal. The latter had destroyed three Roman armies; indeed, the survivors from the most recent catastrophe at Cannae formed a significant portion of Marcellus' army at Nola. Not that Hannibal's reputation would have been sufficient to stop Marcellus; he clearly liked to play against the odds. But he had never, so far as we know, seen the Carthaginian's army in battle, nor had he actually witnessed Hannibal's tactics. It was one thing to be courageous and quite another to be foolhardy. In the context of any larger strategy, forcing a battle in the current circumstances was likely not a sound strategy. At that particular moment, the city of Rome was recovering from Cannae; the consul Varro had returned to the city to give his report; and the senate was deliberating how to rally to the grave challenge Hannibal posed. Many of the most important Greek cities of south Italy had transferred their allegiances to Hannibal. Now the powerful city of Capua had forged an alliance with the Carthaginian. With this arrangement, the allegiance of the entire region of Campania, which it is worth noting again was just south of Latium, was hanging by a thread. Neapolis had remained loyal to the Roman cause, but a Roman failure at Nola could cause the Neapolitans to have a change of heart.[42] Securing Nola, maintaining the Roman position in Campania, and providing the senate with time to recover and plan were paramount among the strategic goals Marcellus entertained, or certainly should have been. None of these goals was served by committing to a pitched battle hastily. And so, the two armies and their commanders apparently waited for days. When Marcellus received word of the nocturnal meetings between Carthaginians and Nolan conspirators, however, he withdrew his army into the walls of Nola and planned to test Hannibal in battle.[43] Marcellus must have judged the benefits of waiting were now outweighed by the disadvantage of giving the Nolan conspirators time to solidify their plans against the Roman army.

Livy and Plutarch report Marcellus' battle plan as follows. The walls of Nola had three gates facing the Carthaginian camp and Marcellus intended to use these gates to launch an attack. The obvious danger, however, was that the Nolan conspirators would close the city gates to the Roman army once it engaged Hannibal, leaving the army trapped between two hostile forces. To guard against any betrayal within the city, the baggage train and camp servants were left within the city walls along with the wounded and a reserve force of soldiers. This group would ensure that the city walls remained in Roman hands while the army engaged in battle. To guard further against any attempt to close the gates behind the Roman army, Marcellus issued an order that none of the Nolans were to come near the walls or gates of the city.[44]

Then Marcellus stationed his best legionaries at the center gate along with the Roman citizen cavalry, while the allied cavalry, light infantry, and newest recruits in the army were stationed at the gates on either side.[45] Either these preparations took some time or Marcellus paused after making arrangements for a few days because Hannibal was caught off-guard by several days of Roman inactivity. Livy and Plutarch suggest he assumed that the Romans had surrendered the field to him completely and gave the orders to bring up siege equipment.[46] At this point when a portion of the Carthaginian army was occupied elsewhere making siege preparations, Marcellus gave the orders to attack. Complete with blasts of the trumpets and shouts intended to startle the enemy, Marcellus ordered the heavy infantry, supported by the cavalry, to close quickly with the Carthaginian forces.[47]

The element of surprise was with the Romans. In such battles it was not necessary that the enemy be caught completely unawares to gain an advantage; introducing any uncertainty and fear into the minds of the enemy combatants could turn the tide. Mental uncertainty translated into less effective fighting, sometimes even chaos, and the collapse of enemy units. The loud initial noises, the continued shouts of the baggage train, and the rush of the Roman army at an unexpected moment successfully disrupted the Carthaginian center. Once the center was clearly thrown into some confusion, Marcellus' lieutenants manning the side gates issued forth with cavalry and light infantry to attack the flanks of the Carthaginian force.[48] Marcellus had executed a well-planned surprise attack designed to disrupt, demoralize, and drive off the enemy. Still, the battle was far more a moral victory than a decisive blow of any sort. Even Livy, who had no experience of military affairs and was not above trusting inflated casualty reports, was reluctant to believe that so many as 2,800 Carthaginians died and only 500 Romans. Plutarch, on the other hand, gave the larger and more even number of 5,000 Carthaginian dead.[49]

Regardless of the actual casualties inflicted, the attack was quite successful. It drove off the Carthaginian army, secured Nola, and demonstrated that there was a Roman field army in Campania that would fight, and could win. Indeed, this victory became a core part of Marcellus' historical reputation. The distinction was so commonplace that 170 years later Cicero compared his spirits raised by a letter from a friend to the Roman people first picking themselves up after Cannae because of Marcellus' victory at Nola.[50] Livy, for his part, waxed poetically a generation later when he said, 'I rather think that the greatest thing in that war was accomplished that day. For not to be defeated by Hannibal was a more difficult thing than it was later to defeat him,' a sentiment uttered later by Valerius Maximus and Plutarch.[51] An exaggeration, to be sure, but it must have been a significant bolster to Roman morale that Marcellus was the first Roman commander to have any success against Hannibal in battle. The Carthaginian was not invincible.

Repulsed at Nola, without hope of easily acquiring the city, and with the constant pressure to supply and motivate his army, Hannibal must have felt he could not afford to spend more time in his current camp. Consequently, his army moved to nearby Acerrae.[52] This town lay between Capua and Nola and was less than ten miles from Neapolis, that port city still arguably a primary objective for the Campanian campaign. The men of Acerrae, and though Livy does not say, presumably the women and children, abandoned the town as Hannibal made preparations to besiege it. Emptied of any resistance, the Carthaginians plundered the city and set it afire.[53]

Meanwhile, now that the danger from the Carthaginian army was momentarily averted, Marcellus turned his attention to the conspirators in Nola. He set up headquarters in the town forum and launched an inquiry into the identities of the Nolans who had met with the Carthaginians. More than seventy, Livy records, were convicted of treason.[54] In a time of war outside the city of Rome, however, conviction hardly implies anything like a formal trial. Though Marcellus may have wanted to conduct a fair investigation so as to secure the loyalty of Nola further, as the supreme Roman military commander there, he technically needed only to satisfy himself that these seventy-plus Nolans were guilty. Once satisfied, the guilty were beheaded and their property forfeited to the Romans – such was the power of consular *imperium* in action.

With that grim business concluded and Nola secured for the future, Marcellus withdrew his forces to a camp north of Suessula. Perhaps this was in response to news of Hannibal at Acerrae, though the precise chronology is not clear. Even if not, the camp was well located. Midway and within a good half day's march of both Capua and Nola, the camp allowed Marcellus to pressure the former and provide support for the latter. From there, he could also guard the leg of the Appian Way that extended from Campania into nearby Beneventum, an important Roman colony in Samnium. Occupying this position allowed Marcellus to restrict Hannibal's movements both by containing him in Campania and putting pressure on his newly acquired and important Capuan allies; Roman cavalry could patrol the countryside and attack foragers while the full army could mobilize if needed for a larger threat. Marcellus' choice of camp was advantageous enough that it was maintained for years later, and dubbed the *castra Claudiana* (or 'Claudian Camp') after its founder.[55]

It appears that encamping above Suessula did put pressure on Hannibal. After the sack of Acerrae, Hannibal was concerned that the Capuans might return to the Roman fold with a Roman army encamped so near, and so marched his forces north to Casilinum, only a few miles distant from Capua, to make sure that Capua kept to its newly struck alliance.[56] Casilinum was held by a small Roman garrison and guarded, as noted earlier, two major roads to Rome. The fact that Hannibal did not march on Rome after Cannae suggests that attacking the city, which most historians agree would have been futile, was not part of his strategy. Nevertheless, taking Casilinum would certainly keep his options open and kept the danger of an attack on Rome – however remote – present in the mind of Marcellus and other commanders. Obfuscation was a critical strategic tool in an ancient commander's kit, and the threat of an attack could serve to pin an enemy commander and force down just as effectively as an actual attack.

Casilinum was garrisoned by a force of perhaps 1,000 soldiers, mostly from the Latin towns of Praeneste and Perusia.[57] Hannibal dispatched a small detachment ahead of his army to negotiate for the surrender of the city and the installment of a Carthaginian garrison. The detachment was driven off by the Casilinum garrison, however, and Hannibal soon arrived with his main force, intending to storm the city.[58] The garrison successfully blunted the Carthaginian attack, however, and Hannibal shifted to siege tactics, attempting to mine the city walls.

What an impressive force those Latin soldiers must have been; no more than 1,000 strong, they held off the great Hannibal and his army. They headed off the Carthaginian mines with their own countermines and stalled the enemy attempts to undermine the walls.

Thwarted for the time being and with winter approaching, Hannibal left a small force in a reinforced camp and took the bulk of his army to Capua to spend the winter months.[59] Marcellus' army, on the other hand, wintered at the *castra Claudiana* above Suessula. Finally, sometime in the autumn or winter of 216, the army that had been hastily assembled at Rome after Cannae – two city legions, composed partly of freed slaves and pardoned murderers – encamped near Casilinum.[60] This force of some 25,000 was under the command of the dictator Marcus Junius Pera and his second-in-command – the position Romans titled 'master of cavalry' – Tiberius Sempronius Gracchus. Gracchus was one of the curule aediles for 216[61] before Pera selected him to be master of horse. Livy notes that these soldiers were levied in the aftermath of Cannae but makes no reference to their destination or activities until the spring of 215, at which point he notes that Gracchus waited in camp with the army, commanded to undertake no action, while the dictator was fulfilling important religious obligations at Rome.[62] Perhaps this simply reflects that it took some time after Cannae to levy troops, form legions, and march to Casilinum, since presumably they could have helped relieve Casilinum if they had arrived earlier. Most likely, this hastily levied force consisting largely of soldiers drawn, from a Roman perspective, from the dregs of society, was intended to remain fixed near Casilinum to guard the roads to Rome while the senate undertook the required administrative recovery after Cannae. It may have been considered far too chancy at this critical stage in the war to commit untrusted troops to battle unnecessarily.

Winter arrived, major military operations ceased with the exception of the blockade at Casilinum, and at Rome a number of loose ends had to be tied. Among the most important of these was the replenishment of the senate. It had been five years since the senate roll had been updated and many had died in the past few years, some from old age, but certainly many more in the battles against Hannibal.[63] A second dictator – pretty much unheard of to Romans – was appointed solely for the purpose of revising the lists of senators.[64] Ordinarily, vacancies in the senate, historians think, were filled by those who had held public office, but in 216 there were far too many vacancies to be filled in this way. Accordingly, the dictator, M. Fabius Buteo, went beyond this standard approach to include Romans who had not held office but who, in Livy's words, 'had spoils of the enemy affixed to their houses or had received the civic wreath'[65] the latter a reward for saving a citizen in battle.

According to Livy, it was after the senate rolls had been revised that the senate instructed Marcellus, the dictator Pera, and his master of horse Gracchus to leave their forces under subordinates and report to the senate at Rome. The three complied, and following their reports, Pera initiated the elections for magistrates for the following year (215).[66] Lucius Postumius Albinus, the praetor who had spent the year in Gaul, was elected consul in absentia and his colleague was Pera's master of horse, Gracchus. The praetors elected for the year were Marcus Valerius Laevinus, Appius Claudius Pulcher, Quintus Mucius Scaevola, and Quintus Fulvius Flaccus, this last one for the second time.[67]

These names in and of themselves should not register with most readers, but the omission of Marcellus' name from among them is surprising until one recalls that the Roman electorate did not limit itself to electing only those with the best military records. In the elections for 216, however, Marcellus had been one of a number of well-qualified candidates that were passed over. His omission from the elections for 215 underscores, however, that even in times of great military need, elections followed the normal lines, whereby there was far more to winning office than a successful record as a commander. Here was the only commander who had won any sort of victory against Hannibal, a man who had kept Campania secure and discharged his duties for the year admirably, to say the least. These were all achievements of the last few months before the elections, yet he was not elected to office.

The best explanation, as hollow as it might seem, is that elections were simply unpredictable affairs then as they are now. The voters simply preferred Gracchus and Albinus. One might have thought that those with the best military records were most likely to win high office. The relationship between a reputation for *virtus*, a martial quality, a victorious military record and election to high office seems commonsensical; in reality, any such connection is very murky to us, and no doubt was to the Romans themselves. Certainly a reputation for *virtus*, that abstract quality of Roman manliness, could qualify one to be selected as a senator; Buteo demonstrated this in 216 when he selected new senators from among those common citizens who had earned honours in battle. Surely, all else being equal, such a reputation might help one win election. Nevertheless, throughout the Republic, Roman voters often did not prefer the candidate with the superior military record. What's more, they seem to have had a marked indifference to holding an aristocrat's military failures against them in any future bids for high office,[68] Instead tending to explain defeat in terms of angry gods and insufficiently virtuous soldiers. It is worth remembering in this context that Marcellus was not the only highly successful commander passed over in the elections. Quintus Fabius Maximus, the dictator of 217 who had waged a successful campaign of attrition against Hannibal, during which the Romans lost no significant battles and kept Italy essentially under their control, was also passed over in the elections.

Indeed, the striking feature of the administrative arrangements for 215 was not that the voters elected others instead of Marcellus; it was that the senate did not plan any military command for Marcellus in the upcoming year, even after disaster struck. The consul-elect Albinus, it seems, led his army into a Gallic ambush in the forest. His army was routed and Albinus himself was killed in the fighting. On a fascinatingly gruesome note, the victorious Boii turned Albinus' skull into a gold-adorned drinking cup for religious ceremonies.[69] After word of the disaster reached Rome, Gracchus, still master of horse, called a meeting of the senate. Gracchus reported on the status of the dictator Pera's troops, Marcellus made a similar report, and the status of the consul Varro's forces in Apulia was ascertained. The senate determined to send the forces under Pera – the city legions, freedmen and convicts – to join Varro. Varro, the commander during the disaster at Cannae, was to remain in command of his forces. Those who had served with Marcellus for the past few months from the army at Cannae, however, were sentenced – indeed Livy's account of the decree reads like a sentence – to serve in Sicily until the war in Italy ended. Other troop redistributions were made. Ultimately, however, there seems to have been no army left for Marcellus. So the senate took Marcellus' army away, decreed that the consul Varro would have his command extended as consul for an additional year, and made no such provisions for Marcellus.[70] This was no accident or oversight. Marcellus had not been elected to office; by not extending his tenure of *imperium* the senate had deliberately arranged for the end of his military command.

It is important to avoid the mistake that is so often made for groups in general, however, of treating the senate as a body of one mind and purpose. Quite the contrary; the senate was composed of proud Roman aristocrats, each of whom not only had their own opinion on how best to manage the affairs of the Republic, but also kept at least some watch on how different courses of action would affect their own reputation and honour and those of their families in an intensely competitive political system. So there was significant room for disagreements in the senate. For practical purposes, however, many of the conflicting opinions on the topics of the day might never be heard, let alone voted upon. Discussion in the senate was led by the consuls, who gave preference of speaking to those of highest rank first: assuredly former consuls and praetors, possibly, according to some historians, former censors and dictators at the front of the line. Though the junior senators could speak when their turn came, and all could vote, if the most powerful men, the lead speakers, reached a rough consensus, that consensus of the few might well become the voice of the senate on the issue in place of a vote.[71] Tradition and the social hierarchy reinforced by tradition dictated that the senate, once senators had arrived at a decision, spoke with a unified voice. When the statement is made from Livy's record that the senate gave no place to Marcellus in the military arrangement for 215 while extending Varro's command, then, what is really being said is that those senators who were most able to control and shape the decisions of that session did not see fit to grant Marcellus a command. They hardly constituted the whole of the senate, however.

Much as it would be illuminating to know if anyone in the senate deliberately moved debate so that Marcellus' command was not continued, there is too little evidence to go on. Fabius Maximus could hardly have been a fan of Marcellus and was a very senior senator with an important role in leading senatorial debate. That is not enough to prove that he made any special effort to end Marcellus' command. In addition, the consul Tiberius Sempronius Gracchus presided over that particular meeting of the senate and could have influenced the discussion.[72] Again, however, there is no evidence that Gracchus opposed Marcellus. Perhaps a better way of envisioning the matter is not that anyone actively opposed a continued command for Marcellus, but that no one who offered opinions during that session suggested his command be continued; without an official extension of his command, it would lapse.

If that had been the end of the matter it would seem the aristocracy had checked the prestige of one of its own, limiting Marcellus' continued political rise by taking no action to extend his command. As it happened, the voters in the assembly, a sufficient number of them in any event, were not willing to stand by while Marcellus was retired from the field. When March came and the new magistrates for the year entered office, the assembly voted Marcellus the command that the senate had not seen fit to give. Here was an instance where Marcellus' reputation worked to his advantage. Ordinarily, prorogation was the result of a senatorial decision and the assembly simply confirmed the senatorial appointments.[73] In this instance, however, the assembly granted Marcellus his command despite the senate leaders who had passed him over that year. That this was something outside the ordinary handling of such affairs is preserved in Livy's wording: 'That Marcus Marcellus should have full military authority as proconsul was ordered by the people, because he alone of the Roman commanders since the disaster at Cannae had met with success in Italy.'[74] In other words, Marcellus received a rare honour from the assembly of Roman voters. This can hardly have endeared him to his detractors, those who had been satisfied with letting his command lapse.

In a very real sense Marcellus had managed to override the decision of the senate or, more precisely, his rivals in the senate. This could not have happened, however, without the support of at least one official. Citizen assemblies were not allowed to meet of their own volition; they had to be summoned by the appropriate magistrate. Furthermore, the assemblies of the Republic, unlike the more democratic Athens of the fifth century BC, were not places of debate and discussion. When the assembly gathered it was presented a motion by the presiding official. It was the right of the assembly to pass the motion, making it a law binding for all Romans, or reject it. For Marcellus to have been granted an extraordinary prorogation of his command by a vote of the people meant that a magistrate, a senator, had taken the initiative to present the motion to the assembly. Apparently, there was a fair amount of disagreement in the senate over

Marcellus' right to command. Enough so, in fact, that a magistrate countered the implied wishes of the senate and proposed an extended command for Marcellus. That magistrate may have been reacting to a critical mass of senators who wished Marcellus to remain in command; as will soon be clear, there were certainly many who felt that way in the senate. Alternatively, the magistrate may have been responding to a popular groundswell of support for Marcellus in the city.

The matter of Marcellus' command was far from settled. The senator and indeed all Romans were bound to follow a motion passed by the assembly; Marcellus was now a proconsul for the year. His first assignment for the year, however, was of dubious importance for a Roman of his stature and authority. The two city legions had been ordered to muster for the year at Cales in Campania. Marcellus was assigned to meet these legions at Cales and chaperone them to the Claudian Camp. From there, the praetor Appius Claudius' subordinate would take the army to Sicily.[75] This was hardly the type of military command those who had voted proconsular authority to Marcellus had envisioned.

Only after Marcellus had left the city on this errand did preparations begin to fill the consulship left empty by Postumius Albinus. This was simply too much for Marcellus' supporters. Livy suggests that murmurs began to rise in the senate, some senators openly suggesting that Marcellus had been removed on purpose to prevent him standing for the consulship.[76] Between the magistrate who had called the assembly to grant Marcellus' command and the murmurings in the senate, although an admittedly vague attribution, it is apparent Marcellus had supporters perhaps no less significant than his detractors. According to Livy, the consul Gracchus moved to quash such grumblings, assuring the senators that the elections would not be held until Marcellus could return from his assignment.[77] Gracchus may have shared the sentiments of Marcellus' supporters, or he simply may have chosen to stop a political squabble that was growing before it became a liability to the war effort. He was certainly not opposed to Marcellus being consul if, as Livy suggested, he told the senate anything remotely along the lines of:

> Both acts were to the advantage of the state, fellow-senators, that Marcus Claudius should be sent to Campania to make the change of armies and that the coming election should not be proclaimed until he, after accomplishing the task which was assigned him, should return thence, so that you might have the consul whom the critical situation in the state requires and whom you particularly desire.[78]

Plutarch, however, suggests that neither Gracchus nor the other magistrates wanted to postpone the election and only did so at the demand of the people. Perhaps, but Livy's account is more plausible in that it recognizes that Marcellus had political support within the senate and explains in a way that Plutarch does not, how it came to be that elections were actually delayed. Either way, the matter was tabled until Marcellus returned. For the moment, those who had opposed a command for Marcellus were stymied.

It would be so very illuminating to know Marcellus' role in these maneuvers, or even his personal feelings on the matter. Suffice to say, while he must have been pleased to find supporters willing to make waves on his behalf, there is absolutely no evidence that Marcellus himself publicly stirred the pot or in any way openly challenged the authority of the senate, regardless of whether it was led by his opponents. Marcellus was consistent in this approach. The consummate political player, he couched his achievements, as essentially every successful Roman aristocrat did, in terms of service to the Republic. The fact that he personally and publicly benefited from the offices and the honours, awards, and glory that accrued from them, to his Roman aristocrat's mind, in no way undermined his claim to be seeking only to serve the Republic. It would strain credulity to suppose Marcellus did not privately voice his frustrations and hopes to trusted friends and associates, and it is only reasonable to suppose he encouraged those who wanted to support his political ambitions. Nevertheless, it would seem that he toed the line of respect for the institutions and procedures of the Republic very carefully and very well, even as he accumulated an unprecedented set of honours.

The extent of Marcellus' ability to challenge powerful institutions and rivals when they limited his ambitions while wholeheartedly claiming – and almost assuredly believing – that his actions were in the best tradition of service to the Republic becomes clearer when one considers that Postumius Albinus was a patrician and Marcellus was a plebeian. When Albinus died, Gracchus was inaugurated; the Republic had its plebeian consul and a rigid tradition dictated that there be one and only one plebeian consul every year – with a patrician colleague. What Marcellus' supporters were proposing, a proposal with which Marcellus clearly agreed, was nothing short of a major constitutional innovation in a society where innovation was often not regarded kindly. If he were elected to replace Albinus, the Republic would have two plebeian consuls. The exact legality of such a thing is murky. It is far from clear that the law opening both consulships to plebeians actually took place in 342 as recorded by Livy; it may have only come to be in the early second century. Nor is it clear there was any explicit law against having two plebeian consuls once the fourth century laws were passed requiring one consul be plebeian.[79] It is abundantly clear, however, from the lists of consuls elected every year that tradition dictated one consul be plebeian and one patrician until the early second century. What was Marcellus thinking in putting his name in for consideration to the consulship? Perhaps he did not; perhaps like the prorogation, his supporters considered him without his direct instigation. Whatever the case may be, others clearly felt Marcellus deserved the office since he was elected by a 'great consensus' of voters, as Livy says. For the first time, two plebeians had been elected to serve as consuls.[80] When Marcellus dedicated the *spolia opima*, seven years earlier, he claimed to have earned a exceptionally rare honour to be sure, but one that had some precedent. There was no precedent for two plebeian consuls and good reason to suspect that many would be upset by the innovation.

Strange as it may seem to modern readers, just as Marcellus entered office, thunder was heard, a well-recognized omen from the gods. It was not for just any Roman to determine whether the gods had sent a bad omen when it pertained to the welfare of the Republic as a whole. The college of augurs was the body of priests charged with determining whether the signs from the gods had been negative, usually during sacrifices, but also in cases like thunder and other celestial messages. They were summoned, considered the omen, and declared that there had been a flaw in the election, though it appears they did not specify exactly what the cause of the flaw was. It is tantalizing to note that Marcellus himself was an augur. Questions arise: Did he take part in the discussion of the thunderclap? It certainly fell under his jurisdiction as an augur. Had he heard the thunder? So long as someone of sufficient authority had heard the thunder or persuasively claimed to have done so, it did not matter. Did he agree with the consensus opinion of the other augurs that the thunder represented a flawed election? He had established a reputation of attending carefully to the gods and he may have persisted in that stance. Or perhaps the augurs silenced his objections? Regardless of how the augurs came to their conclusions, if indeed they did not specify exactly why the gods were upset, a number of senators were happy to offer an obvious interpretation: The gods were angered by the election of a second plebeian consul.[81]

It is important to understand the nature of their objection. In the days of the foundation of Rome there were two classes of Romans: patricians, who were the nobility, and plebeians, who were everyone else. When the Republic was created, it was essentially the result of the patricians chafing under the restrictions of a monarchy and wanting to establish a political system where they wielded greater power and influence. Hence in the earliest Republic the patricians alone were eligible for the highest magistracies. For the first century and a half of the Republic or so, there were a number of social and political conflicts between the plebeians and patricians. While the exact nature of the conflict is as hazy as everything else in that early period, it appears that the poorest plebeians wanted a set of legal protections, particularly involving matters like debt, so that they could not be oppressed by wealthier creditors. The wealthier plebeians – and there were a number who had wealth but chanced not to be born into the noble patrician families – wanted a share in the political power and prestige that the patricians had gained. In other words, they wanted access to the political offices. The details of this struggle need not detain us here.[82] What is most important is that somewhere in the middle of the fourth century a law was passed guaranteeing that one of the consuls every year from then on would be plebeian. This was a major concession from the patricians for it meant that their supply of consulships was cut in half.

By Marcellus' day the distinctions between patricians and plebeians that held political office had faded to a certain extent, and a patrician-plebeian aristocracy of office holders and senators had been well established.[83] The practice that one consul would be patrician and one plebeian, however, was a tradition. Or to look at it another way, there had never been two plebeian consuls. The Romans, like all ancient peoples, took their traditions seriously. After all, the world was a dangerous place. In the absence of modern industry, science, technology, and medicine, bad weather could kill by destroying crops, childbirth was far too frequently lethal to mother and child, and minor bacterial infections could prove fatal. With so many fewer solutions to the problems that all humans face, the effective practices of ancestors, tested and confirmed through the centuries, were the generally accepted means of making sure individuals and the commonwealth survived in a dangerous world. Many of these practices revolved around placating the gods. By observing the proper rituals, prayers, and sacrifices, the Romans generally hoped to maintain the goodwill of the gods as protection against the dangers of the world. Failure to respect the gods could turn them against the commonwealth with devastating effect.

So, it was no small thing for Marcellus to win election as the second plebeian consul for the year, and when the augurs indicated that the gods were angry, something had to be done. His critics had him over a barrel. Ultimately, there was no debating that Marcellus' election violated precedent – no one could deny that. As such, there really was little Marcellus could do. Violating the received will of the gods was not a viable option, certainly not when the augurs had identified a problem and the interpretation that Marcellus had caused the offense had gained momentum. It is noteworthy in this context that Cicero would much later refer to Marcellus as *augur optimus* ('the best of augurs') while writing at the same instant that '[Marcellus] used to say that, if he wished to execute some maneuver which he did not want interfered with by the auspices, he would travel in a closed litter.'[84] This was not an illogical claim on Cicero's part. The gods and humans, the Romans seemed to believe, played a very strictly legalistic game. If one did not see the signs of the gods' displeasure, they, strictly speaking, did not exist.[85] The obverse of this reasoning was also true – the augurs agreed an ill omen from the gods had been delivered. Marcellus had shown himself to be interested in following the will of the gods and following tradition of a sort – hardly the sort to cross them now. 'He abdicated the office' was Livy's only comment on the outcome. The patrician Quintus Fabius Maximus became consul to replace Albinus.[86]

What are we to make of this episode? Certainly, it strains the credulity of those with modern political sensibilities to assume the whole episode – from the hearing of the thunderclap to Marcellus' abdication – was completely above board. Surely, one might suspect, Marcellus' enemies – those who had initially managed to prevent him having a military command for the year, those who had inspired complaints that Marcellus had been given busywork to keep him away from the elections – must have manipulated the religious beliefs of the Romans to engineer his embarrassment? It hardly calms suspicions to note that Fabius Maximus was an augur too,[87] the very one whose family monopoly of ties to the cavalry and whose very temple to Honos were undermined by the claims of Marcellus less than a decade earlier. He was an augur and he replaced Marcellus as consul. Did Fabius, a senator of considerable influence, take a lead position in determining that a bad omen had indeed been sighted and that the omen was because of Marcellus' election? The timing of the thunder seems very convenient. Was the whole episode a plan by Marcellus' opponents to stop him from a major innovation in the constitution?[88] It is illuminating to remember that Fabius was a patrician and by simple arithmetic, Marcellus had taken an office that had always been reserved for patricians. If allowed to stand, Marcellus' innovation could potentially limit the number of consulships available to patricians severely. This was not a precedent that Fabius would likely have willingly tolerated. Certainly not from a rival who had already shown his willingness to claim what might be seen as unorthodox privileges in the past. None of this proves conclusively, of course, that Fabius had a hand in this, but he had means, motive, and opportunity.

In this instance, Marcellus had broken with convention and opponents rallied to stop him. They had leverage in their obstruction. Regardless of the reality of the omen, a questionable enough electoral innovation would have made many pause. Omens indicating flaws in elections, not to mention flaws in all sorts of public business, were not that rare. The Roman state, as far as Romans were concerned, depended on the good will and material support of the gods for its prosperity, and it was critical that the laws of the gods be obeyed for that good will to be maintained. It is a bit misleading to cast the objection solely as the plot of a group of politically motivated rival senators potentially taking advantage of a religious technicality. Such a view runs the risk of misunderstanding the inseparability of the public religion and politics in the Republic and, indeed, in all ancient societies. The public religion protected the commonwealth; pleasing the gods helped ensure a prosperous state, angering the gods meant courting disaster. There is no need to suppose any distinction between the political and religious stances of Marcellus's enemies on this point. His enemies did not want him to be consul or even to have a military command. They assumed, as do most of us in such situations when we feel animosity to others, that they were justified in their opinions of Marcellus. Why, then, would they think the gods disagreed? Rather, the thunderclap for Marcellus' enemies simply confirmed what they already believed; Marcellus was unworthy. In the end though, it is highly unlikely that all the senators who raised the point that the gods were angered were enemies of Marcellus.

Still, a citizen assembly had granted Marcellus the authority of a consul for the year and there had been no irregularities in that procedure. The senate dispatched Marcellus to the army at the Claudian camp in order to keep Nola secure. Fabius took command of the dictator Pera's forces and Gracchus of the slave volunteers, both of which were wintering at Teanum.[89] In this, the fourth year of war, the Roman military efforts in Italy continued to focus on Campania and on a series of marches, countermarches, sieges, and relief efforts focused on controlling the critical strategic forts and towns that dominated the countryside. Casilinum had fallen to Hannibal's siege in the winter or early spring. There seems to have been no major effort to recover the city this year, however. Marcellus' primary activities that summer focused on garrisoning Nola and launching punitive raids from the city into neighboring Samnite and Hirpini territory, both peoples having allied with Hannibal after Cannae.[90] The raids were highly effective, according to Livy, driving both peoples to complain to Hannibal that he was leaving them wholly defenceless.[91] According to Livy, Hannibal returned to the region of Nola to check Marcellus' predations on the lands of his allies and another indecisive battle was fought between the two commanders. This second battle at Nola, however, has been doubted by a number of historians who suggest Livy or his sources had mistakenly duplicated the authentic battle episode from the year before. Whatever the case may be, at the end of the summer Nola held, the Samnites and Hirpini were perhaps doubting the wisdom of siding with Hannibal, and Marcellus, in compliance with the consul Fabius' orders, released all his soldiers for the winter except those needed to garrison Nola.[92]

At the end of the year, Fabius came to the Campus Martius field outside the city of Rome and announced the elections for next year's officials. The consular elections this year produced another curious irregularity. In the late third century, the century that voted first for consuls was chosen by lot; it was considered a distinction to vote first, and it was not uncommon for the first century's picks for consul to be elected. Perhaps subsequent centuries liked the idea of picking a winner. The young men of the Aniensis tribe – as opposed to the century of older men from that same tribe – picked Titus Otacilius Crassus and Marcus Aemilius Regulus to be consuls. Fabius, the presiding consul, however, strongly rebuked the tribe for selecting these two men. If Livy's constructed speech is boiled down to its essence, Fabius criticized the military qualities and successes of both men and ordered that the junior Aniensis century be called upon to vote again for more suitable candidates. This was not a common phenomenon, to say the least. Interfering in consular elections, particularly by the presiding consul, would have been a habit dangerous to the Republic, for it would put too much power into the hands of the consuls. It appears Otacilius at least was aware of Fabius' grave impropriety and sputtered that Fabius was trying to architect an extended consulship. Fabius, however, would not brook any challenge to his consular authority. He reminded Otacilius that they were both outside the city limits of Rome, and as such, that his lictors still carried the axes in their *fasces*. To translate: Fabius as consul outside the city could lawfully execute a Roman citizen, even Otacilius, with just a word of command to his axe-carrying lieutenants. Otacilius ceased his public protest, the junior Aniensis tribe voted again, and Fabius and Marcellus were elected consuls for 214.[93] It would be interesting to know how Fabius felt about Marcellus being elected this year. Did his plan backfire? Likely Fabius was pragmatic about these matters. If he did wish Marcellus to be kept from the highest honours, he must have realized with the events of the previous year that he could not do so with any certainty. Marcellus, for his part, cannot have played any large part in Fabius' manoeuvre. He was with the army in Campania and elected in absentia.[94]

Marcellus had remained in the field in the winter and returned to protect Nola early in the spring of 214 when the city leaders requested his help.[95] Most of Marcellus' time and energy for the season were invested in Nola again, since Hannibal had returned to the region from the south and there continued to be concerns about the city's loyalties. Fabius, on the other hand, prepared to retake Casilinum. He sent word to Marcellus asking whether he could assist or Fabius should seek aid from Gracchus at Beneventum. Marcellus left part of his force to guard Nola and joined Fabius at Casilinum. The two Roman armies must have tested the city walls for assault, for some Roman soldiers close to the walls of Casilinum were wounded. According to Livy, Fabius and Marcellus hotly debated whether to continue the siege in light of the Roman causalities. Fabius advocated lifting the siege rather than committing additional time and resources. Marcellus, on the other hand argued that withdrawing in failure would needlessly tarnish their reputations.[96] The whole debate seems a bit formulaic since, conventionally, the historical tradition emphasized that Marcellus was audacious and Fabius cautious. This may have been an instance where the Livy chose to illustrate the sword and shield of Rome metaphor through an improvised debate. Certainly, Casilinum's location along the Appian and Latin Ways was hardly insignificant, the Romans had persevered despite suffering terrific casualties in the past, and there is no clear evidence of great casualties here other than a vague reference. Most importantly, though, the commanders maintained the siege regardless of whether there had been any formal debate on doing so.

Subsequent events, however, suggest that the two commanders did have a decided difference of opinion about how to conduct operations at Casilinum. Livy's account is a bit puzzling in that he seems to be compressing events: 'While sheds and all other kinds of siege-works and apparatus were being brought up, and the Campanians were begging Fabius for permission to go to Capua in safety, after a few had left the city, Marcellus occupied the gate by which they were leaving.'[97]

Probably the best way to untangle this rushed account is to separate the three parts in time. Therefore, while the Roman forces began to prepare the siege works needed to take the city, some of the Campanians within the garrison at Casilinum seem to have negotiated with Fabius that they be allowed to leave the city and travel under safe conduct to Capua. Presumably, Fabius agreed, else it is difficult to explain why the Campanians began leaving the city. Why he would have done so is not clear since these Campanians were returning to Capua, still an ally of Hannibal. Perhaps Fabius reasoned that the defection of these Campanians would weaken Casilinum more than they would strengthen Capua. Certainly, this would make sense of Livy's report that Fabius thought the city too difficult to be worth taking at that moment in time. Marcellus, however, seems to have been left out of these negotiations, or at least did not receive any word of them. Any number of scenarios might explain this. Marcellus must have been elsewhere – there was much to do to prepare for a siege after all – when Fabius was approached. Perhaps Fabius did not see fit to communicate the arrangement to Marcellus. Perhaps events happened so quickly that Fabius did not have time to communicate with Marcellus. Or perhaps Fabius did communicate with Marcellus and counted on him to obey, since Fabius was an elected consul for the year.

Regardless of whether and how the arrangement was communicated, though, Marcellus clearly had very different ideas about how the Campanians should be handled. To their horror, Marcellus and his soldiers occupied the gate from which they began to depart and began slaughtering those inside the city gates indiscriminately. Marcellus felt no sense of mercy for those in the city. Indeed, his force moved from the gate into the city and continued to attack. Meanwhile, a few Campanians escaped the city – perhaps fifty – and sought the protection of Fabius. Fabius, true to his word, sent them under armed escort safely to Capua.[98] He must not have been part of any plan with Marcellus to betray the Campanians. Rather, it seems that the two commanders acted without any sort of cooperation. This episode suggests several important things about Marcellus. First, that he had little remorse for enemies. Though Livy hides it in the brevity of his description, Marcellus had decided to subject the inhabitants of Casilinum, a rebel city, to a rampage of killing, making them an object lesson in the penalties for disloyalty to Rome. He was hardly alone among Romans in believing that no fate was too harsh for an enemy and that all who resisted in any way during a time of war were enemies. At the same time, though, Fabius did not share these ideas about Casilinum, so it appears that this stance may have been part of Marcellus' particular world-view. Second, Livy's brief description of the episode at Casilinum seems likely to have glossed over a serious inability of the two men to work together. Not only did the left hand not know what the right was doing, the left actively challenged the right. Combined with the other traces of problems between the two men, it becomes increasingly reasonable to conclude that Marcellus and Fabius were, if not complete political enemies, probably bitter rivals.

*   *   *

A careful analysis of Marcellus' activities from the aftermath of Cannae to 214 indicates that his political career was supercharged by the demands of the war. He had built a strong reputation based upon military achievements before the beginning of the Hannibalic War. This reputation was greatly magnified by his victory over Hannibal at Nola. By 215, he was powerful enough to challenge the restriction against two plebeian colleagues in the consulship. Yet despite his abilities and growing prestige, he suffered delays in his early career and attempts to exclude him from a command and elections in 215. Even the exceptional success of winning election as the second plebeian consul of 215 was ultimately checked when the augurs declared a flaw in the auspices. There was a limit to how much even as successful an aristocrat as he could innovate to his own advantage. As we shall see, the years from 214 to 210 would catapult Marcellus even farther past his peers in terms of honours and prestige, yet he would face even greater political challenges designed to limit his laurels.

Chapter 3

Syracuse

For the Mediterranean world there were few places more strategically important than Sicily. Its central location and proximity to Africa and Italy made it a gateway between the eastern and western Mediterranean. However important Sicily was to Roman and Carthaginian interests in the First Punic War, it was of even greater strategic value in the second war. The western part of the island was the logical choice for staging any Roman invasion of Carthage itself; the eastern part was just a brief sail to Italy for Carthaginian troop transports, and control of naval supply routes to all of western Italy could be influenced by whoever held the island. Re-establishing control over Sicily was critical if the Carthaginians had any hope of regularly supplying Hannibal with troops and supplies by sea. Still, the Carthaginians were unwilling or unable to commit any effort to regaining Sicily when Hannibal first invaded Italy, and the Roman province remained quiet for several years. The Romans were clearly prepared for an attempt on Sicily from early in the conflict, however, since they maintained a substantial garrison there, one that included the survivors of Cannae.

When Syracuse was plunged into chaos by an internal revolt, however, the Roman situation in Sicily degenerated rapidly. The Roman conflict with Syracuse began when Hiero, who had ruled Syracuse effectively for half a century, died of old age, probably sometime in early 215.[1] Hiero's grandson Hieronymus, only 15 years of age, took the throne. A considerable amount of political maneuvering and in-fighting took place during Hieronymus' short reign as rival elements in Syracuse sought to gain control over the city. Additionally troubling to the Romans, Hieronymus initiated talks with the Carthaginians, providing them with the potential leverage to return to the island. Hannibal sent to Hieronymus as advisors the Carthage-born Epicydes and Hippocrates, both connected to Syracuse through their grandfather, who had been exiled from the city. Appius Claudius, the praetor stationed in Lilybaeum on the western end of Sicily, heard word of these political shifts and sent negotiators to Hieronymus. His reminders of the longstanding friendship between Rome and Hiero and attempts to patch the alliance met with rough handling; consequently Appius or his legates gave Hieronymus a warning and withdrew to observe how events played out.[2] Soon, Hieronymus completed a treaty with Carthage that would divide Sicily roughly in half at the River Himeras, Carthage controlling the west and Syracuse the east. Shortly after, Hieronymus made claims to the entire island; the Carthaginians must have been humouring him. Additional Roman envoys came to Syracuse in response to this treaty, and though some of the royal advisors advocated maintaining their commitments to Rome, those wishing to join Carthage prevailed. Accordingly, the brash young king sent word to the Romans declaring that he would preserve Syracuse's ties to Rome if the Romans granted all of eastern Sicily to Syracuse and paid Hieronymus back all the gold his grandfather Hiero had given as gifts to the Romans.[3] It hardly needs to be said that this was something of a slap in the face to the Romans.

Hieronymus was assassinated after ruling for about thirteen months, according to Polybius,[4] and this would have been some time in the summer of 214.[5] He had been with his army in nearby Leontini, a dependent of Syracuse, when conspirators struck him down in the city streets. With the death of Hieronymus, Syracuse descended into revolution, if not outright anarchy. Two of the lead assassins, Theodotus and Sosis, hurried from Leontini back to Syracuse in order to establish a new, elected government before the allies of the deceased king clamped down. Adranadorus, the uncle of the Hieronymus, however, heard of the assassination of his nephew and pre-empted Theodotus and Sosis by sending troops to occupy strategic points throughout the city. The conspirators were undeterred, however, and gained the support of the city council and citizenry to form an elected government. Bolstered, they quickly persuaded Adranadorus to relinquish control over the strategic positions in the city and submit to the authority of the city council. Elections were soon held for executive magistrates, and Adranadorus was granted a leading office along with a number of the conspirators against the king.[6]

But the threads continued to unravel. When Hippocrates and Epicydes, the primary diplomatic links between Hannibal and Hieronymus, heard of the Syracusan king's death, they followed the conspirators to Syracuse. Once there, Epicydes held open the possibility of maintaining the alliance with Hannibal, even finding that there was a significant level of anti-Roman sentiment in the city. Though we cannot uncritically accept Livy's assertion that Epicydes started to entertain the idea of seizing control of Syracuse at this point, it certainly is plausible.[7] Livy also suggests, however, that Adranadorus entertained his own coup at this point. Apparently, reports of Adranadorus' plans reached the Syracusan city council, whose members brought Adranadorus to their meeting chambers and murdered him.[8]

The city council quickly held elections for a magistrate to replace Adranodorus. It came as something of a surprise, however, when some in the electoral assembly called for both Epicydes and Hippocrates, neither Syracusans by birth, to be named as magistrates. The disruption caused the council to dissolve the assembly. The two had sufficient support, however, that the council feared further revolution if some concession were not made. Accordingly, Epicydes and Hippocrates were named magistrates.[9] At about the same time, the council sent envoys to Appius Claudius seeking a truce that would lead to a reaffirmation of the Roman-Syracusan alliance. It would hardly have been surprising if Appius Claudius was a bit stunned by these rapid changes in the political alignments at Syracuse.

By this time, no later than the end of 214,[10] Marcellus arrived to take over Roman negotiations. While consul (214), Marcellus had returned to Nola after capturing Casilinum. He had become ill, however, and was incapacitated for a period of time.[11] Once he had regained his health, the senate assigned Marcellus the command in Sicily to deal with the growing problem at Syracuse.[12] Marcellus arrived on the island after the Syracusan envoys had reached Appius Claudius, and the latter dutifully sent them on to the consul. Marcellus spoke with the envoys, believed peace to be possible, and sent his own legates to speak directly to the magistrates of Syracuse.[13] Not surprisingly, Epicydes and Hippocrates, both of whom were deeply connected to Hannibal and thus unlikely to find anything favourable in a Roman–Syracusan alliance, agitated against siding with the Romans. The fact that Appius Claudius had stationed warships at the mouth of the Syracusan harbour as a precautionary measure had also proved a useful propaganda tool against the Romans. Nevertheless, the Syracusans held an assembly and voted to renew their relationship with the Romans rather than risk an immediate Roman invasion.[14]

To the dismay of the Romans – perhaps even to the exasperation of some readers at this point – the government of Syracuse reversed course yet again. Soon after the Syracusans voted to join Rome, Leontini requested a force of Syracusan soldiers to defend its border. The Syracusan council sent Hippocrates with a force of Roman deserters in order to both meet the demands of Leontini and drain Syracuse of dissidents at the same time. Hindsight, of course, is 20/20, and it is unreasonable to condemn those in the past for not seeing the future. Still, what were the leaders of Syracuse thinking, sending off Hippocrates with an army? If one hopes to attribute any sort of sensibility to the city council, it seems necessary to assume that Hippocrates and Epicydes were exceptionally talented politicians who managed to persuade the council that, despite their Carthaginian origins and their reintroduction to Syracuse as ambassadors for Hannibal, they were, nevertheless partisans of Syracuse firmly committed to supporting the pro-Roman decisions of the assembly. Or perhaps, as one might suspect from Livy's account, the city council was at its limits and simply picked the lesser evil by removing Hippocrates from the city in a way that did not involve murder and the potential for even further factional strife. Perhaps they reasoned that there was little Hippocrates and 4,000 soldiers could do that could not be checked by the combined might of Syracuse and Rome.

In any event, Hippocrates quickly took advantage of his new freedom of action and used the troops to raid Roman territory near Leontini. In response, Appius Claudius sent additional troops to guard the farms in the area; a number were killed by one of Hippocrates' raids. When Marcellus heard of the attacks on Roman territory and Roman soldiers, he sent a message to Syracuse. The peace was broken, he noted, and there was no remedy except to remove Hippocrates and Epicydes from Sicily entirely. Marcellus also queried whether attacking Leontini, ostensibly under Syracuse's authority, would further disintegrate the treaty between Rome and Syracuse. Epicydes, probably realizing that he would soon be in an untenable position at Syracuse due to his brother's predations on the Roman province, swiftly left Syracuse and joined Hippocrates in Leontini.[15] The Syracusan city council, now with both of the brothers out of the picture, declared to Marcellus that Leontini was in rebellion and Syracuse could not be held accountable for that town's actions. Marcellus could attack Leontini, and Syracuse itself would provide support troops so long as the town, once conquered, was returned to Syracusan authority.[16]

Having reached a diplomatic agreement with Syracuse, Marcellus led his forces to Leontini while instructing Appius Claudius to approach the opposite side of the city. The forces of Leontini offered no significant resistance to the Roman soldiers, who Livy asserts sought revenge for the attacks on their comrades. Still, according to Livy, other than those slain in the initial assault, the soldiers in the town were spared and the property seized during the attack was restored to its rightful owners. Epicydes and Hippocrates, however, managed to escape the city. Meanwhile, the auxiliary troops promised by Syracuse were on the march to Leontini, unaware that the Roman forces had already seized the city. Rumours reached the force that the Romans had massacred the adults of Leontini and plundered the city itself. This news stunned the Syracusan commanders, who were unsure of how to proceed. The complexities of actions taken within the Syracusan army next need not detain us here.[17] What is critical is that during this time of confusion, Epicydes and Hippocrates made contact with a contingent of Cretan archers in the Syracusan force. By continuing to manipulate the rumour of Marcellus' cruelty at Leontini, they took command of the whole force. Then, supported by this army and taking advantage of inflamed anti-Roman sentiments in Syracuse, Hippocrates and Epicydes engineered a coup in the great city itself, seizing control and winning election to be generals of the city.[18]

The speed with which Hippocrates and Epicydes carried out this stratagem must have amazed Marcellus, who was still encamped at Leontini. When he received the reports, however, he moved his forces to Syracuse. The Roman army encamped less than two miles away from Syracuse at Olympium, a site that overlooked both the city itself and the harbour. At about the same time as the Roman army was arriving, apparently, Appius Claudius had sent legates to the city by ship, but the ship was captured and the legates were hard pressed to escape. Though this hostile treatment of diplomats probably did not bode well for peace, Marcellus made a last effort at diplomacy. He sent legates to the city, but rather than allow them into the city, Epicydes and Hippocrates met them at the gate. Since one of the Roman terms was that the leaders of the coup be surrendered, intercepting the Roman envoys essentially guaranteed the failure of further diplomacy. The legates were rebuffed, and Marcellus' forces set about the business of taking Syracuse, probably in early 213.[19]

The siege of Syracuse is one of the striking episodes of Roman military history in the Republic, one that imprinted itself on the minds of many later authors. In part, this is due to the scale of the deed. Syracuse was one of the great cities of the third century Mediterranean, and it would not yield easily to any attempts to take it. When dealing with the siege itself, the historian is very fortunate in that Polybius, whose account of events after Cannae vanished sometime between its authoring and today, has left us an intact account of the operations. As one who had commanded soldiers and had experience of war, his assessments, though not to be taken at face value, are invaluable. Polybius gave this assessment of the city defences: 'The strength of Syracuse lies in the fact that the wall extends in a circle along a chain of hills with overhanging brows, which are, except in a limited number of places, by no means easy of approach even with no one to hinder it.'[20]

This requires some elaboration. The mainland portion of the city itself consisted of three distinct sections. The oldest part of the city was in the south-east section. This contained the citadel of Syracuse and was called alternately Nasos ('the Island' in Greek) or Ortygia; it guarded the harbour of Syracuse and was defended by its own wall. Achradina was next, the heavily populated mainland section of the city, located north of the island and on the coast. Finally, to the west of Achradina, the large plateau of Epipolae was included in the main defensive wall of Syracuse. Though both districts were encompassed by the defensive wall, the fourth-century wall of Dionysius, they were also separated from one another by internal walls and thus able to be defended independently. The Epipolae quarter itself may have been largely uninhabited, but including the plateau in the defensive circuit made Syracuse that much more formidable as a defensive position since many segments of the wall were built on heights and difficult to approach directly. At the western tip of the triangle created by the walls of Epipolae stood the formidable Euryalus fortress, as solid a defensive position as could be desired.[21]

The obdurate walls themselves were formidable enough, but at that particular time the defences of the great city were supervised by none other than the famous mathematician and engineer Archimedes. This Greek engineer was said to have claimed he could move the very earth with a lever if he had the right fulcrum; his feats of calculation and formulation are still important in modern mathematics. Archimedes had designed a daunting series of missile engines and other machines to defend the landward and seaward walls of the city.[22] Still, the Romans, according to Polybius and Livy, were confident they would take the city quickly by assault.[23] Polybius would have it that the Romans gave the consul Marcellus command only over the naval forces, while Appius Claudius was appointed as the independent commander of the land forces.[24] This is assuredly either a mistake on Polybius' part, or yet another effort to lessen Marcellus' prestige, in this case by making his command seem less powerful than it was. Appius Claudius' praetorship in Sicily was for the year 215, and he must have been granted an extension, presumably as a propraetor, for the year 214, since he continued on in an official capacity, attempting to negotiate with the Syracusans when Marcellus arrived. As the consul, and thus by far the ranking commander, Marcellus had authority over the province of Syracuse and all Roman forces in it. This province was re-established when the senate extended his command and made him proconsul for 213, with a province delimited by the boundaries of Hiero's former kingdom. In short, Appius Claudius was Marcellus' subordinate in this attack, regardless of Polybius' effort to mask it.

What forces did Marcellus have at his disposal for the attack on Syracuse? This is a bit of a thorny issue. Since 215, the regular Roman garrison force for Sicily – two legions – consisted of the so-called *legiones Cannenses* ('Cannae legions'). These soldiers were the survivors who had fled the battlefield at Cannae. As punishment for their failure to die holding their ground against the enemy, the senate sentenced them to a punitive form of service as a mark of disgrace. As Livy, Plutarch, and the first century AD recorder of military stratagems, Frontinus, recorded it, the Cannae legions were to serve in Sicily for as long as the enemy was in Italy.[25] Generally, it has been understood by historians that, as part of this punishment, the soldiers of the Cannae legions were barred from active duty in field armies, required to serve only as garrison troops. This is because Livy suggests that in the winter of 213/2, a year after the attack on Syracuse had begun, the soldiers of the Cannae legions received permission from their commander in Sicily, Publius Lentulus, to send their most distinguished centurions and cavalrymen to petition Marcellus, a petition that Marcellus forwarded in a letter to the senate.[26] Livy attributes a particularly lengthy and elaborate speech to the delegates that seems wholly out of place for soldiers addressing their general; he even seems to forget the location of the speech when he has the soldiers address the 'conscript fathers' – the title for the senators – though they were far away at Rome. After a recount of relevant ancient and recent history, the petitioners end with the request, 'Let us engage the enemy and by fighting earn freedom... We demand all the worst hardship and danger, in order that what should have been done at Cannae be done as soon as possible, since every day that we have lived since has been marked for disgrace.'[27]

While the speech itself is surely a fabrication, the core request is believable enough; the Cannae legions wished to serve under Marcellus in his attack on Syracuse. Marcellus was apparently not unsympathetic to their cause but was no renegade; he followed a reasonable protocol under the circumstances, promising nothing, but writing to the senate for a decision on the matter. The response from the senate repeated the general principle that the men of these legions could not be trusted; however, Marcellus might employ the soldiers as he saw fit. The prohibitions nevertheless remained in place: none could be decorated for service in battle, exempted from duty, or allowed to return to Italy until the war was over.[28] Plutarch adds the detail that Marcellus chafed at the restrictions placed upon him and several years later reprimanded the senate for not allowing him to reward these soldiers for their service. It seems, then, that Marcellus did in fact incorporate these legions into his army.

Livy's timing of this episode poses a problem for historians. Were the Cannae legions actually prohibited from serving as active field troops until they had petitioned Marcellus? Did they only petition him at the end of 213? If so, Marcellus and Appius Claudius had to attack Syracuse without the aid of these legions, a prospect considered unlikely by some. After all, why would Marcellus fail to use every soldier available on the island when attacking so mighty a city?

Livy's chronology of events in Sicily as a whole has long been considered problematic by historians.[29] He seems to have conflated the events in his account from 214 to 213 and presented them as if everything from the death of Hieronymous to the attempt to assault Syracuse occurred in 214 and nothing at all happened in Sicily in 213, a highly implausible scenario. It is certainly possible that he or his source dated the petition of the Cannae legions to Marcellus incorrectly or perhaps even passed on a fabulous account of the petition. The question is, what other evidence can be found that suggests a more plausible reconstruction of the relationship between Marcellus and Cannae legions?

When historical problems like this present themselves, it is necessary to see if other sources can corroborate the events. As it happens, Plutarch also refers to the petition of the Cannae legions. According to the Greek biographer:

As Marcellus took over [Appius Claudius'] force [in Sicily], he was beset by many Romans who were involved in a calamity now to be described. Of those who had been drawn up against Hannibal at Cannae, some had fled, and others had been taken alive, and in such numbers that it was thought the Romans had not even men enough left to defend the walls of their city. And yet so much of their high spirit and haughtiness remained that, although Hannibal offered to restore his prisoners of war for a slight ransom, they voted not to receive them, but suffered some of them to be put to death and others to be sold out of Italy; and as for the multitude who had saved themselves by flight, they sent them to Sicily, ordering them not to set foot in Italy as long as the war against Hannibal lasted. These were the men who, now that Marcellus was come, beset him in throngs, and throwing themselves on the ground before him, begged with many cries and tears for an assignment to honourable military service, promising to show by their actions that their former defeat had been due to some great misfortune rather than to cowardice. Marcellus, therefore, taking pity on them, wrote to the senate asking permission to fill up the deficiencies in his army from time to time with these men. But after much discussion the senate declared its opinion that the Roman commonwealth had no need of men who were cowards; if, however, as it appeared, Marcellus wished to use them, they were to receive from their commander none of the customary crowns or prizes for valour. This decree vexed Marcellus, and when he came back to Rome after the war in Sicily, he upbraided the senate for not permitting him, in return for his many great services, to redeem so many citizens from misfortune.[30]

Plutarch's version differs from Livy's in several important ways. Most importantly, he suggests the soldiers approached Marcellus when he arrived in Sicily, which would have been late in 214 and a year before Livy's dating.

To make matters more confusing, Frontinus, a writer in the late first century AD, the period of the Empire, seems to split the difference between the two authors. In a book of military stratagems that happened to include the encounter between Marcellus and the Cannae legions, Frontinus explicitly places the event in the consulship of Quintus Fulvius Flaccus and Appius Claudius, 212. In the same sentence, however, he says that the soldiers petitioned the 'consul Marcellus', which would have referred to the year 214. What are we to make of this? Did Frontinus mean 212 and simply mistakenly indicate Marcellus was consul, or was Marcellus actually consul when he was petitioned and the actual year was 214 (or early 213), and the dating to 212 a mistake? It would seem that mistakenly labeling Marcellus consul, particularly by a writer from the Empire, when consuls were far less powerful, would be a far easier slip to make than writing out the phrase, 'In the consulship of Quintus Fulvius and Appius Claudius' (*Q. Fulvio Appio Claudio consulibus*). This is hardly decisive proof, however.

It seems, if anything, that the testimony of these three sources compared more strongly suggests late 213 or early 212 was the time when the Cannae legions petitioned Marcellus. It is not enough, however, to compare the sources and establish a simple majority. The question is this: Does stipulating that, firstly, the petition took place in late 213 or early 212, and, secondly, the Cannae legions were not allowed to serve in anything other than a garrison capacity before this, allow a plausible reconstruction of the military operations before the end of 213? Quite simply, no.[31] Consider that the two Cannae legions were the only legions, historians generally believe, stationed in Sicily in 215. Traditionally, Sicily was protected by two legions, and when the Cannae legions were penalized and sent to Sicily, the two legions already there were transferred to back to Italy for operations against Hannibal.[32] Marcellus presumably brought two legions and the accompanying allied troops with him to the island, the normal army for a consul. One of those legions, however, apparently did not arrive for months after Marcellus did, perhaps late in 213.[33] Essentially, then, Marcellus seems to have brought only one legion and its allied complement with him initially to Sicily, so perhaps 10,000 men.

If the Cannae legions were prohibited from active duty and Marcellus did not use them until late 213 or early 212, two more solid points of evidence become very difficult to reconcile. The first is that Marcellus planned to assault Syracuse with only 10,000 troops at his disposal for the landward attack. Consuls normally had two legions and their allies with them, double the size of the force Marcellus had. It is more than a bit incredible to think that Marcellus would estimate this force to be sufficient to attack one of the great walled cities of the ancient Mediterranean, and be willing to let an additional 10,000 to 16,000 soldiers sit idly by. The second point of evidence that is difficult to reconcile comes from a campaign after the assault on Syracuse. This episode will be treated in more detail later. For now, what is important is that Marcellus, after failing to take Syracuse by storm, left two thirds of the army under Appius' command and took one third with him into the field. He declined to engage a Carthaginian force of 28,000 but surprised, engaged, and defeated a Syracusan army of 10,500. If Marcellus did not draw on the Cannae legions at all, his army would have numbered perhaps 3,000 or 4,000 men at this point, and it becomes improbable, even with the element of surprise, that Marcellus accomplished this deed. Assuming the Cannae legions were part of his total available forces soon after he landed on the island, however, provides a reasonable figure for Roman troops available. The total army would be more than 30,000, and the detachment Marcellus used to rout the Syracusan force somewhere in the neighborhood of 10,000 – still small enough to explain why Marcellus dared not challenge a Carthaginian army of 28,000.

So while the testimony of Livy is clear about when these events happened, Plutarch is equally clear. The ramifications of each date for the rest of the evidence are the deciding factors. Though there can be no certainty in these matters, the requirement that all the known military operations of the year in Sicily be plausibly explained suggests that Plutarch was correct and the legions petitioned Marcellus in late 214 or early 213, before he began the attack on Syracuse. Marcellus was still consul then, which would make Frontinus' reference accurate. Of course, this leaves unsolved the problem of why he dated the event to a later consulship, but Frontinus clearly made an error one way or another, and we have to choose which chronological marker was erroneous, the reference to Marcellus being consul, or the reference to Appius Claudius being consul. If Plutarch's version is to be preferred, the prohibition on the Cannae legions can be accepted, Marcellus' request to use the troops from time to time and the senate's reluctant acquiescence fit, and all in a way that does not require us to believe that Marcellus thought it better to assault Syracuse without these troops, but then added them to his forces for a siege only at their request.

It is worth making one additional point in favour of Plutarch's dating – or at least consistent with it – that has generally been overlooked. Though historians have generally assumed, based on the petition Livy describes, that the Cannae legions were prohibited from active service, none of the sources actually says any such thing. Consistently, when the Cannae legions are mentioned, the only punishment stated is that they had to serve continuously until the war in Italy ended.[34] None of the sources directly states that the legions were barred from actively serving in field operations. That that was the case is inferred from Livy's grand, and assuredly embellished rendition of the soldiers' petition:

We should have approached you, Marcellus, when you were consul, in Italy, as soon as that severe if not unjust resolution of the senate was passed concerning us, had we not hoped that after being sent into a province thrown into confusion by the death of its kings, to take part in a serious war against Sicilians and Carthaginians combined, we should have made reparation to the senate by our blood and our wounds in the same way that those who were taken by Pyrrhus at Heraclea, within the memory of our fathers, made reparation by fighting against Pyrrhus afterwards. ... But we, against whom no charge can be brought except that it is through our fault that a single Roman soldier is left alive after the battle of Cannae – we, I say, have not only been sent far away from our native soil and from Italy, but we have been placed out of reach of the enemy, we are to grow old in exile, with no hope, no chance, of wiping out our shame, or of appeasing our fellow citizens, or even of dying an honourable death. We are not asking for an end to our ignominy or for the rewards of valour, we only ask to be allowed to prove our mettle and to show our courage. We ask for labours and dangers, for a chance of doing our duty as men and as soldiers. This is the second year of the war in Sicily with all its hard-fought battles. The Carthaginians are capturing some cities, the Romans are taking others, infantry and cavalry meet in the shock of battle, at Syracuse a great struggle is going on by land and sea, we hear the shouts of the combatants and the clash of their arms, and we are sitting idly by, as though we had neither weapons nor hands to use them. The legions of slaves have fought many pitched battles under Tiberius Sempronius; they have as their reward freedom and citizenship, we implore you to treat us at least as slaves who have been purchased for this war, and to allow us to meet and fight the enemy and so win our freedom. Are you willing to make proof of our courage by sea or by land, in the open field or against city walls? We ask for whatever brings the hardest toil and the greatest danger, if only what ought to have been done at Cannae may be done as soon as we can do it, now. For all our life since has been but one long agony of shame.[35]

It is important to remember first of all that this speech is assuredly in no way an attempt to capture verbatim what was said, even if Livy had that information available. Second, Livy almost assuredly was mistaken in his dating of the soldiers' petition, since it makes little sense that the Cannae legions stayed out of the battle for Syracuse, given what is known about the numbers of the forces involved. So, focusing only on the expressed complaints of the soldiers, strictly speaking, all that Livy really suggests they claimed is that they had been stationed far away from the main theater of war and wanted to play an active part, not that the senate had forbidden them to play such a part. This fabricated speech is the closest Livy comes to any suggestion that the senate had forbidden the troops to fight anymore, and even here he does not actually say this. Once again, every reference elsewhere in Livy and the other relevant sources states that the punishment for the legions, the mark of disgrace, was that they would be forced to remain in service until the war was over, not that they would be prevented from serving in battle. Plutarch's account in this regard fits very well within this context; Marcellus arrived on the island and was asked by the Cannae legions if they could play a significant role in the attack on Syracuse. He agreed, wrote a letter to the senate, asking if he could draw on these troops, and the senate agreed, while maintaining the stigma it had laid on those troops. The practical issue at stake may have been simply that soldiers who fell under Marcellus' command could potentially, if not clearly identified as members of the disgraced Cannae legions, leave the island as members of Marcellus' army before the war was over and their sentence completed.

Assuming, then, that the Cannae legions were part of the total Roman force at Marcellus' disposal, Marcellus had approximately 30,000 troops available in addition to a fleet of some ships. With these forces at hand, he planned a combined attack by land and sea to take Syracuse by storm. This was in late 214 or, more likely, early 213. Appius Claudius' land forces made for the Hexapylon, the strong gate complex on the north wall of the city. At the same time Marcellus commanded an amphibious attack against the seaward wall of Achradina first.[36] The latter was certainly an ambitious undertaking. Amphibious assaults were rare enough in antiquity, and the Romans, in general, were far more experienced at fighting on land than at sea. Still, the core idea of using a large army to apply pressure to disparate points along a city wall was sound enough. But why not simply attack multiple points on land? Perhaps because breaching the Epipolae defences would still have left the Roman army facing the walled Achradina quarter, effectively a second city requiring besieging, and the location of most of the population. If the Romans were confident about their chances in taking the city quickly, it certainly was most expedient to seize both Epipolae and Achradina simultaneously, reducing the largest of the two city quarters at once.

The strategy may have been overly confident, but Marcellus certainly was not rash in his planning. Quite pragmatically – indeed, one might almost say in a Roman fashion – Marcellus planned a naval assault that in its essence was a land assault. He had sixty *quinqueremes* at his disposal, warships with five rowers per oar that were the core of the Roman fleet. Eight of these ships were lashed in pairs side-by-side so that they could provide catamaran-like stability for the construction of assault towers known as *sambucae*. These were so called because they resembled those ancient stringed musical instruments. One can hardly do better than to paraphrase Polybius' description of these devices. Each *sambuca* consisted of a ladder four feet wide and as high as needed to reach the ramparts of the Achradina walls. The base of the ladder was attached near the prow of the ship, perhaps with some sort of pin. On each side of the ladder at the front of the ship was a tower, presumably to protect both the ladder and climbers. The top of the ladder was suspended by cables through pulleys attached to the masts of the ship. Finally, the top of the ladder had screens on the sides and front to offer some protection. In practice, four soldiers rode at the head of the ladder as the ships approached the walls. When the ship came sufficiently close, the four jumped onto the top of the wall. Though Polybius does not explicitly say so, it is reasonable to suppose the task of the first four, other than to fight off the defenders at the wall, was to secure the top of the ladder for the subsequent assault troops that climbed it.[37] While the four *sambucae* tried the walls, the remaining *quinqueremes* held back, their decks full of missile troops whose job was to keep the seaward walls clear of defenders.[38] While the navy assaulted the sea walls, Appius Claudius executed a landward assault west of the Hexapylon gate with ladders to mount the walls and screens to protect the Roman soldiers as they brought and placed the ladders.[39]

The ancient authors agree, however, that Archimedes' defences stopped the Roman assault cold. There were several components to the defence systems constructed by the famous Greek engineer. First, he had positioned stone throwers and ballistae along the seaward walls of Achradina. The heaviest of these were capable of harrying the Roman ships at a distance, and the smaller engines kept up the attack when the ships passed under the minimum range of the large engines. According to Polybius, these defences alone were sufficient to halt the Roman advance and persuade Marcellus to try an attack at night. They were hardly the only tools Archimedes had placed at the Syracusans' disposal. Arrow-loops along the base of the wall also allowed archers and small missile engines to harass the Roman soldiers as their *quinqueremes* closed with the city walls.[40]

By far the most spectacular countermeasures, however, were those used against the Roman ships and *sambucae*. These were of two types. The first were wooden beams with boulders or heavy weights of lead at the end. These were pivoted out and over the walls and their weights dropped on the Roman *sambucae* as they approached. More dramatic still were the beams with grappling devices, which, once affixed to the prow of any Roman ship, used counterweights to draw the prow straight into the air then released, dashing the ship down and stunning the crew when not capsizing the boat outright.[41] Through these combined defensive measures, the Roman seaward assault was simply crushed. Indeed, Polybius, who was not overly inclined to make jokes in his work, attributed a moment of levity to Marcellus amidst the destruction. The commander was said to have quipped after the horrendous refusal, 'Archimedes uses my ships to ladle sea water into his wine cups, but my sambuca band is flogged out of the banquet in disgrace.'[42] Claudius, meanwhile, fared no better on the landward side. There, Archimedes' engines rained stones and bolts onto the advancing Roman soldiers, preventing them from reaching the walls. Claudius, too, was forced to call off the attack. Syracuse, it appeared, would not be taken by storm. The Roman commanders shifted to siege preparations.[43] Essentially, this meant encircling the city with a set of outposts and guards in order to prevent anyone or anything, especially food supplies, from getting in or out. A city as large as Syracuse, however, would not fall quickly to siege, as Marcellus no doubt knew well.

Once the siege had begun, there was little to do at the city but wait. In an effort to demoralize Syracuse and strengthen the Roman position in the region, Marcellus left Appius Claudius with the task of monitoring Syracuse with two thirds of the Roman army while he took the remaining third and campaigned against several cities in Syracuse's sphere of influence that had supported the Carthaginian cause. His exact route is not clear; Livy only provides us a list of his successes. The citizens of Helorus, a coastal town south of Syracuse, surrendered, as did Herbesus, a town west of Syracuse between it and Leontini. Marcellus took Megara by storm, no more than 10 miles north-east from Syracuse, and gave it to his soldiers to plunder and destroy as an object lesson to the rebellious Syracusans.[44]

Whatever effect Marcellus' victories may have had on persuading the Syracusans to surrender, it vanished almost immediately as news arrived that a Carthaginian force had landed in western Sicily near the important southern city of Agrigentum. The commander, Himilco, had brought a force, according to Livy, of 25,000 infantry, 3,000 cavalry, and twelve elephants.[45] Livy provides numbers for the Carthaginian force that are large but certainly within the realm of plausibility. Marcellus attempted to head off the Carthaginian invasion and marched westward. By the time the Roman army arrived, however, the Carthaginians had already seized control of Agrigentum. Apparently judging that his forces were insufficient for the task of ousting the much larger Carthaginian army, Marcellus ordered his army to march back to Syracuse.[46]

The return of a Carthaginian army to the island spurred on the many cities opposed to Roman control, including Syracuse. Somehow, Hippocrates managed to leave Syracuse and run the Roman cordon with 10,000 infantry and 500 cavalry. With this portion of Syracuse's forces, he marched west toward the town of Acrillae, presumably planning to join his forces with the Carthaginians. As it happened, however, Marcellus had adopted a cautious stance for his army on the return march to Syracuse and managed to catch the Syracusan soldiers as they had dispersed to pitch camp. The Roman force seized the upper hand and quickly defeated the Syracusan infantry. The cavalry held out slightly longer, but eventually Hippocrates retreated with them to Acrae, several miles to the east.[47] Soon, Hippocrates made his way to join Himilco's forces as they approached Syracuse, apparently in pursuit of Marcellus. Himilco was unable to close with Marcellus' force before he reached the safety of the Roman fortifications and the bulk of the army near Syracuse; by then, it was too late.[48] Still, it appeared that the Roman position around Syracuse was in danger. Not only was Himilco's army positioned only a few miles away at the River Anapus, but also a fleet of fifty-five Carthaginian *quinqueremes* managed to enter the Great Harbour of Syracuse. The Romans received reinforcements of their own, however, as Marcellus' second legion finally landed on the island and made its way to the Roman camps.[49]

Himilco opted – and there is no reason to second guess his estimates – not to challenge the siege of the city directly but to destabilize Roman control of the island by encouraging cities that hoped to revolt against Rome. The citizens of Murgantia, perhaps 50 miles inland from Syracuse, ousted the Roman garrison and took control of the supplies and food the Romans had stored there.[50] In Henna, however, a city in the center of Sicily with a citadel on a high cliff that dominated the surrounding countryside, the Roman garrison preemptively slaughtered the men of the city rather than risk falling prey to rebellion. When word was sent to Marcellus of the deed, he condoned the act by authorizing the garrison to plunder Henna. This may have been another of Marcellus' object lessons to intimidate the Sicilians into submission, but it apparently had the effect of only further fanning the flames of revolt in Sicily and removing any psychological advantage gained from his recent victory over Hippocrates.[51] By the end of the campaign season, a number of towns had joined the Carthaginian cause. With winter closing in (late 213), Himilco returned with his forces to Agrigentum, and Hippocrates traveled to Murgantia to join the rebellion there. Marcellus, meanwhile, had his soldiers construct a new fortified winter camp several miles from the Hexapylon gate on the north side of Syracuse. With the election season approaching, Marcellus discharged his legate Appius Claudius, who was intent on running for consul; Titus Quinctius Crispinus assumed the role of Marcellus' new legate in charge of the fleet and the soldiers stationed at the old camp, near the Temple of Jupiter south of the city and approximately one mile from the Great Harbour.[52] From these positions the Roman forces settled in to focus completely on the siege of Syracuse.

Appius Claudius and Quintus Fulvius Flaccus were elected consuls for 212, and the military commands in Sicily for that year were arranged as follows. Marcellus' command was extended for the year within the limits of King Hiero's former territories. Publius Lentulus was made propraetor and remained in charge of the rest of Sicily. Titus Otacilius, meanwhile, was placed in command of the fleet at Sicily.[53] Marcellus' spent his time enforcing the siege at Syracuse. It became apparent at some point that the city was simply too large to be starved into submission by the Roman forces available. The better part of a year spent attempting to stem all supplies from reaching the city seemed to have accomplished very little. Marcellus tried a different tack. Among the Romans were some of the more influential and powerful men of Syracuse who had been compelled to leave the city because of their pro-Roman leanings. Marcellus instructed these exiles to inform any supporters they might have inside the city that Syracuse would be left to govern itself if it surrendered to the Romans. Somehow, the exiles managed to get one slave accepted back into the city, claiming to have fled from the Romans. The slave made contact with Roman sympathizers in Syracuse. In return, some sympathizers slipped out of the city hidden on a fishing boat and made their way to the Roman lines. Through such clandestine meetings a number of Syracusans – Livy says eighty – were primed to betray the city to the Romans. A whisper of their plans was brought to Epicydes, however, and the conspirators experienced a painful death.[54]

Providence, however, seemed to be on the Roman side. Syracuse had sent an envoy named Damippus, a Spartan, to treat with King Philip of Macedon, against whom the Romans had declared war in 215. Damippus did not make it to the Balkan Peninsula; Roman ships patrolling the coast of Syracuse had captured him. Epicydes sent word to Marcellus that he wished to ransom the Spartan, and Marcellus was willing. A parley was arranged near the Trogili Harbour, to the north of the city, and negotiators met there several times to discuss the terms for ransom. One of the Roman negotiators, through sheer cleverness or the instructions of a superior, surreptitiously estimated the height of the northern walls of the city by estimating the size of one of the tiers of stone and counting the total number of tiers. This section of the city wall, in the estimation of the negotiator, was significantly lower than previously thought and indeed the lowest part of the whole defensive circuit. Therefore, the Romans wagered they could use reasonably sized scaling ladders to overcome the walls here.

The Syracusans apparently were aware of this weakness in their defences, however, for they kept this section of the wall under extra guard.[55] Again, Providence seemed to favour the Romans. A Syracusan who had recently abandoned the city informed Marcellus that inhabitants were in the midst of celebrating the feast of Diana and that festivities would continue for three days.

Epicydes, the Syracusan reported, had furnished extra wine to the whole populace to make up for the restrictions on food. In short, much of the adult populace was likely to be drunk and relatively senseless; this might just prove to be the opportunity the Romans needed.

Marcellus called his military tribunes together for a meeting and formed a plan. One maniple of soldiers would carry quickly constructed ladders to the short section of the walls, and a picked detachment of 1,000 men would mount the walls. The attempt would be made late at night at a time when, it was hoped, the inhabitants would have had their fill of wine and be drifting to sleep. Frontinus reported that Marcellus himself scaled the walls of Syracuse, killed the guards nearby and opened the gate to his forces.[56] Perhaps, but it does seem a stretch. Polybius and Livy provide a far more plausible account. The tribunes picked the soldiers they thought best for the task, and when the time came, the scaling crews did their job effectively. The initial forces occupied a section of the wall and made their way to the Hexapylon gate undetected, the few Syracusans on the towers asleep or passed out. While additional troops climbed the walls, the initial raiding party targeted a small access gate nearby the Hexapylon and broke it open to allow easier access to the Roman forces outside. A sizeable Roman force was soon within the walls and at the agreed-upon blare of a trumpet began to occupy Epipolae near the gate openly. The Syracusans in the area reeled from the shock of the invasion, but the farther reaches of the enormous city were unaware that anything was amiss.[57] When morning came, the Hexapylon gate was dismantled and Marcellus entered with the whole of the Roman army. Several miles away on the Island, Epicydes mustered a force of soldiers and moved to drive out the invaders. He had been wholly misinformed about the size of the invading force, however, and when he learned that the whole Roman army had entered Epipolae, he relinquished control of that city quarter and retired behind the walls of Achradina. The Romans shortly had control of Epipolae.

At this point, Livy and Plutarch relate, tradition recorded that Marcellus, when he stood on high ground and surveyed the city that would, sooner or later, fall to Roman hands, wept both at the magnitude of his achievement and at the greatness of the city that would soon be subjected.[58] A great literary moment, to be sure, but likely a fabrication. Even were there any reason to suspect he was more sentimental than the average Roman aristocrat – unlikely given his treatment of other enemy cities – he had hardly taken the city. True, Epipolae was under his control. But the formidable Euryalus fort at the apex of the triangle of Syracuse's walls, the westernmost point of the city, was still in the hands of a Syracusan garrison commanded by one Philodemus.[59] Marcellus opened negotiations with Philodemus, but Philodemus did not immediately agree to surrender the fort; according to Livy, he was biding his time, waiting for Himilco to arrive from Agrigentum, a not unreasonable assumption. How long he waited is not clear, but it cannot have been long, and either just before, or more likely just after the Roman plundered the occupied portions of the city, Philodemus surrendered Euryalus in return for safe conduct to Epicydes.[60]

Marcellus moved his army to camp in a less-populated section of the city on the south side and made plans to plunder the captured portions of the city. Plundering a captured city, the Roman way, was an exercise in organized violence and destruction that, despite the organization, must have included a great deal of chaos. When a city's walls were first breached and the Roman soldiers entered the living areas, there was a real danger that looting and plundering would compromise the military objectives, not to mention result in the destruction of locations that the Roman commanders would rather have preserved – treasuries and the houses of allies, among other places. Instead, it was a common practice to prohibit soldiers from any looting when they were taking the city in return for the guarantee of a time reserved for plundering once the military objectives had been met.[61] The Syracusans knew the Roman rituals; the occupied portions of the city sent representatives to discuss the terms for the Roman seizure with Marcellus, or rather to plead that the loss of life be kept to a minimum. Marcellus issued the order that while no free person in the city should be injured, everything else was rightfully the spoils of the soldiers. Then he gave the necessary instructions to secure the camp from attack while the soldiers were away, ordered that the signal be given, and let loose the soldiers on the city. According to Livy, they looted freely but followed the orders to spare all free-born life – one can imagine the fate of slaves was left up to the discretion of the soldiers, no doubt with often horrific consequences.[62]

With the plundering of the occupied sections complete and Euryalus now in the hands of a Roman garrison, Marcellus gave the orders to besiege Achradina. Three camps were set up and the quarter was hemmed in. Shortly thereafter, however, the Syracusans and their Carthaginian allies, made a counter-attack. Himilco and Hippocrates arrived from the west; Hippocrates moved with what must have been a detachment of troops against the old Roman camp at Olympium commanded by Crispinus. He was bolstered by troops that issued forth from Achradina. At the same time Epicydes led another segment of the Syracusan defenders to attack Marcellus' guard posts in the city. Where exactly Himilco's army was in these raids is not clear, but it appears he was hanging back cautiously, establishing a camp near the city. In any event, the raids did not achieve any particularly important strategic objectives.[63] Now, however, the Roman armies were in a precarious position between Himilco's forces to the west and the walls of Achradina to the east. At this point, catastrophe struck both the Roman and Carthaginian armies. Disease, that destroyer of armies and cities in antiquity, beset Roman, Carthaginian and Syracusan indiscriminately. Either due to chance or, more likely, to the Romans, experience at building functional camps, the Carthaginian army was the worst hit, disintegrating in the face of the deadly illness, its Sicilian allies forced to scatter back to their homes.[64] Not even Himilco and Hippocrates were spared. The teetering Roman position had been righted.

Still the siege was not yet complete; the most heavily populated sections of the city, Achradina and Ortygia, remained outside Roman control. In addition, the remnants of Hippocrates' Sicilian forces had occupied several fortified towns near Syracuse and gathered allies and supplies. At about the same time, the Carthaginian commander Bomilcar returned to Carthage to seek reinforcements for Syracuse and returned with a fleet of warships and troop transports. The fleet was stalled by unfavourable winds, however, and unable to sail round the south-eastern tip of Sicily, Pachynum, and arrive at Syracuse. Word of the fleet had apparently reached both Epicydes and the Romans. Epicydes, for his part, boarded a ship, and left the city to meet with Bomilcar. Marcellus, on the other hand, sent his smaller fleet to engage the larger Carthaginian one. For reasons that are unknown – Livy does not even venture a guess – Bomilcar caught sight of the Roman fleet and, despite his greater numbers, quit Sicily for Tarentum in southern Italy. The transports he ordered to return to Africa. It was a stroke of luck for the Roman forces, to say the least. At this point Epicydes showed his practical estimate of Syracuse's future by abandoning the city and continuing on to seek safety in Agrigentum.[65]

With Epicydes fled and the hope of Carthaginian reinforcements dashed, the Sicilian armies sent messengers to discuss terms for the surrender of the remaining sections of Syracuse. Marcellus agreed with them that the Romans should directly control all that Hiero had controlled, but the rest of Sicily should retain its own local laws and magistrates. The lead Sicilian negotiators then asked permission to enter the rebel sections and include those inside the city in negotiations. Once inside, they rose up against the lieutenants Epicydes had placed in command and killed them. These negotiators then persuaded the Syracusans to look favourably on a settlement with the Romans. The Syracusans elected representatives to seek terms from Marcellus.[66]

When all seemed resolved and the formal surrender of the city but a step away, the Roman deserters in Syracuse, who feared the capital punishment which would certainly be imposed on them when the city surrendered to the Romans, reacted. They persuaded the mercenary forces in the city that the Romans would treat them just as harshly – unlikely, but persuasive enough to soldiers who had fought the Romans for years. Together, the deserters and mercenaries rebelled against the newly elected magistrates of Syracuse, indiscriminately slaughtered civilians within their reach, if Livy is to be trusted, and seized control of Achradina and Ortygia.[67] Once again, Marcellus had to look for a connection within the city to make further progress. As it happened, a Spanish mercenary by the name of Moericus was one of the mercenary leaders in charge of the forces at Ortygia, and he was open to dealing. Marcellus' negotiators focused much of their energy on persuading Moericus that the mercenaries, in Marcellus' mind, were a wholly different matter than those who had deserted from the Roman army and would not meet the deserters' fate.[68] No doubt, they also assured Moericus that he would receive a handsome award. Satisfied and likely seeing no good alternative, Moericus agreed to aid the Romans in seizing the city.

Livy is a bit unclear about several details of the final operation to capture the great city. Moericus arranged to surrender Ortygia to a small force of Romans who crossed the Great Harbour late in the night by transport and gained entry within the walls. When the sun rose, the forces directly under Marcellus assaulted Achradina's walls in an effort to draw the attention of the enemy forces there away from the Island. Apparently, their efforts were so successful that a number of the defenders from Ortygia left the island to aid their comrades in defending Achradina. Now that the attention of the defenders was fully drawn toward Marcellus, a squadron of Roman ships deposited additional soldiers on Ortygia. These troops gained entry into that quarter through the very gates the mercenaries on the island had opened to leave for Achradina.

What is particularly odd about this account is that the initial small force that entered the city in the night is not mentioned. Though there might be any number of solutions to explain Livy's inconsistency here – he may have misunderstood his source or his source itself made the confusion – it is reasonable to suppose that, in reality, the advance squad had played a role in securing access for the larger force that tried the walls of the island later in the day.[69] Another oddity; without further detail, Livy asserts that Marcellus received word that both the island and a part of Achradina had been occupied. Again, it is not clear how this happened in Livy's account; presumably, the force that occupied Ortygia made its way to Achradina. It is also possible that some of Marcellus' force gained access to Achradina, though that would certainly have been a much harder task since it would involve scaling the defended walls of the quarter from the landward side. Whatever the exact tipping point, once Marcellus learned that his forces had seized access to the last resisting section of the city, he recalled his forces in order to prevent the looting of Hiero's treasury.[70]

There were no options left for the Syracusans. Their attempt to seek peace after a long rebellion had been thwarted by the coup of the deserters and mercenaries. Part of Achradina was occupied by Roman forces and there were no walls left to shield the inhabitants of the city. They had nothing with which to bargain, nothing they had could not be readily seized by the Romans. Aware of the reality, envoys from the captured city met with Marcellus, asking only that the lives of the city inhabitants be spared. Marcellus acquiesced; if the Syracusans had dared hope for more, they certainly were disappointed. Marcellus, according to Livy, sternly rebuked the defeated at this point, to the effect that the wrongs Syracuse had committed against the Roman people far outweighed the services, but that those who had been the ringleaders had already received their punishments. Then, according to Livy, he noted that the

Syracusans could have resisted the deserters and mercenaries as Moericus had.[71] Regardless of whether his exact words are known, it is difficult to believe that after years of siege, Marcellus refrained from any admonishment of the citizens at this most opportune moment when they had surrendered.

Arrangements were made yet again for Roman troops to plunder, this time the older, wealthier district of Achradina. The precision of the plundering operation is striking to modern eyes when one considers the ultimate goal was to ravage the city. A quaestor was dispatched with a unit of Roman troops to guard the royal treasury of Hiero; after all, plundering did not extend to robbing the Republic of its rightful spoils. Then guards were positioned to protect houses and possessions of all those who had defected to the Romans before the city fell. Once these critical points were secured, the army was sent in to loot and plunder the city freely.[72] Livy, as that gentle man of words often did, reproves the behaviour of the Roman soldiers by noting 'many shameful examples of anger and many of greed were given.'[73] He does not elaborate on the horrific details, but given references by sources to other cities taken by Romans, assault, rape, and murder would have been at the top of the list. In the midst of the pillaging, some Roman soldiers found the great Archimedes. Some say he was intent on studying a mathematical problem and either refused to go with a Roman soldier or failed to hear him altogether. Either way, one of the Roman pillagers murdered him during that chaotic day.[74]

Roman tradition had it that the spoils from Syracuse were unbelievably rich, a match perhaps, Livy speculates, for the wealth of the great enemy Carthage itself. Statues and paintings, countless works of art, all were carried off by the Romans and brought back to their city. Marcellus apparently used a number of artworks plundered from Syracuse to decorate public areas in Rome, especially the future temple to Honos and Virtus. Indeed, he apparently had not built the temple and used the spoils from Syracuse to finance the actual construction.[75] These spoils served to commemorate the magnitude of his achievement in taking the grand city of Syracuse. Interestingly enough, a tradition was preserved or invented by Cicero much later that Marcellus took nothing of the loot for himself, with the exception of a globe constructed by Archimedes.[76] All other sources are silent on the matter, however, and it remains up to the reader to decide the likelihood of this.

After the surrender and sacking of the city, the time came to hammer out the details of the peace. Typically, in such situations where the Romans had defeated an enemy, it fell to the highest magistrate on site to make the provisional arrangements for peace with the defeated. These arrangements were termed *acta*, the 'deeds' of the general, and it would remain for the senate and people to ratify any major arrangements made by a field commander into formal treaty provisions. In this case, the proconsul Marcellus established arrangements not only with the Syracusans but with the other city states of Sicily, which sent envoys to set terms with the Romans. The details of the arrangements Marcellus made with these various peoples are essentially lost to us. In general, Livy suggests that Marcellus reaffirmed the status of *socius*, or ally, for those states that either had not rebelled against Rome or had returned to the Roman side before Syracuse was taken. Livy asserts that those states that attempted to join the Roman cause only after Syracuse was taken were treated as defeated enemies receiving terms from a conqueror.[77] Livy, with his usual moral hyperbole, asserts that Marcellus was a model of integrity and fairness as he arranged matters in Sicily. Even so, there is no reason to suspect his arrangements were corrupt either.

The capture of Syracuse brought the eastern half of Sicily firmly back into Roman control, but the west was still in a state of revolt, aided by Carthaginian forces. The Syracusan renegade Epicydes and the Carthaginian commander Hanno at Agrigentum, that southern port city a little more than 100 miles from Syracuse, were now joined by a new commander sent by Hannibal, Muttines. He was a Libyophoenician, one of the North African peoples brought under the rule of the Carthaginians over the centuries. He had served with Hannibal and learned the business of command in the process. He initiated a series of raids at the head of a force of Numidian cavalry.[78] Numidian horsemen were renowned as light cavalry. They were masters of the horse and able to maneuver and move precisely and quickly, often to the dismay of slower infantry and cavalry forces. These soldiers were ideal for quick raids, and with them Muttines harassed the territories of the Romans and their allies as part of an effort to sway more Sicilians to leave the Roman alliance. Likely the preoccupation of many of the Roman forces at Syracuse made it even easier for Muttines to move freely around the countryside. His raids created enough uncertainty in the political alignments of the countryside that Hanno and Epicydes led their army out to the River Himera, a natural border between western and eastern Sicily, and pitched camp, presumably on the western bank of the river.[79]

News that the Carthaginian army had left the safety of Agrigentum and marched towards Syracuse reached Marcellus and he responded by bringing his own army within four miles of the Carthaginians so that he could wait and observe. Muttines' Numidian cavalry crossed the Himera and harassed the Roman guard posts almost immediately. The next day he followed up with more raids. Livy says that during the second day Muttines almost fought a 'proper battle' and forced the Romans to retreat within the fortifications of their camp. It is not exactly clear what Livy meant by this. If Muttines only had the Numidian forces at his disposal, while they would have been the ideal force to harass and terrorize a larger slower Roman army, they would hardly have been sufficient in numbers or strength to commit to anything like a pitched battle. Muttines, on the other hand, may have been drawing from some or all of the Carthaginian army – which would explain the comment that a proper battle almost began.

Either way, his successes came to an end when a number of Numidians began to mutiny at their base camp; several hundred reportedly left the camp and travelled to Heraclea Minoa, another southern coastal city west of Agrigentum.[80] Muttines allegedly left to win back the withdrawing Numidians. According to Livy, there was friction among the Carthaginian commanders at this point. Muttines instructed Hanno and Epicydes to wait for his return. Hanno, indignant that a Carthaginian subject should dictate orders to a Carthaginian, decided to cross the river and offer a full battle while Muttines was away.[81] It is certainly reasonable to suppose that Hanno and Muttines were not on the friendliest of terms. The one had been formally placed in command over the Carthaginian forces. The other was a recent addition, supplied by the commander Hannibal, and it would have been difficult for Hanno to avoid the conclusion that Muttines had been sent to him because Hannibal at least, did not have full confidence in his abilities. Certainly, this would not have been the first or last time that tensions between commanders of a joint force had led to a split in commands.

Subsequent events in Livy's record suggest that there was a considerable amount of disorder in the Carthaginian forces, both among soldiers and commanders. Marcellus was game for a decisive engagement and indulged Hanno's desire for a pitched battle. As he set in motion the orders for his soldiers to adopt their formations and assume the correct positions, a handful of Numidian cavalry approached and reported the defection of their comrades. They also passed on that Muttines had left the camp. Consequently, the Numidian cavalry who trusted their commander were unwilling to fight and would keep out of the impending battle. When the Carthaginian forces advanced into battle, the Numidians remained in their initial positions on the wings, refusing to support the main army. This, in and of itself, must have been a major blow to the morale of the Carthaginian infantry, who had suddenly and unexpectedly lost the security of skilled cavalry protecting their flanks.[82] The Roman forces knew in advance of the Numidian defection. They had suffered at the javelin points of the African cavalry over the past few days. No doubt it boosted Roman morale greatly to know that the Numidians would stay out of the battle and, in doing so, deliver a nasty surprise to the Carthaginian army.[83] Livy reports that the battle was decided in the first clash of the front lines. The Carthaginian soldiers had no stomach for battle that day, particularly now that they felt the sudden shock of betrayal and since the soldiers on the flanks were left vulnerable without their cavalry. The main army retreated to Agrigentum while the Numidian forces dispersed to any number of nearby cities.[84] That day, Livy reports, the Romans killed thousands of Carthaginians, and captured thousands more in addition to eight war elephants.[85]

*   *   *

This was Marcellus' last battle on the island. With the year coming to an end and consular elections for 210 approaching, he left the island and returned to Rome.

If he had traveled to Rome occasionally during winter respites or lulls in the fighting, there is no record of it, and so it appears that Marcellus had spent more than three years on the island living the life of a field commander. During that time he humbled rebel Syracuse through perhaps the greatest siege in living Roman memory and acquired riches that he would soon spread throughout the city of Rome. He had also defeated several Carthaginian field armies. Most importantly for the Republic, he had quelled the rebels, and tightened Roman control over the eastern portion of Sicily – though as will soon be apparent, the island was still to be a source of struggle. As a successful general who had accomplished such distinguished achievements, it was time to return home and seek the immediate rewards that could accompany such exploits; a military triumph, formal praise for his deeds from the senate and people, perhaps an additional consulship. Marcellus no doubt expected these rewards were rightly his and would come easily; he was, after all, the general who had matched Hannibal, and taken mighty Syracuse. As he would soon find, however, his most recent victories, grand as they were, only inspired his opponents further to obstruct his claims for honours.

Chapter 4

The Political Battle for Syracuse

Late in 211 or early in 210, Marcellus returned from Sicily. He left his troops there under his successor, though apparently unwillingly, since he hoped to bring them home at least in part to serve as witnesses to his deeds.[1] The timing of his return to Italy can only mean he intended to seek the consulship; otherwise, his command would not have expired until the new consuls were inaugurated sometime in March of 210. Clearly, Marcellus also intended to claim a triumph for his victory over Syracuse. Accordingly, he did not enter the city in observance of an important religious restriction. According to Roman custom, a proconsul, one who held the military powers of a consul by special appointment of the senate, no longer retained his *imperium* once he crossed the *pomerium*, the sacred boundary of the city. Once lapsed, the proconsul's term of command was formally over. Since the army marched along with the general in a triumph, the celebration was technically an exercise of command, and thus it was necessary for the commander to retain *imperium* up to the day of the triumph. Then a vote of the assembly was secured so that, for the day and purposes of the triumph, the commander could hold *imperium* within the *pomerium*. Thus a commander seeking a triumph, in practice, would wait outside the city walls until he could be granted the victory celebration by the senate and an exemption to the normal loss of *imperium* by the people.[2] And so, Marcellus waited until the senate could approve his request. The praetor Gaius Calpurnius facilitated the process by summoning a meeting of the senate at the Temple of Bellona, outside the *pomerium* on the outskirts of the city.[3]

Though the capture of a city as great as Syracuse may have made a triumph seem like a foregone conclusion, Marcellus may have thought he needed to mount a special argument. In part, this may have been because his soldiers had remained in Syracuse at the command of the senate. Ordinarily, a general's soldiers were the critical witnesses of his deeds and to that extent were important in approving his victory celebration. Livy illustrates this most powerfully in an episode from more than forty years after Marcellus took Syracuse. A military tribune, Servius Servilius Galba, had a grievance against Aemilius Paulus, the commander who spectacularly defeated King Perseus and reduced Macedonia to a subject state. Galba endeavored to block Paulus' triumph by inciting the commander's soldiers to vote against granting him a triumph. Many of the soldiers appear to have been more than willing, resenting the fact that Paulus had not given them greater shares of the Macedonian loot. According to Livy, Galba noted that the plebeian assembly would surely follow the lead of the army and refuse to grant honours to Paulus if his own soldiers would not.[4] Though it is far from clear that hesitant soldiers could always block the triumph of a general in such a way, the testimony of those Romans who had actually observed their general's conduct in battle must have been a powerful incentive to award or deny a triumph. After all, they were the ones best positioned to judge the general's performance.

Marcellus seems to have believed that he might be at a disadvantage with his army still in Sicily; at least this is suggested by the account of the meeting that day. Marcellus protested, gently according to Livy, as much for his soldiers as for himself, that they had been ordered to remain in Sicily even though they all had completed the mission assigned to them in their province.[5] One wonders whether Marcellus meant all of his soldiers should have been allowed to return home, even those from the Cannae legions who had served with him but were forbidden by the senate to leave Sicily. If so, Marcellus was testing the authority of the senate. He may, however, simply have been referring to his two legions that had come to the island over the course of 214.

Marcellus also requested – perhaps, as Livy says, demanded – to be awarded a triumph for his victory. A lengthy debate ensued in the senate. The main outlines Livy provides are plausible enough. On the one hand, Marcellus, while still in Sicily, had been awarded a public thanksgiving by the senate for his successes. This was an official time of prayer and sacrifice to the gods that could precede the granting of a triumph. Might it not seem outrageous to deny him a triumph now after such a thanksgiving? On the other hand, Marcellus had been ordered to transfer his army to a successor. This was done explicitly because there was still a war in the province. How could he triumph, then, if the war in the province was not over and his army was not with him to witness his right to celebrate this grandest victory celebration?[6]

There are some thorny issues here that beg to be investigated. If Livy accurately represents the technical details of the senate's debate, there were competing definitions of Marcellus' province being cast about in the temple that day. The term *provincia* ('province'), it is worth noting, did not always correspond to modern ideas of imperial or national provinces. In the Republic, particularly during times of war, a province was often simply the region to which a commander was assigned to prosecute a war – though the term could also refer to a more peaceful assignment, such as governing a pacified territory or even administering justice in Rome itself. In this particular case, Marcellus' province was clearly a military assignment, and the senate debated whether he had finished the war there. What exactly was Marcellus' province, and did it remain the same throughout his time in Sicily? It is hazardous to place too much stock in Livy's precise wordings of senatorial military assignments, but it is a start to untying this knot. Livy, as noted in the last chapter, reported in his entry for the senate's assignment of commands in 213 that Marcellus had been assigned by the senate 'Sicily with the boundaries that Hiero's kingdom had had,' while Publius Lentulus, with the rank of propraetor, was assigned 'the old province', the area of Sicily under Roman control since the First Punic War ended.[7] For 212, Livy asserts that Marcellus' proconsular command was extended again by the senate; his province was 'Syracuse and up to the former boundaries of Hiero's kingdom.' Lentulus continued as propraetor within 'the limits of the old province in Sicily.'[8] Perhaps this change in phrasing reflects the extension of Marcellus' command to include Syracuse, which would be reasonable if the final revolt and siege of Syracuse did not take place until somewhere between March of 213 and March of 212. March, after all, was the month when the first senate meetings of the new political year were initiated and commands were normally assigned. That would explain why Livy or his source added Syracuse explicitly to the province when that city was already within the old kingdom of Hiero. In 211, though, Marcellus' command was extended again so that 'as proconsul in Sicily he might finish the remainder of the war with the army which he had.' The newly elected praetor Gaius Sulpicius was assigned to 'Sicily' – no mention of the old province here – and took command of the two legions under Lentulus' command.[9] If the addition of Syracuse was purposeful in Livy's account, what should be made of Marcellus' assignment in 211, which appears broader in scope than those of the previous years? First off, by any chronology seriously entertained by historians, Syracuse must have been taken well before the spring of 211. Consider that Appius Claudius, Marcellus' subordinate, must have left for Rome at the end of 213 in order to be elected consul for 212. Polybius says that the city was besieged by Appius and Marcellus for eight months.[10] If indeed Appius was there for the entire siege, and assuming Polybius was only referring to the time up to the breaching of the Epipolae walls, then the first stage of capturing the city was complete by the end of 213. Livy associates the final siege of Achradina and the arrival of the plague with the fall,[11] which must be the fall of 212. If the city had fallen at any time before the early spring of 211, when the senate would assign commands for the year, this would explain why the senate omitted Syracuse and included the task of finishing up what was left of the war in 211. Marcellus could have fought his last significant battle in Sicily late in 212, as Livy suggests, or sometime during 211; since no one at the time could know it was to be Marcellus' last battle, neither dating would undermine the suggestion that Syracuse was considered taken by March 211 and Marcellus' province for that year was to mop up.[12]

Clearly, Marcellus had sacked Syracuse and soundly defeated the largest known Carthaginian force on the island before he returned to Rome. To arrive at

Rome early enough to seek the consulship for 210, he presumably departed Sicily in late in 211 or perhaps early in 210. Subsequent events in Sicily, however, revealed that there was a Carthaginian military presence on the island after he had left. This was beyond Marcellus' ability to predict or control: Carthaginian transports had landed infantry and Numidian cavalry reinforcements on the island after Marcellus left. These forces persuaded the towns of Murgentia and Ergetium to rebel against the Romans as well as Hybla and Macella, all in the eastern part of the island. Not for long; the praetor Marcus Cornelius Cethegus now commanded the Cannae legions and with those forces returned the rebels to the Roman fold. [13]

Returning to the debate over Marcellus' triumph, some senators noted, according to Livy, that Marcellus had been ordered to turn his troops over to a new commander, something that was done only when a province was not completely pacified.[14] Indeed, later in the same chapter, after describing the debate, Livy jumps back to Sicily and narrates briefly the need for Cethegus to extinguish the rebellion. Though his structure here implies a connection between the debate in the temple and the new uprising in Sicily, it is highly doubtful that any word of the new rebellion could have reached Rome. If, as Livy suggests, this small Carthaginian invasion force came to Sicily after Marcellus set sail for Rome,[15] and Marcellus met with the senate upon his arrival from Sicily, it is highly unlikely that Cethegus could have received word of a new Carthaginian invasion and informed the senate before it met with Marcellus.

While this entire debate could be seen as simply an honest and earnest discussion of the technical qualifications for celebrating a triumph, this was only the tip of the iceberg. At the heart of this debate was the struggle between Marcellus and those of his rivals who sought to limit his prestige and achievements. It was one of the many examples of the broader tensions that existed between the senatorial aristocracy and any of its members, especially successful generals, who rose too far above the rest in honour and prestige. The political system of the Republic, complete with its unwritten rules on competition for offices and honours, was intended to, among other things, give a variety of aristocrats access to powerful offices and the chance to win military victories. These opportunities for offices and victories in turn allowed those aristocrats to win the glory and fame that were the currency for the political elite. So, it was generally accepted that a consul would achieve measures of glory unavailable to other senators, possibly a military victory of sorts, perhaps a triumph; after all, the office circulated to new holders every year and others would have their chance for fame. When someone like Marcellus was the commander, the situation changed. Here was an individual whose record already dwarfed almost every other senator. He had already held several consulships and triumphed, which put him in an exceptionally small group. Now he had to his credit the conquest of mighty Syracuse. But if he was denied a triumph for this victory it would diminish his honour or at least check it from growing further at the moment. There must have been many senators who simply felt that Marcellus had had more than his fair share of glory, a deeply Roman and, indeed, deeply human sentiment. Thus the subtext to these arguments about the technical requirements for a legitimate triumph was essentially about limiting the amount of glory any individual could win.

Indeed, any sense that senators that day were pointing out fixed criteria for triumphs vanishes when the general practices for granting triumphs in the period are considered. In the Samnite wars at the beginning of the third century, Roman commanders were awarded triumphs explicitly against the Samnites for five of the six years from 295 to 290.[16] Quintus Fabius Maximus Rullianus celebrated the first of these in 295, even though the Samnites invaded Etruria after Rullianus led the army out of the region.[17] The next year's consuls both celebrated triumphs against the Samnites by taking several cities, though there were still other cities in the region left untouched.[18] Triumphs in the third century, in short, were awarded for great military successes, not because they marked permanent ends to any given conflict in a region.

Perhaps though, some requirement to pacify a region was instituted only after the Samnite Wars, as Roman armies were drawn further afield and could not as easily return home in the winter months. During the First Punic War, however, a conflict in which Marcellus and many other senior senators fought, there is no evidence of any rule requiring an enemy to be defeated permanently if a general was to win a triumph. Commanders celebrated triumphs for victories on land over the Carthaginians in 263, 259, 258, 257, and 250.[19] Indeed, at the beginning of the war, Marcus Valerius Maximus Messala celebrated a triumph over the Carthaginians and the king of Sicily.[20] True, Hiero was no longer a threat to Rome, but the Carthaginians, regardless of Messala's triumph, remained a force on the western part of the island for another twenty years.[21] It strains credulity too far to suppose that the Romans awarded triumphs to commanders in these years on the premise that Carthage had been driven from Sicily and the island had been wholly pacified. Rather, as in the Samnite Wars, triumphs were granted for significant victories, not ultimate victories. This practice continued during the Gallic wars that were of recent memory for many senators. Lucius Aemilius Papus' victory over the Gauls, according to Polybius, encouraged the Romans to think they might soon drive the enemy completely out of the Po Valley[22] clearly, they had not done so yet when Papus was granted a triumph in 225. Gaius Flaminius then triumphed over the Gauls in 223,[23] and while the Gauls made peace overtures in the subsequent year, the Romans opted to remain at war.[24] Finally, as seen in the first chapter, Marcellus won his triumph over the Gauls for Clastidium.[25]

These trends in granting triumphs suggest that there was nothing like a requirement for total victory at the time the senate debated Marcellus' claim.

Rather, the award of such a celebration depended upon the general consensus of senators and the assembly that the victories of the general in question were worthy of such recognition. It was Marcellus' detractors, then, that brought up this alleged rule because it helped their case. Not uncommonly, most rivalries between senators were played out in this fashion, with each side suggesting that the traditions and rules favoured their point of view. Though there were undoubtedly exceptions, most of the time, the introduction of rules was probably not an act of outright fabrication – not in the modern sense. In an age without extensive records and fact checking, without even extensive written rules – there was no written Roman constitution – it was up to the collective consensus at any given time to determine what the rules and traditions exactly were. Traditions and memories about those traditions varied then just as they do now, and one Roman's sacred custom could be another's spurious fabrication. Ultimately, it was up to the collective to determine which rules were truly sanctioned. Accordingly, individuals and groups could often challenge their rivals by suggesting they were breaking the rules. With this in mind, Plutarch's account of the senate debate becomes particularly helpful. According to him, Marcellus' enemies opposed his triumph both because war still existed in Sicily and because another triumph would arouse envy.[26] A self-serving phrasing in a sense, since presumably it would only arouse envy in those very rivals who felt Marcellus did not deserve it. As noted earlier, though, a tension existed when any individual aristocrat went beyond the bounds of normal honour and fame, and it was not at all uncommon for a significant portion of the aristocracy to work collectively, consciously or not, to limit or even humble one of their own who aspired to too many honours. Marcellus certainly fit the bill. Truly, celebrating a single triumph was a rare achievement for any Roman aristocrat. Celebrating two triumphs was almost unheard of. Celebrating two triumphs in addition to the probably controversial celebration for winning the *spolia opima* was simply without precedent.

The debate in the senate that day illustrates quite well the competition at which the aristocracy played for centuries. Previously, it was suggested that the system of political competition in the Republic could be helpfully conceptualized as a game. Again, the goal for players was to gain prestige, fame, and a reputation for *virtus*. Winning election to offices and achieving memorable deeds while in office, particularly military deeds, were the critical means by which players moved toward their goals. In addition, aristocrats could win additional fame and glory by claiming special rewards for their deeds. Success bred success; if an aristocrat managed to carve out the kind of reputation that made him appealing to peers and voters, he would continue to hold higher offices, possibly even repeating the consulship. Marcellus' career exemplifies how successful one could be at this practice: crowns for single combat, the *spolia opima*, one triumph celebrated and now a second one claimed. As for his political career, by the beginning of 210, he had been elected consul three times, once as the first ever plebeian to hold a spot reserved for patricians. He had been named proconsul for years, and the one year the senate chose not to grant him that power, the popular assembly asserted its will and voted him a command anyway.

What the debate in the Temple of Bellona illustrates so well is another of the plays senators could make to keep their rivals in check. It was fully recognized and condoned by practice that one could raise objections to an individual's efforts to gain posts, honours, and power by casting them in terms of points of law, points of religion, points of tradition, really points of propriety. So Livy and Plutarch's versions need to be combined to get a complete picture of what happened that day and why. There were senators envious of Marcellus earning another triumph who used the language of procedure and propriety to express their objections. They did so not because that technical language was superficial or disingenuous, but because it was a vocabulary that spoke to the recognized need the Romans felt to follow the traditions and procedures that had brought them favour from the gods, and success in this world.

When all was said and done, the move to block Marcellus' triumph succeeded – at least in part. True, he would not be granted a formal triumph. A decisive group of senators, however, must have found it unreasonable that he receive no recognition for the victory over Syracuse, a victory that, as his supporters that day had noted, had earned him a public thanksgiving. This argument must have had traction with undecided senators; in the end, Marcellus had rendered a critical service to the Republic by subduing the keystone of eastern Sicily and virtually guaranteeing Roman control of the region. Senate meetings were times of deliberation, not necessarily voting; so far as we know, only when the leading senators had debated the issues thoroughly and reached no consensus did matters come to an actual vote. A compromise was reached. Marcellus was granted the right to process in Rome in an *ovatio* ('ovation'), a form of parade junior in grade to the triumph.[27]

The choice of compromise was a striking one. The celebration itself was extremely rare. Plutarch describes it as similar to the triumph, but 'in conducting [the ovation] the general does not mount upon a four-horse chariot, nor wear a wreath of laurel, nor have trumpets sounding about him; but he goes afoot with shoes on, accompanied by the sound of exceedingly many flutes, and wearing a wreath of myrtle.'[28] So far as the historical record goes, Marcus Fabius Ambustus was the last to celebrate an ovation in 360. The anonymous fourth century AD writer of *De Viris Illustribus Urbis Romae* ('About Famous Men of the City of Rome') suggests one ovation was celebrated in 290 or 289, but this is not corroborated elsewhere, and it is likely this was some other kind of celebration. Either way, Marcellus was granted the right to celebrate a ceremony that either had not been used for 150 years or had been used twice in 150 years, the last time 80 years earlier. For practical purposes, he had revived an archaic ceremony to suit his needs.[29] Nor, it should be recalled, was this the first time. Historians have noted regularly that Marcellus seemed to have been fond of archaic ceremonies and antiquated rituals. It may be that Marcellus fancied himself an aficionado of antique ceremonies, perhaps in part viewing himself as a representative of the traditional Roman *virtus*, which earned favour from the gods.

Any intrinsic interest Marcellus had in such rituals, however, cannot be separated cleanly from the fact that these rituals formed a critical part of his political persona and were a formidable tool of competition. The rhetoric of competition among aristocrats in the Republic – much as it still is today among all sorts of legislators – was cast in terms of what was and was not beneficial to the Republic. Where modern politicians assert – at times it seems with reckless abandon – that their positions represent the will of the people, the general claim of the Roman aristocrat, the standard by which the public measured his actions, was that his behaviour and character were consistent with the best Roman traditions and his deeds were all in the service of the Republic. Taking this a step further, consider that the well-being of the Republic, in Roman eyes, generally depended on following the *mores maiorum*, the customs of the ancestors. This meant following the proper rituals and practices, and observing the customs that had been demonstrated over centuries to win the favour of the gods and keep the Republic strong. In these respects Roman society, like essentially all ancient societies, tended to value the old and established, the traditional and proven far more than the novel and innovative.

Marcellus' skill at resurrecting moribund customs allowed him to trumpet his victories, emphasize the favour in which the gods held him, and, no less importantly, show that he particularly respected the ancestral customs. It was a classic packaging: accomplish the extraordinary under the mantle of following the traditional. Sincere belief may have moved him deeply; a fascination with and reverence for the antique customs of his elders may have inspired him; there is no question, however, that this ability to revive old customs served him personally. If nothing else, an ovation could have been more noteworthy because of its novelty. Presumably, to any Romans' mind, the triumph was the supreme honour, but if that was to be denied Marcellus, people would well remember an unusual ceremony that had not been used in their lifetime but had the patina of tradition.

Marcellus' next steps only reinforce the conclusion that he was a particularly shrewd player of politics. The day before he was scheduled to the enter the city for his ovation, he celebrated a triumph *Monte Albano*, 'on the Alban Mount'.[30] This sacred peak in nearby Alba Longa was used to celebrate triumphal processions several times by generals who had been denied formal triumphs in Rome. Interestingly enough, these alternative triumphs, though they lacked the formal approval of senate and people, were officially recorded on the Fasti, suggesting they were considered legitimate ceremonies.[31] According to later

Romans, the first to celebrate such a triumph was Gaius Papirius Maso, slightly over two decades before Marcellus. It has been suggested, however, that Maso was actually reviving a tradition that had lapsed in the distant past, perhaps a triumph celebrated by Latins rather than Romans.[32] Certainly, this would fit with Marcellus' penchant for reviving ancient customs. In this way, Marcellus circumvented his opposition in the senate. And what a way: Marcellus was the first, so far as we know, ever to hold two victory celebrations for the same achievement. So while obeying the dictates of the senate, Marcellus still managed to claim exceptional honours for himself.[33] He also did so in a way that must have seemed shockingly novel to many, even as his actions had the mantle of venerated custom. Marcellus' rivals and detractors must have been disturbed, if not incensed, by the way he had snatched an extraordinary victory from the jaws of defeat.

Whether the triumph on the Alban Mount followed the same outlines and used the same props as the ovation is lost to us. What is clear is that Marcellus was determined to make his ovation, regardless of its junior status, appear more magnificent than any triumph. Livy describes the ceremony:

An enormous quantity of spoil was carried before [Marcellus] together with a model of Syracuse at the time of its capture. Catapults and ballistae and all the engines of war taken from the city were exhibited in the procession, as were also the works of art which had been accumulated in royal profusion during the long years of peace. These included a number of articles in silver and bronze, pieces of furniture, costly garments and many famous statues with which Syracuse, like all the principal cities of Greece, had been adorned. To signalize his victories over the Carthaginians eight elephants were led in the procession. Not the least conspicuous feature of the spectacle was the sight of Sosis the Syracusan and Moericus the Spaniard who marched in front wearing golden crowns. The former had guided the nocturnal entry into Syracuse, the latter had been the agent in the surrender of Nasos and its garrison.[34]

While the splendor of the celebration in general is most the important point to note, it is also striking that rather than limit the promotion of his achievements to Syracuse, Marcellus also made sure to claim a victory over the Carthaginians. This was a bold display.

The spectacle was not yet complete, for Marcellus lavished Rome with the riches he had stripped from Syracuse. The sources agree on these points: the wealth, especially objects of art, taken from Syracuse was greater than any seized before by the Romans, and Marcellus spread it around. As a result, a great deal of Greek art was put on display throughout the city. Much of it was used to decorate the temple to Honos and Virtus. In fact, the riches from Syracuse were used to enable Marcellus to complete this vowed victory temple. It had not yet been built when Syracuse was taken; historians have often assumed, based on a passing reference in Plutarch,[35] that Marcellus renewed the vow at Syracuse. Whether this is the case or he simply followed through on the original vow from 222, the temple to Honos and Virtus began to be constructed and decorated with Syracusan art.

There is no compelling evidence that Marcellus' contemporaries were either unexposed to Greek art and culture or categorically upset by the importation of such rich spoils. However, his rivals did seem to make use of the amount of spoils Marcellus brought from the city to argue that he had acted with a profound lack of restraint in his treatment of the city. Later writers adopted the stance – though here modern readers must be very skeptical – that the importation of such wealth was corrupting. Polybius offers the earliest surviving sermon on this matter no more than a century after the event. He first notes, 'A city is not adorned by external splendors, but by the virtue of its inhabitants,' and later suggests:

> There were indeed perhaps good reasons for appropriating all the gold and silver [from Syracuse]: for it was impossible for them to aim at a world empire without weakening the resources of other peoples and strengthening their own. But it was possible for them to leave everything which did not contribute to such strength, together with the envy attached to its possession, in its original place, and to add to the glory of their native city by adorning it not with paintings and reliefs but with dignity and magnanimity.[36]

Livy, writing yet another century later, preached:

> As regards the adornments of the city, the statues and paintings which Syracuse possessed in abundance, [Marcellus] carried them away to Rome. They were the spoils of the enemy, to be sure, and acquired by right of war. Yet from that came the very beginning of enthusiasm for Greek works of art and consequently of this general license to despoil all kinds of buildings, sacred and profane, a license which finally turned against Roman gods and first of all against the very temple which was magnificently adorned by Marcellus. For temples dedicated by Marcus Marcellus near the Porta Capena used to be visited by foreigners on account of their remarkable adornments of that kind; but of these a very small part is still to be seen.[37]

Plutarch provides the fullest description of the kinds of decorations Marcellus transferred from Syracuse to Rome:

> When Marcellus was recalled by the Romans to the war in their home territories, he carried back with him the greater part and the most beautiful

of the dedicatory offerings in Syracuse, that they might grace his triumph and adorn his city. For before this time Rome neither had nor knew about such elegant and exquisite productions, nor was there any love there for such graceful and subtle art; but filled full of barbaric arms and bloody spoils, and crowned round about with memorials and trophies of triumphs, she was not a gladdening or a reassuring sight, nor one for unwarlike and luxurious spectators. ... Therefore with the common people Marcellus won more favour because he adorned the city with objects that had Hellenic grace and charm and fidelity; but with the elder citizens Fabius Maximus was more popular. For he neither disturbed nor brought away anything of the sort from Tarentum, when that city was taken, but while he carried off the money and the other valuables, he suffered the statues to remain in their places, adding the well-known saying: 'Let us leave these gods in their anger for the Tarentines.' And they blamed Marcellus, first, because he made the city odious, in that not only men, but even gods were led about in her triumphal processions like captives; and again, because, when the people was accustomed only to war or agriculture, and was inexperienced in luxury and ease, but, like the Heracles of Euripides, was 'Plain, unadorned, in a great crisis brave and true,' he made them idle and full of glib talk about art and artists, so that they spent a great part of the day in such clever disputation. Notwithstanding such censure, Marcellus spoke of this with pride even to the Greeks, declaring that he had taught the ignorant Romans to admire and honour the wonderful and beautiful productions of Greece.[38]

Plutarch offers the most complete moral indictment, suggesting that the Romans had known nothing other than crude art and the rough decorations of war before Marcellus imported Syracusan art collections. He places the beginning of the Roman exposure to the luxuries of Greek art and decoration with Marcellus' importation of spoils from Syracuse. He also suggests that these finer objects of art softened the Romans. In bringing such great and, by implication, morally corrupting art to the city, Marcellus allegedly gained favour with the average citizen while receiving the disapproval of the city elders. Again, though, it must be stressed that these sermons fundamentally misrepresent the familiarity Romans had with Greek culture at this time. There simply is no certain and compelling third century evidence suggesting contemporary Romans felt corrupted by the Syracusan art.

Later preaching aside, Marcellus' calculations for his victory celebrations had been highly effective. Some senators at least were likely disgruntled that he effectively circumvented the senate's denial of a triumph by his extraordinary celebrations. Clearly, whatever animosity he might have aroused was insufficient to prevent his election to yet another consulship sometime soon after the celebration of his triumph – not that anything as mercurial as the moods of a voting assembly could be predicted with any certainty. Indeed, the *centuria praerogativa*, the century chosen by lot to cast its public vote for consul first, did not select Marcellus at all. Instead, it voted for the old and distinguished Roman noble, Titus Manlius Torquatus and for Titus Otacilius, at that time commanding the Roman fleet in Sicily. Torquatus' eyesight was failing, however, and when the initial vote was cast, he addressed the assembly and demanded that it vote again for a different candidate.[39] This episode suggests again that at least during the war years, one did not have to declare one's candidacy in order to be elected consul, for it is difficult to see why Torquatus would have petitioned to be consul and then challenged the vote when it went his way. Further, it reinforces the reality that despite any efforts to believe otherwise, these elections were not pre-determined or predictable, not even necessarily rational. Livy's assessment of what happened next, some two centuries after the fact was likely little better than ours. In his account, the prerogative century, on this day the juniors of the Voturian tribe, requested time to confer with the senior century of their tribe. Livy says they were granted space for a secret meeting and in the next breath, without any sense of irony, reports the discussion in that meeting: the elders suggested that there were three choices, Marcellus and Fabius among the established nobles and Marcus Valerius Laevinus, who had been conducting the war against Philip of Maecedon, if they desired a less established but capable candidate. Leaving aside the implausibility that Livy would know the three names discussed in an ad hoc secret meeting conducted on the day of elections, these were hardly the only men that could have been elected consul, particularly when the customary restrictions on intervals between successive consulships were largely ignored in this period. More likely, Livy simply noted that when the junior century voted again, Marcellus and Laevinus were chosen and all the remaining centuries concurred. He inferred then that these men were named in the secret discussion and considered it reasonable that the elder statesman Fabius would also be in the running as a matter of course. Ultimately, Livy was most interested in using the episode to illustrate the superior morality of the Romans of old, compared to those in his own day, noting with the affected air of a curmudgeon, 'that a century of the younger men wished to confer with their elders on the question to which persons they should, by their vote, entrust a high command, should seem to us scarcely credible – this is due to the cheapened and diminished authority even of parents over their children in our day.'[40]

Despite his victory at the polls, political trouble was brewing for Marcellus. Sicilians who had grievances against Marcellus had traveled to Rome and were staying in the various villas of his rivals in the suburbs of the city. By the time the Ides of March had come and Marcellus was inaugurated consul, according to Livy, he claimed to know that these Sicilian envoys were making the rounds of the city and that they wished to levy an accusation against him. Here it is worth reading Livy's account in full:

[Marcellus] knew ... that a large number of Sicilians were near the city at the country-places of his detractors; that so far was it from being true that these men were not permitted by him to noise abroad openly at Rome the charges emanating from his personal foes, that he would himself immediately have given them a hearing in the senate but for their pretending no little fear to speak of the consul in the absence of his colleague. When indeed his colleague should arrive, [Marcellus] said, he would not allow any business to be taken up prior to the question of bringing the Sicilians before the senate. It was almost a levy that Marcus Cornelius [Cethegus] had conducted all over Sicily in order that as many as possible might come to Rome to complain of himself. [Marcellus] added that Cornelius had also filled the city with letters falsely stating there was a war in Sicily, in order to detract from the praise of the speaker. After winning a reputation for moderation on that day, the consul [Marcellus] dismissed the senate.[41]

Livy uses the vocabulary of political conflict when describing Marcellus' statement: Marcellus said that his *inimici* ('formal enemies') had accusations to make against him and that he was ready to receive those charges, but felt it improper to do so until the other consul Laevinus, who was still abroad and recovering from an illness, had returned and taken up his consulship.

Livy's account is plausible enough, as was Marcellus' claim that his personal enemies were behind the suit, hosting the envoys and encouraging them to plead their case to the senate. Without such patronage the Sicilian envoys would have made very little headway, and those senators who entertained the Sicilian claims were opposing Marcellus by that very act if they had not done so before. That Marcellus had formal political opponents of this level is practically certain. It was the nature of the Roman political system, if not of politics in all times and places, to produce such formal rivalries. More precisely, though, there had to have been substantial opposition to Marcellus on the day his claim for a triumph was rejected, substantial enough to block the claim. Surely not everyone who opposed Marcellus was simply a categorical enemy, but for some there was a clear connection to be made between the debate over Marcellus' triumph and the encouragement of the Sicilian envoys. Marcellus' actions in Sicily were controversial enough that they inspired opposition from those who wished to see him humbled or their own careers promoted.

This time, though, instead of some general reference to enemies in the sources, one of Marcellus' rivals is named: Marcus Cornelius Cethegus. He had succeeded Marcellus as commander in Sicily. During his time there, Cethegus had apparently persuaded – actively encouraged, claimed Marcellus – Sicilians with grievances against the sacker of Syracuse that they would find supporters at Rome. Again, this is plausible enough. Cethegus had also apparently sent letters – a flood, Marcellus noted – reporting that Sicily was far from pacified. There is no question that encouraging the Sicilian envoys and writing such letters would actively undermine Marcellus' accomplishments on the island. Cethegus cannot have been unaware of this; the alternative would be simply incredible, that such a complete political naïf had played the game of politics successfully enough to make it to the praetorship.

None of this requires supposing, however, that Cethegus sought to discredit Marcellus simply for the sake of doing so. The letters about Sicilian affairs may have been no more than status reports based on Cethegus's assessments, and he would hardly have kept quiet about the realities in the field simply to spare another commander's feelings. Perhaps, too, Cethegus did nothing more than suggest to any complaining Sicilians he encountered that their grievances should be properly received by the senate in Rome. The embassy dispatched to complain about Marcellus and the publicity it received, however, were both substantial. They lend credibility to Marcellus' accusation that Cethegus had actively stirred up trouble.

Why? Some possibilities suggest themselves. First, the debate over Marcellus' triumph and over the end of the war in his province was still quite fresh. It can hardly have been more than a few months since he celebrated his ovation and triumph on the Alban Mount, perhaps six at the most. Those who seriously resented Marcellus then would have found Cethegus to be a useful instrument or ally for continuing the debate on Sicily. Perhaps they collaborated with Cethegus. Certainly, Cethegus, in general terms, had things to gain. His own command in Sicily and his own deeds would become more important if the general consensus was that Marcellus had not finished the job. Since senators were already divided about the completion of the war there, Cethegus had an opening to increase his own prestige at Marcellus' expense. It is worth noting that in the Roman political system, people of lower rank could and often did attempt to increase their own stature simply by promoting their *inimicitia* ('enemy status') with a more famous and distinguished politician.[42] The greater the fame of the enemy, the more status could be gained, particularly if the lower-status rival checked his enemy. This is a logic still at work today when junior legislators denounce established politicians or new prosecutors tackle cases against high-profile defendants – regardless of their motives – and gain media exposure. Certainly, Marcellus would be an excellent target for an ambitious rising aristocrat. He was unsurpassed by his contemporaries, matched only by Fabius Maximus, yet he was not unassailable. Perhaps a combination of these factors moved Cethegus.

However much Marcellus may have claimed Cethegus' reports were mere lies, the reality was more complicated. Sicily's strategic importance to both Carthage and Rome ensured that the Carthaginians would not surrender it easily. The relatively short distance between the western half of the island and Carthage itself meant that new forces could be dispatched to continue the struggle there with relative ease. Roman senators at the time must have been fully aware of this. Did Marcellus really claim that there was no fighting on the island? It seems more likely that he would have argued, instead, the more defensible and, for him, relevant point: there was no war in his former province. To a certain extent, he had a point. Cethegus had quickly pacified the revolt of the Sicilian cities, and since he would have been a primary source of information about affairs on the island, it might have appeared to Marcellus that Cethegus' reports were lies. Ultimately, since Marcellus had already celebrated his ovation, triumphed on the Alban Mount, and won the consulship, Cethegus' letters posed the lesser problem. The greater political challenge was the accusation that Marcellus had conducted himself improperly as the agent of Rome in Sicily. The perceived conduct of an aristocrat on campaign played a critical role in his reputation for *virtus* and honour or a lack thereof. Marcellus had cultivated an exceptional reputation for superior conduct and superior *virtus* on the battlefield. The accusations of the Sicilians threatened to undermine his great source of political strength, and a humiliation now could end his ascendancy.

Whether he would be condemned or vindicated would soon be seen. Laevinus recovered from his illness and returned to Rome. Soon after, the senate determined that the two consular provinces for the year would be 'Sicily and the fleet' and 'Italy with the war against Hannibal'. When the lots were cast to determine which province each consul would have, Marcellus received Sicily. Apparently, the Sicilian envoys, who had not yet had the chance to put their case before the senate, were present when the lots were drawn or at least received the news quickly. Seeing that Marcellus would again hold *imperium* in Sicily, they protested elaborately, donning the clothes of mourners and making the rounds to the houses of senators. Such a dramatic course of action suggests that Marcellus had a point when he charged that the Sicilians were being supported by his enemies. Perhaps by some stretch of imagination foreign embassies were regularly allowed to wander on their own between senators' houses publicly lamenting and petitioning, but it is far more likely that such tactics would only be permitted, let alone successful, if the delegates had powerful friends within the senate. According to Livy, 'these complaints of the Sicilians, at first circulated in the homes of the nobles and repeated in conversations inspired partly by pity for the Sicilians, partly by envy against Marcellus, even reached the senate.'[43] If Livy chose his words precisely and based them on a valid source, his reference to the nobles suggests that those who encouraged the Sicilians were among the highest ranking of Roman senators.

The campaign was successful; the senate convened and asked Marcellus and Laevinus to discuss the appropriateness of the year's provincial assignments. In particular, the consuls were asked by some to exchange their provinces so that Marcellus no longer would hold *imperium* in Sicily. Marcellus could have treated the request as a grave insult, but simply agreed that since the Sicilians had not yet presented their grievances to the senate it would be appropriate to discuss an exchange of provinces. He was surely well aware that failing to swap provinces would spur speculation that the Sicilians had feared to raise legitimate complaints because they feared reprisals from the consul. The consuls asserted, however, that they could discuss the matter themselves; there was no need for a formal senatorial decree exchanging provinces, and indeed, any such official action would be highly, publicly insulting to Marcellus. The senate concurred, Marcellus and Laevinus conferred, and the consular provinces were transferred for the year.[44] Really, it was a win-win situation for Marcellus. Though command over Sicily and the fleet was strategically important, the opportunities for glory were greater in Italy, where Hannibal, now having spent almost a decade in the peninsula, was still the primary threat and was certainly the symbolic heart of the enemy.

With the provinces reassigned, the Sicilian envoys could present their grievances to the senate without any hint of coercion. The substance of their complaint seems to have been these points. Hiero had been a steadfast ally of the Roman people. Therefore, the defection to Hannibal under the short-lived king Hieronymus and the tyrants Epicydes and Hippocrates was no more than a policy aberration and one hated by the Syracusans at that. Marcellus himself was partially responsible for this change in policy. The tyrants were able to seize power because of Syracusan resentment at the way Marcellus had brutally sacked Leontini – though it was never clear that this was more than a rumour. Furthermore, when the Syracusans plotted to assassinate the tyrants and made arrangements with Marcellus to put pressure on the walls of Syracuse, he had delayed in positioning his army. That delay caused the assassination plot to be exposed and the assassins executed. After this, secret emissaries from leading citizens at Syracuse repeatedly tried to surrender the city to Marcellus, but he was set on taking the city by force and insisted on working with the mercenaries in the city rather than the leading citizens. Finally, came what was likely the core of the complaint: Marcellus' troops had despoiled the city, stripping temples and private houses, looting the city of all its riches. Furthermore, much of the land owned by the wealthiest Syracusans had been seized by the Romans and given away. The envoys requested that, insofar as it was possible, the Syracusans have all possessions returned to their verifiable owners.[45]

Once they had finished their complaints, the Syracusan envoys were asked to leave the senate chambers by Laevinus. Marcellus, however, countered the order, wishing to make his response in front of both the senators and the envoys. It is impossible to determine the extent to which Marcellus was enraged, astounded, defensive, or simply calculating when he responded to the charges. What can be said is that he acted yet again in a politically savvy way by rhetorically emphasizing his role as a loyal servant of the Republic. Responding to the charges in front of the envoys was as good a way as any to show that he believed he had done nothing dishonourable.

Though the sources agree that Marcellus was a model of restraint that day, it strains credulity to think he felt sanguine during the Syracusan charges. There is no reason to doubt that from his point of view, the Syracusans had been mercurial, treacherous, and dishonourable. On several occasions Marcellus had negotiated a peaceful end to the conflict in Syracuse only to have political disorder in the city smash all arrangements. When all was said and done, no professed good intentions on the part of these leading citizens had changed the fact that Syracuse resisted surrendering to the Romans until the very end. From his point of view, their claims must essentially have amounted to: 'We do not think we should have lost all our possessions just for defying and resisting the Romans.' That these envoys could now come before the senate at all and make these claims must have been galling. What right did Rome's enemies, once vanquished, have to complain about the terms of their defeat?

When Livy constructed Marcellus' response from the available evidence, he clearly was thinking along similar lines. Though Livy assuredly fabricated the exact wording of Marcellus' response, he just as likely preserved the substance of the response passed on by earlier sources. It is a good speech and worth reading:

Not so forgetful have I been of the majesty of the Roman people and of this authority of mine, conscript fathers, that if it were a question of a charge brought against me, I would have pleaded my case with Greeks as my accusers. But it is not what I have done that is to be inquired into – for whatever I did in the case of enemies is defended by the law of war – but what they deserved to suffer. If they have not been enemies, it makes no difference whether it was recently or in the time of Hiero that I desolated Syracuse. But if they rebelled against the Roman people, if they attacked our ambassadors with sword and arms, closed their city and walls, defended them against us with an army of Carthaginians, who is indignant because they suffered hostile acts, when they have committed them? When leading men among the Syracusans tried to surrender the city, I rejected them; I preferred [the mercenaries] Sosis and Moericus the Spaniard as the men to whom I would entrust so important a matter. You are not Syracusans of the lowest rank, inasmuch as you reproach others with their humble station. Who is there among you who promised that he would open the gates to me, that he would admit my soldiers under arms into the city? You hate and curse those who did so, and even here you do not refrain from uttering insults against them. So far is it from the truth that you also would have done anything of the sort. [Sosis and Moericus'] humble rank, conscript fathers, of which those men make a reproach, is itself the strongest proof that I did not turn my back on any man who wished to serve our state. Before I laid siege to Syracuse, I endeavored, now by sending embassies, now by going to a conference, to secure peace; again, it was not until after they showed no shame in injuring ambassadors, and no answer was given even to myself when I met with their leading men at the gates, that, having endured many hardships on land and sea, I at last captured Syracuse by force of arms. Of what befell the captured it is more reasonable for them to complain in the presence of Hannibal and the defeated Carthaginians than in the senate of a victorious nation. For myself, conscript fathers, if I had been intending to deny the despoiling of Syracuse, I should never be using its spoils to adorn the city of Rome. But in what I as victor either took from individuals or gave to them, I am quite sure that I acted both according to the law of war and according to each man's desert. Whether you confirm these acts, conscript fathers, or not, concerns the state more than myself. For my duty has been fully discharged; it is to the interest of the state that you do not make other commanders less energetic for the future by annulling my acts. And seeing that you have heard face to face the words of the Sicilians as well as mine, conscript fathers, we shall leave the temple at the same time, so that in my absence the senate can deliberate with greater freedom.[46]

The themes of service to the Republic and the justness of humbling Rome's enemies are certainly consistent with the rhetoric of the time, and it is difficult to imagine Marcellus taking a different tack in his formal defence. Plutarch captures the speech much more briefly:

Marcellus made answer that in return for many injuries which [the Syracusans] had done to the Romans, they had suffered nothing except what men whose city has been taken by storm in war cannot possibly be prevented from suffering; and that their city had been so taken was their own fault, because they had refused to listen to his many exhortations and persuasions. For it was not by their tyrants that they had been forced into war, nay, they had elected those very tyrants for the purpose of going to war.[47]

While Plutarch leaves out the focus on service to the Republic, he corroborates Livy on what must have been the core complaint of the Syracusans, that they had been mistreated. Both sources agree that Marcellus's defence essentially was that the Syracusans had been enemies in a time of war and thus a Roman commander could legitimately treat them however he saw fit.

When his rebuttal was complete, both parties left the senate chambers, the consul to conduct the necessary levies of soldiers for the year, the ambassadors to await the decision of the senate. Laevinus, as the presiding consul, opened the debate on the Syracusans claims. Livy suggests that the senate was divided on the issues. No doubt this was the case since the Syracusans had had the support of some influential senators since at least their arrival in Rome. He names Titus Manlius Torquatus in particular as the leader for the 'great part of the senate' that found fault with Marcellus. The substance of their argument, apparently, was that the war should have been against the tyrants of Syracuse not the Syracusan people, who had been oppressed by the tyrants. Accordingly, Marcellus should have liberated the city as a recovered ally, not conquered and sacked it.

It was ultimately the propriety of Marcellus' behaviour that was questioned by Torquatus and those who were like-minded. Torquatus noted rhetorically, according to Livy, that:

> If Hiero, that loyal supporter of the power of Rome, could rise from the dead, with what face would any one dare to show him either Rome or Syracuse? In the one – his own city – he would see universal spoliation and a large part of it burnt, and as he approached the other he would see just outside its walls, almost within its gates, the spoils of his country.[48]

While Torquatus' exact words are irrecoverably lost, the substance of this critique likely came directly from his speech that day. Marcellus had used a great deal of the spoils from Syracuse to construct and adorn his temple to Honour and Virtue outside the Capena Gate of Rome. That made the temple an easy target for anyone critiquing the general's handling of Syracuse.

As with the earlier debate at the Temple of Bellona, various levels and motives for opposition can be identified. Certainly, some senators must have believed that Marcellus had treated the Syracusans poorly. It was a debatable point whether they were properly considered enemies or victims of the rebel government's policies. This can hardly have been the main sticking point for most senators however. Shortly after this debate, the senate heard the complaints of the Capuans, whose city had been sacked by Fulvius Flaccus. Arguments similar to those of the Syracusans were made and the senate did return possessions and land to a number of the citizens, even though the city had revolted from Rome.[49] Clearly then, even though our sources sometimes hint otherwise, the Romans were not limited to simple binary categorizations of people as either enemies or friends. The Capua parallel, however, also illustrates that Romans had no qualms about treating enemies harshly. A number of Capuans were ordered sold into slavery after their petitions, some were kept in chains awaiting future decisions on their fates, and possessions were not restored to those deemed undeserving. In this case, however, no debate was recorded in the senate when it ordered that some Capuans to be sold into slavery and others clapped in irons. Even if there were some debate that escaped the sources' notice, the senate apparently did not think the Capuan protests warranted calling the commander Quintus Fulvius Flaccus back from Capua to account for his actions as Marcellus had. It is difficult to suppose, then, that there was universal agreement in the senate that the Syracusans had been treated too harshly, that, categorically, rebellious cities should be treated better than Marcellus had Syracuse.[50]

In Livy's version Marcellus' opponents took advantage of the opportunity presented by the Syracusan protest to generate envy (*invidia*) against the consul. They were certainly successful insofar as they managed to orchestrate the hearing at all. That the senate even received the Syracusan deputation and required Marcellus to respond formally called into question the consul's actions in Sicily and could easily have been seen as a slight to his dignity.[51] Certainly, Livy says as much in his recreation of Marcellus' speech: Flaccus had not been required to answer his accusers, but Marcellus stood on trial.[52]

Why did the sacking of Syracuse provide an opportunity for Marcellus' opponents in a way that the taking of Capua did not? As seen earlier, Livy indicates, with considerable exaggeration, that the sacking of Syracuse marked a transition in the Republic, ushering in the Roman penchant for Greek art – but of course Livy was fixated on trying to track the decline in Roman morals from the founding of the Republic to his own day.[53] Plutarch provides an interesting relevant detail: the older citizens in Rome were offended by Marcellus' excessive use of Syracusan loot to adorn the city, particularly the use of gods – statues of gods, it should be noted – seized from that city. They grumbled that his introduction of so much Greek art would corrupt the Roman people, making them soft and unwarlike.[54] While there certainly may have been those who felt so, as with Livy, one must be on guard for the tendency of Plutarch, and his sources, to introduce an anachronistic moralizing that was not clearly present in the third century.

The important kernel of truth in the statements Livy and Plutarch report is their testimony to the copious amount of wealth that Marcellus had seized from Syracuse, the beauty of the spoils, and the uses to which he put it, adorning temples and public spots. The Romans were not unfamiliar with Greek art, but still, Marcellus had apparently imported this art on a previously unknown scale, so much from one city at one time. These works were bound to spark the curiosity of the city dwellers, high and low status alike. When they saw the works, they would know that Marcellus had seized them from the enemy and brought them to enrich Rome. It was an example of the most permanent and powerful kind of advertising a Roman aristocrat could have. Marcellus was neither the first nor last to use the spoils from a captured city this way, but the scale of his conquest meant the scale of the spoils he had at his disposal were extraordinary for the time.

This context helps explain why Torquatus may have opposed Marcellus so adamantly. Certainly, he may have honestly felt that the Syracusans had been ill-treated. But there was likely also a more personal element in play. Torquatus was one of the great aristocrats of the time, a man who had had a highly distinguished career and enjoyed great influence in the senate. Marcellus was an active or potential rival whose prestige and successes were far beyond those of a normal aristocratic career. He had been central to the Roman war effort for the past six years in a way Torquatus had not. He had certainly eclipsed him in the offices, honours, and scales of victories he had earned. An untarnished political victory in the Syracusan debate would only enhance Marcellus' reputation further and potentially undermine Torquatus' own position. It was not even a stretch for an envious senator in a society that paid such homage to tradition and character to proclaim that Marcellus' display of Syracusan wealth was immodest, immoral.

Furthermore, Torquatus had a special reputation for being a staunch traditionalist. After the defeat at Cannae, he had delivered a scathing speech, persuading the senate to refuse ransom for those legionaries captured by Hannibal. In the Livian account, he raised issues of traditional military virtue. Later that year, when Spurius Carvilius proposed the possibility of enrolling Latins in the senate to fill the gaps, Torquatus' speech was recorded for the opposition. He began by alluding to his famous ancestor who had fought the Latins in the fourth century. At the end of the speech against letting Latins fill the holes in the senate, Torquatus threatened that there was 'still one man of the stock to which that consul belonged who once in the Capitol threatened that he would kill with his own hand any Latin whom he saw sitting in the senate.' Clearly, Torquatus was both a man of prestige and influence at Rome, and one who was quite vocal in promoting traditional values.[55] If he continued to operate from the stance of a traditionalist, he could have had many reasons to object to Marcellus' behaviour. Marcellus had claimed the *spolia opima*; what he framed as the warranted revival of ancient glory, Torquatus could have just as easily seen as a spurious invention. From the patrician Torquatus' view, it would take no stretch at all to disapprove of the fact that Marcellus sought and won election as the second of two plebeian consuls and sparked a warning from the gods. Just in the past few months Marcellus had challenged the will of the senate and celebrated an antiquarian triumph on the Alban Mount. Now he brought wealth into the city perhaps on a scale never before seen. Perhaps Torquatus was even aware that, back in Sicily, the Syracusans had originally offered to make themselves clients of Marcellus, something unprecedented for a Roman.[56] In short, there are many reasons why Torquatus might have felt Marcellus flouted custom and propriety.

In any event, none of these concerns was sufficient for the senate to reprimand Marcellus or countermand his decisions in Sicily. The senate formally approved by decree his conduct and arrangements. And while Marcellus' opponents had scored a limited victory in that they had managed to cast doubt on the commander and question the propriety of his actions, the end result could not be considered anything but a confirmation of Marcellus' standing. When the Syracusan envoys heard the senate's ruling, they took the stance of supplicants, begging Marcellus to protect them and their city. Marcellus readily agreed, reassured them that he would not seek vengeance, and sent them on their way.[57]

The magnitude of what the Syracusans actually offered to Marcellus that day should not be underestimated. They essentially promised to place their city under the permanent patronage of Marcellus and his descendants. What's more, they voted honours to him and his descendants worthy of a god-king. When he or any of his descendants set foot on the island, the Syracusans pledged they would wear garlands and offer sacrifices to the gods.[58] A festival and games were established to celebrate the divine glory of Marcellus, an honour that was common enough for rulers in the Greek world but, so far as can be determined, had never yet been bestowed on a Roman. It's worth repeating: the Syracusans established yearly games called the *Marcellia* to celebrate their patron. These games continued to be held in Cicero's day well over a century later. In short, the city of Syracuse at least and, according to Cicero, who certainly would have known, the entire island were fully associated with the Marcelli from that day forward.[59] Though he had faced a number of substantial political challenges from the moment he had returned to Rome, Marcellus had essentially overcome them all and reached a pinnacle of success, now capped with patronage over a city and island, that had not been matched by any Roman in the past.

Chapter 5

The Final Italian Campaigns

While Marcellus had been away in Sicily, the war against Hannibal had continued much the same as it had since Cannae. Hannibal continued to wander southern Italy testing the loyalties of various towns, and Roman armies continued to monitor his movements and attempted to counter any damage he inflicted on their alliance system. This had been going on for years, and war weariness lay particularly heavy upon the Romans when Marcellus and Laevinus were inaugurated as consuls for 210.

Certainly, the Roman strategic situation in Italy had improved dramatically since the dark days after Cannae: Syracuse had been recaptured; Capua and Campania with it secured; and the Romans were no longer in any immediate danger of losing the war. These improvements in the Roman strategic position, however, had come at a heavy cost. Tens of thousands of Romans had lost their lives serving in the legions and fleets, cities and towns had been destroyed, farmlands devastated, and peasants displaced from their homes. So it was that the levies for 210 were bitterly received by citizens at Rome. After the infantry soldiers were conscripted, it came time to select rowers for the fleet. In response to a shortage of both manpower and state money, the consuls decreed that citizens themselves should supply rowers along with their pay and rations rather than funding this through the state treasury. This was not a completely novel suggestion; in the Greco-Roman world it generally fell to citizens to supply these kinds of military services, though not necessarily the accompanying pay and supplies. The demand agitated the populace, however, which had been subjected to extra financial and personal burdens for the better part of a decade. Complaints arose openly in the forum and reached the point where the consuls were unable to quell them. The senate met to discuss the issue but seemed unable to come up with a solution; the state treasuries were empty and it simply had to fall upon the citizen body to supply the necessary funds. A much needed solution soon came from Laevinus and Marcellus, who discussed the matter at great length. They, as befitting their station as consuls, would take the lead in giving virtually all of their personal holdings of precious metals, in whatever form they might be, to the state so that rowers could be properly furnished. The senators in return would follow the example of the consuls. The senate agreed without making any formal declaration, and each man brought his liquid assets to the state treasury. As usual, there was a competition to be seen serving the Republic, but this time it was by donating wealth rather than providing military and political service. In response to the show of dedication on the part of the senators, the wealthy cavalry class followed suit, as did the rest of the population.[1]

As for Hannibal, his strategic situation in Italy had certainly deteriorated. He had captured the important southern port of Tarentum but failed to secure the citadel, which remained in the control of a Roman garrison. Capua, the capital city that was critical to controlling Campania and fueling the flames of resistance against Rome, had fallen. After the Roman success at Capua, other Italians believed the tide had shifted and switched their allegiance to Rome. Unable to garrison effectively all the remaining loyalist regions, Hannibal adopted a policy of devastating disloyal areas in central and southern Italy in order to deny them to the Romans.[2]

Since Marcellus had traded his province of Sicily to Laevinus, it fell to him to prosecute the war against Hannibal. He had been in this situation six years earlier. The enemy was still loose in Southern Italy, engaging Marcellus in a military and diplomatic struggle for the loyalties of the various Italian city states in the region. An important victory for Marcellus came from Salapia, a city in Apulia near the Adriatic that had served as an important logistical post for Hannibal.[3] The leaders of the city, after some internal wrangling, decided to surrender Salapia to Marcellus, who had been in communication with Roman partisans there throughout the process.[4] The city was important in and of itself, but also because a detachment of Numidian cavalry were stationed there. The loss of these skilled horsemen was a serious blow for Hannibal. After securing the city, Marcellus turned his attention to other regional nodes in Hannibal's system of supply depots and fortified towns. First among these were the towns of Marmoreae and Meles in nearby Samnite territory. They contained considerable supplies of grain and were defended by a Carthaginian garrison several thousand strong. Marcellus' forces seized these towns and confiscated 240,000 *modii* of wheat and 10,000 of barley, a large haul corresponding to perhaps 3,600,000 pounds of wheat and 150,000 of barley. Other loot from the towns Marcellus distributed to his soldiers.[5] The gains made by Marcellus' forces were followed shortly by a Roman defeat at Herdonea, perhaps twenty miles distant from Marmoreae and Meles. Tradition blamed the proconsul in command, Gnaeus Fulvius Centumalus. Centumalus hoped to pressure Herdonea to return to the Roman alliance, especially after Marcellus had recovered Salapia. Supporters of Hannibal's cause in the city sent word to the Carthaginian, however, and Hannibal's army dropped its baggage and conducted forced marches until it reached Herdonea. Centumalus, Livy reports, was surprised and somewhat hastily drew up his forces. His plan was to send the fifth legion and the left wing of allied soldiers and cavalry first, with the sixth legion and right wing in reserve.

He had apparently not chosen a particularly secure spot for his camp, however, and Hannibal's cavalry, as their commander instructed, flanked the Romans quickly after the fifth legion and left wing engaged in close combat. The cavalry attacked both the Roman camp and the reserve forces, throwing them into disarray. They then turned their attention to the front line and routed the Roman forces. Thousands of Roman soldiers – how many exactly is unknown – died that day, Centumalus and a number of officers along with them.[6] The remnants of the army made their way to Marcellus.

The way in which Hannibal dealt with Herdonea after the victory illustrates the logistical and operational difficulties he faced at that stage in the war. After years of campaigning in Italy, he simply lacked the forces and the loyalty of sufficient Italian city states to enjoy a secure position. Rather, his army continued to play the role of a formidable band of marauders, certainly safer in southern Italy than elsewhere, but hardly secure. It may have been a sound strategy, therefore, though it certainly seems desperate, that Hannibal deported the population of Herdonea to Thurii and Metapontum and then razed the town.[7] Its loyalties were suspect; its position was strategically important; and Hannibal's forces were too few to garrison it.

Soon after the Roman defeat at Herdonea, Marcellus drafted a letter to the senate intended to bolster its courage: he would engage Hannibal and exact revenge for Herdonea. His army left its position in Samnium and marched south over the rugged hills to the town of Numistro in Lucania, perhaps sixty or seventy miles away. There Marcellus found Hannibal's army encamped on a hill and ordered his soldiers to pitch camp on a nearby plain within sight of the Carthaginian. Once the camp was established, Marcellus taunted Hannibal to battle, forming his lines facing the enemy with the left flank anchored by the town. The first legion and right allied wing occupied the front lines while the third legion and left wing made up the reserve. Hannibal accepted the challenge and arranged his forces with the right wing extended up the hillside and the Spanish infantry in the front.[8]

The two armies engaged in what must have been an exhausting struggle. Livy says that the Roman left and Carthaginian right first clashed at the third hour, roughly 9.00 am by modern reckoning, and fought until dusk, with Hannibal adding war elephants to the fray at some point in the fight. Make no mistake; individual soldiers were certainly not fighting for their lives for nine or ten hours straight without relief. By any reckoning, there must have been numerous pauses in the fighting as the men clashed then fell back, even if only a pace or two to recover and test the mettle of the enemy through shouts and threats – if they had sufficient breath to do so.[9] As it happened, the forces were well matched that day, and there would be no quick victory. Indeed, as dusk approached, Marcellus relieved the front lines by sending in the third legion and left wing; Hannibal also cycled in fresh troops. The battle reignited with a fury, but nightfall quickly put an end to any thought of continuing the battle. The next day, Marcellus arranged his forces for battle again, but Hannibal kept his army inside its camp on the hill. The Romans, though no doubt with scouts carefully watching the hill, took advantage of the de facto truce to despoil the enemy corpses from the previous day and burn their own dead. Hannibal, though, must have judged that he had nothing to gain by continuing the battle when the armies were so evenly matched; he struck camp that night and withdrew east to Apulia under cover of darkness.[10]

For Hannibal, close battles such as these drained manpower that he could ill afford to lose. Marcellus was fighting under no such limitations; even after the catastrophic defeats early in the war, the Romans could still sustain losses far more readily, especially when those losses contributed to the ultimate defeat of the invader. It is no surprise then that the consul opted to pursue the Carthaginian army. He left the Roman wounded at Numistro under the protection of a detachment then marched after Hannibal. The Romans, or at least their commander, must have been more motivated to re-engage the Carthaginians than the latter were to escape, for the Roman army caught up with Hannibal outside the colony of Venusia, approximately twenty miles distant from Numistro. The two armies camped again and tested one another with their infantry and cavalry vanguards. Presumably, Hannibal would have committed his armies to a full engagement if the skirmishes had revealed any weaknesses in the Roman position. They did not. After a few days, the Carthaginians again struck camp at night and moved to Apulia. Marcellus' forces doggedly followed Hannibal's army over the next few days, scouting well during the day for traps along the route that Hannibal had marched the night before.[11]

The pursuit must have continued until the end of the campaigning season, since Marcellus drafted a letter to the senate late in that year or early in the next reporting that he continued to pressure the Carthaginian to fight. Presumably, Marcellus indicated in that letter that it would be better for him not to leave his troops to hold the consular elections at Rome. In any event, the senate decided to summon Laevinus, still in Sicily, so that Marcellus could keep his post.[12] It would appear that Hannibal continued to avoid engaging Marcellus that year, however, for no battle was reported, and the next thing we know from Livy, it was spring of 209 and Marcellus had been granted proconsular *imperium* to continue his operations in Apulia. He was assigned the legions he had commanded as consul, but the several thousand survivors of Centumalus' army at Herdonia were sent in disgrace to bolster the Cannae legions in Sicily.[13]

The war strain experienced by the Romans had only worsened with the passage of another year. Where Roman citizens had complained the year before, now dissatisfaction had sparked among the allies. Beyond the simple fact that Rome's allies had provided no fewer, and likely many more, troops to the war effort than the Romans themselves, the precipitating event seems to have been the news that the survivors of Herdonea, many of them allied troops, were being exiled to Sicily. Moved to protest, twelve of the thirty Latin colonies' delegates at Rome declared to the consuls that they simply could not provide any additional troops or funds for the war effort. This was a serious stand – the twelve were violating their formal treaty obligations with the Romans and setting a precedent that could decimate Rome's ability to prosecute the war. The news hit the senate hard. Without any clear solution to the problem, the senate instructed the consuls to act as they saw fit in the Republic's interests. Accordingly, the consuls checked the mood of the remaining eighteen colonies. The delegates from each of these assured the Romans that they were ready to meet their annual troop requirements and, according to the version Livy preserves, that they would patriotically supply even more if called upon. The senate officially thanked and praised the eighteen colonies, and even two centuries later Livy dutifully preserved the names of the towns. The twelve treaty violators were shunned, neither reprimanded or dismissed.[14]

The meeting of the senate and the decisions made at the beginning of this consular year are particularly interesting because they are recorded in some detail by Livy and give a better-than-usual picture of some of the types of issues the senate faced in the middle years of the war. First of all, there were still more signs of war strain. The spontaneous donation of precious metals by the aristocracy in the previous year had not fully relieved the Republic's financial straits. Consequently, the senate decreed that the gold supplies the Republic collected from a five per cent tax on freed slaves be drawn upon to continue funding the war effort. Since the gold, apparently 4,000 pounds of it, was distributed to each of the consuls and proconsuls, and 100 was allocated for the citadel of Tarentum, under Roman control, it would seem these funds were used primarily to pay and supply soldiers.

The senate's efforts to keep the Republic upright and fighting for the year could not be complete, however, without addressing the various signs of the gods' displeasure. Livy reports an interesting mix of prodigies this year, too good to pass up, if for no other reason than that they illustrate some of the possible signs the Romans believed the gods could present. (Note that the *pulvinaria* referred to were the couches and cushions set aside in the temples for the gods to sit upon.)

On the Alban Mount a statue of Jupiter and a tree near the temple had been struck by lightning; and at Ostia a basin, and at Capua the city wall and the temple of Fortune, and at Sinuessa the wall and a gate. Also some persons testified that the current of the outlet of the Alban Lake was blood red and that at Rome inside the cella of the Temple of Fors Fortuna a small image on a garland fell of itself from the head of the statue into the hand. And at Privernum it was established that an ox spoke, and that in the crowded market place a vulture flew down upon a shop, and that at Sinuessa a child was born of an uncertain sex, as between male and female … also that it rained milk there, and that a child was born with the head of an elephant. These prodigies were atoned for with full grown [sacrificial] victims, and prayers were ordered at all the *pulvinaria* and entreaties for one day.[15]

Reading the list of omens presented by Livy, which were hardly unique to this year, is an excellent corrective for any who think of the Romans as modern rationalists simply dressed in ancient garb. It never hurts to be reminded that, for the Romans, maintaining the proper, balanced relationship with the gods was considered a critical duty of the government, even more so in times of war.

Most illuminating of all in the report of the initial senate meeting for the year was the fact that Roman aristocrats continued at their usual business of political competition. The continued presence of an invader in Italy, the strain to Roman funds, the small-scale rebellion of twelve Latin colonies, and the abundance of bad omens from the gods for the year did nothing to stop the wrangling for prestige and position. The consul Flaccus conducted the elections for censors; Marcus Cornelius Cethegus and Publius Sempronius Tuditanus were elected. One of their first orders of business was to choose the *princeps senatus* ('first man of the senate'), a great honour for an aristocrat. They did not have to agree on the candidate; perhaps it was because two censors would usually not agree on whom to bestow the honour that it was normally decided by lot which censor had the right to choose the *princeps*. The lot, which for Romans represented the will of the gods, fell to Tuditanus. Cethegus apparently did not agree with his colleague's inclinations and demanded Tuditanus follow custom and choose the senator among them all who had first been elected censor: Titus Manlius Torquatus. Tuditanus shot back that the lot showed the gods wanted him to make the choice and, therefore, he was free to make whatever choice he wished. He chose Fabius Maximus, whom he believed to be the premier citizen of the state, regardless of custom. The censors argued vehemently about whom to award the honour, but Cethegus finally yielded and Fabius, Tuditanus' choice, was honoured with the title *princeps senatus*.[16] This is yet another example of how the rules and customs of the Republic could be quite malleable when applied to the competition for offices and honours.

The censors next attended to the business of revising and updating the roll of senators, passing over several eligible men who had not been steadfast in their commitment to Roman victory. Finally, the senate moved to punish those whose contributions to the war were deemed less than satisfactory. First came the punishments for the Cannae legions, still the scapegoats of choice for the Republic. Those cavalry troopers among the Cannae legions who had been serving with a state-supplied horse were now stripped of those horses and required to serve their full ten years of required military service with their own horses, regardless of the years they had already served – a little arithmetic shows that these soldiers had served at least seven years, including their fight at Cannae. Then the senate directed its attention to those of the cavalry class who had been at least seventeen at the beginning of the war – and thus liable to provide military service – but had not served. These citizens were stripped of their political status and made into *aerarii*, those who had no right to vote or hold office, and had no military obligations.[17]

After concluding these various official matters, the consuls headed south, Fulvius to Capua and Fabius to Tarentum in hope of relieving the Roman garrison holed up in the citadel and taking the port city. It appears, going by Livy's account, that the capture of Tarentum ranked highest on the list of Roman objectives. Accordingly, Fabius, who commanded operations in the region of Tarentum, asked Marcellus to keep Hannibal occupied. No doubt Marcellus, who had spent the better part of the previous year pursuing the Carthaginian forces, readily agreed, perhaps even feeling what Livy attributed to him: '[Marcellus] had come to believe that no Roman was so good a match for Hannibal as himself.'[18] When spring came, Marcellus led his forces from their winter quarters – presumably in Apulia – and made contact with Hannibal's army at Canusium. Hannibal was at work turning the town to his cause. The arrival of the Roman army changed his plans, however, and he led his troops away from the plains around Canusium toward more wooded ground. The Romans followed, and initially it must have looked to them as if another season would be spent marching round the Apulian countryside with little to show for it. Still, Marcellus hoped to draw his enemy into battle or perhaps catch him in some mistake. Camping close to the Carthaginians after every march, he drew his forces into battle lines. Hannibal, however, though willing to send out cavalry and infantry skirmishers, would not commit to a full battle.[19]

The situation changed one evening when the Roman army finally caught its enemy on the march. It must have been a chaotic affair as soldiers clashed in the failing light, but the Romans successfully prevented the Carthaginians from building a regular camp. When the encroaching darkness separated the armies, both hastily constructed whatever encampments they could in the open plain. The proximity of the enemy likely made it far too risky for Hannibal to disengage fully. Perhaps, too, the morale of his soldiers was not high enough to risk refusing battle yet again. Whatever the case, when Marcellus ordered his soldiers into their positions the next morning, Hannibal followed suit. There was to be a battle that day.[20]

That particular day, Marcellus stationed the allied right wing in the front line along with the *extraordinarii*, those soldiers hand-handpicked for exceptional fitness and ability. The line persevered through two hours of fighting, but eventually showed signs of wavering. Marcellus commanded his reserve legion to the front to relieve the troops. The reserves were moving into position as the front line yielded. Then, something went terribly wrong. Livy's version suggests that the troops handled the maneuver poorly; the quickly yielding front lines were relieved too slowly by the plodding reserves.[21] Plutarch, however, suggests that Marcellus made a poor decision and that the very decision to send in reserves at that point and in that way caused the disruption, not any failure on the soldiers' parts.[22] While assessment of blame would prove important in the following months, the immediate practical effects remained the same. Confusion bred fear, fear sparked panic, and the Roman battle line collapsed. Even were our sources for the battle eyewitnesses and multiplied in number, it would be impossible to know the exact sparks that led to the rout. The physical and psychological stress of the battlefield could build one person's fear into a wave of chaos. An individual's uneasiness raised the apprehension of others, which in turn increased that individual's stress in a feedback loop that could disintegrate armies.[23] On that particular day, in that particular catastrophe, several thousand Romans died in the rout, six military standards were lost, and the army retreated to its camp.[24] Though they differ in the attribution of responsibility, both Livy and Plutarch agreed that Marcellus chastised his troops' cowardice that evening. Whether that was the course he chose, Marcellus must have been frustrated that things had gone so terribly wrong.

Here an interesting problem appears in the sources. Livy and Plutarch suggest that Marcellus gave orders to his soldiers to prepare for battle again on the next day. In this second battle, the defeated troops of the allied wing and the Roman cohorts that had been routed returned to the front line to redeem themselves. The eighteenth legion occupied the right wing, seemingly held back in reserve according to Livy's description. According to Livy, Marcellus indicated that he would personally lead the troops that had lost their standards the day before. This is followed by a reference to Marcellus at the center of the battle line, encouraging his soldiers and witnessing their performance.[25] Though he essentially agrees on the details of the battle, however, Plutarch makes no reference to Marcellus in the front ranks. His only relevant comment is that the general saw a point of confusion in the Carthaginian line and ordered his cavalry to charge at the weak spot.[26] The Roman front line, according to the sources, engaged Hannibal's Spanish infantry, tough veteran soldiers. The centers of the two battle lines fought in close combat for some time without reaching any decision. Hoping to tilt the scales, Hannibal ordered war elephants to be brought to the front. The elephants and their drivers assaulted a spot in the line and caused considerable panic among the Romans at the center. A junior officer, Gaius Decimus Flavus assessed the situation and acted swiftly to restore his soldiers' morale. He grabbed the standard from a unit of *hastati* not yet panicked by the elephants and ordered the soldiers to follow him. At his command the *hastati* cast their *pila* at the elephants. The creatures, shocked and maddened by their injuries and likely wishing they were grazing peacefully on an African plain, not engaging in the follies of humans, turned and stampeded. They rampaged through their own battle lines, disrupting the Spanish formations as they fled through their own ranks to escape the noise and pain of the battle. The Carthaginian line collapsed in the panic and confusion, egged on by the Roman cavalry that Marcellus dispatched to the center when he observed the failing enemy line.[27] The Carthaginian forces fled to their camp pursued by the Romans, elated by their success. Between the continued damage wreaked by the elephants, and the vengeance sought by the Romans, the Carthaginian forces were slaughtered. Perhaps 8,000 died that day on the Carthaginian side. The Romans suffered high casualties as well, considering they were the victors; perhaps close to 3,000 soldiers died and many others were wounded.[28] Indeed, the number of wounded was substantial enough that it prevented Marcellus from pursuing Hannibal when he led his army away that night. The best the Roman commander could manage was to send scouts to track Hannibal's movements; they gave word that the commander had led his forces south to Bruttium, the 'toe' of the Italian peninsula.[29] Marcellus, however, returned his army to its winter quarters at Venusia, though it was still only the middle of the summer.[30]

The accounts of this second battle provide a terrific tale of an army and its commander bouncing back from defeat and winning back on the second day what it had lost on the first. This has caused some historians to doubt seriously whether it ever happened. It has the suspicious marks of a glorified fable constructed both to show Roman determination in the face of defeat and to minimize the harm to Marcellus' reputation. Livy's version even includes two outstanding moral examples: the first of Marcellus personally leading the troops, fighting in harm's way, and the second of the brave tribune saving the day. Two critical pieces of evidence, however, suggest that the second battle was either wholly invented or, equally as likely, not such a victory, and that the defeat in the first battle was the critical event for Marcellus' army that year.

First, Livy later in his history states that Marcellus suffered two defeats this year to Hannibal,[31] but only mentions these two battles during his account for the year. It is hard to imagine where and when Marcellus would have had the opportunity to lose another battle that year. Equally as important, it is difficult to see why, if the Roman army had indeed inflicted almost three times as many casualties on the Carthaginians as it had received, Marcellus was forced to enter winter quarters immediately but Hannibal was able to march off without harm. Finally, the number of Roman casualties on the alleged second-day victory is very large, more consistent with a defeat than a victory. If, though, the defeat on the first day was decisive, perhaps even the Roman casualties listed for the second day were actually from the first. Then Marcellus' need to seek winter quarters early would make more sense. Whatever the truth of the matter, what is clear is that Marcellus did cease his efforts to engage Hannibal that year. The early end of the campaign season must have been forced by the sheer number of wounded

Roman soldiers. Marcellus had shown no hesitation in pursuing Hannibal in the past and would not have ended the campaign season months early unless he judged the fighting condition of his army to be poor indeed.

The defeat of Marcellus' legions was not a complete strategic loss for the Romans by any means. Hannibal's preoccupation with Marcellus had given Fabius the time he needed to besiege Tarentum. As was so often necessary in sieges of great cities, Tarentum ultimately fell through treachery. A Roman infiltrator worked his way into the confidence of the garrison commander in Tarentum and persuaded him to betray the city to the Romans. When the army gained access to the city, they engaged in the usual initial slaughter intended to break any resistance, followed by the formal plundering of the city.[32] The accounts of the haul from the city include hints of the continued political friction between Marcellus and Fabius or, at the very least, between those sources who preferred Fabius and those who preferred Marcellus. According to Livy, Fabius authorized the plundering of 30,000 slaves, a massive weight of silver, over 3,000 pounds of gold, and works of art that 'almost rivaled the adornments of Syracuse.' Still, Fabius 'showed more magnanimity in refraining from plunder of that kind than did Marcellus. When a clerk asked what he wished to have done with statues of colossal size – they are gods in the form of warriors, but each in his own attitude – Fabius ordered that their angry gods be left to the Tarentines.'[33] Plutarch offers the same comparison – where Marcellus did not even hesitate to capture gods at Syracuse, Fabius showed moderation at Tarentum.[34]

Was this really the case? Other evidence suggests Fabius too was not above seizing gods from the Tarentines. Plutarch himself, in his biography of Fabius, says that Fabius did take the colossus of Hercules from Tarentum and not only installed it on the Capitoline hill, but also built an equestrian statue of himself to set near it, showing in this way less restraint than Marcellus.[35] Pliny, that compiler of encyclopedic information in the early Empire, also preserves a tradition that Fabius wished to take the colossus of Jupiter from Tarentum but was unable to move so massive a statue.[36] Once again, as with the descriptions of Marcellus' haul from Syracuse, we cannot escape the conclusions that the ancient historians of Rome in general openly embraced history-writing as an exercise in exemplifying moral behaviour, rather than an attempt at providing reasonably objective interpretations. In this case, the truth seems to be that both Marcellus and Fabius fully exercised their rights as victorious generals by plundering whatever possessions of the defeated they wished. It was left to the later recorders to wage a new battle over which commander had been more virtuous.

With Tarentum retaken, Fabius' proposed strategy for the year was successful. Still, Marcellus' decision to billet his troops for a substantial part of the fighting season exposed him to political attack at Rome. Gaius Publicius Bibulus, a tribune of the plebs for 209 and, according to Livy and Plutarch, an enemy of Marcellus, began a campaign indicting the general's decisions and conduct for the year, especially the decision to enter winter quarters early. Regardless of the military necessities that may have dictated such a choice, it simply looked bad to the citizens at Rome, far removed from the realities in the field, to have their army resting while Hannibal's army was intact and on the move.[37] Bibulus capitalized on these perceptions and proposed that Marcellus be stripped of his command. Livy says Marcellus' relatives persuaded whoever it was that needed persuading – the senate presumably – that the commander was entitled to return to Rome to defend himself against Bibulus' charges.[38] Though he is not explicitly named, Marcellus' son, who had served as aedile and was, presumably, already enrolled in the senate would likely have taken the lead in defending his father and his family's reputation – unless he was serving as an officer, as he did in the subsequent year. In any event, the family's appeal was successful, word was sent to Venusia, and Marcellus left the army under the command of subordinates, returning to Rome around the time that the elections for 208 were to be held.[39]

The debate over Marcellus' command took the form of a great trial held in the open air of the Flaminian Circus. The level of curiosity, if not outright excitement, in the city must have been very high. Here was arguably the greatest of Rome's living generals – for Scipio Africanus had not yet achieved the glory of decisively defeating Hannibal – on trial for failing as a commander. A much younger man of much lower rank, the tribune Bibulus, would attempt to strip the commander of his office and strike a blow of dishonour that would be difficult to overcome. Bibulus, apparently, did not fail to put on a show for interested observers. He did not limit his criticisms to Marcellus, but found fault with the governing class for failing to bring the war to a successful conclusion after almost ten years. This was certainly a tactic that would resonate with many, judging by the signs of war strain from the previous few years. After indicting the ruling class, he shifted his attack to Marcellus. For Bibulus, Marcellus' defeat and decision to stay encamped at Venusia exemplified the failure of the aristocracy to win the war swiftly and decisively.

The particulars of Marcellus' defence are lost. Livy says only that he gave a statement of his achievements. This could mean that he simply assessed the campaigns of recent years and justified his decisions in them. More likely though, given the habits of the Roman aristocracy, his defence focused more on his moral qualities, his *virtus*, than on any of the technical details of his campaigns. Perhaps he even went so far as to indulge in the time-honoured tradition of displaying the battle scars he had acquired over the years. There is a fair amount of evidence that Roman aristocrats, when their *virtus* and honour were challenged publicly and politically, would not infrequently engage in this spectacle, recounting each of their campaigns and noting the various scars from wounds received in those battles. The purpose of these displays was to illustrate one's superior courage, valour, and toughness – one's *virtus*. In doing so the accused showed that he had served the Republic with his spirit and body and that any moral challenges levied against him were unwarranted.[40]

This sort of defence may seem illogical when the precipitating event of Marcellus' trial may well have been the result of a tactical error, a failure in exercising command decisions. In reality, it was wholly consistent with the Romans' view that the victory or defeat of their armies was not primarily an issue of the commanders' tactical competence. Rather, conventional wisdom held that military success depended upon three crucial factors: the favour of the gods, obedient and brave soldiers, and commanders that displayed the proper courage on the battlefield. Though it may seem counterintuitive that the tactical decisions of the general were rarely called into question, it made great sense to elite Romans within the system of aristocratic competition. The Roman political system essentially made it highly likely that those who were elected consul, those who would generally be entrusted with the weighty task of commanding a citizen army in the field, had no prior command experience. True, they would have, in the early and middle Republic at least, years of military service, but not experience commanding armies, unless the candidates had happened to do so as praetors during those infrequent occasions when praetors commanded field armies. The Roman army of the middle Republic was an army of citizen soldiers, not professionals, and the commanders of the army were amateurs. There were no military academies for young aristocrats to attend, and indeed, if they were involving themselves in a political career they had no time to attend them anyway.

With this in mind, consider that if military defeats were routinely blamed on the general's tactical failures, and indeed, exceptional skill as a commander became a primary criterion for election, access to the prized consulship, and even praetorships, would be closed off for all those who were not gifted with that skill. In short, competition was already hot enough for these offices when the main claim to office was one's pedigree and character; adding the factor of command skill would disrupt the competitive balance. And so it was very much within the interests of the aristocracy collectively to promote the idea that any aristocrat was technically fit to command armies, any possessed sufficient skill to do so. In rare cases, when a defeat was blamed on the commander rather than on the *virtus* of the soldiers or the will of the gods, that blame was based not on whether he had made any technical errors in command, but how he comported himself during battle. A true aristocrat, one worthy of the position of commander and worthy of continued respect, would, the Romans generally agreed, show valour on the field of battle and after, refusing to give up and never despairing, even in the face of defeat. He would make the proper sacrifices to the gods, serve as the font of morale for the troops and in all other ways be a moral exemplar.[41] Indeed, this was the sum of Bibulus' charge. Marcellus, along with the other leaders of Rome had dissembled and delayed. To top it off, here he was cringing in winter quarters rather than fighting. He lacked the moral competence to command, Bibulus harangued.

By recounting his achievements, and perhaps showing his battle scars, Marcellus certainly could make the claim that he did. All that he needed to do to defend himself was emphasize that he had an unparalleled record of bravery in the face of the enemy, all in the service of the Republic. He was no delayer or dissembler. Whether it was through the details or delivery of his defence, or both, Marcellus was elected consul the very next day by a large number of voting centuries. Titus Quinctius Crispinus won the other consulship.[42] Pressing matters, however, delayed Marcellus' return to Venusia. A letter had arrived in the senate from the propraetor Gaius Calpurnius warning that the citizens of Arretium in Etruria were considering a break with Rome. The senate tasked Marcellus to travel to Arretium and investigate the matter; should the situation warrant it, he could request an army be sent to Etruria. Apparently, the presence of the venerable warrior was enough to quell any eagerness for revolt, however, and the sources mention no more of the matter.[43]

When Livy says the new consuls Marcellus and Crispinus took office in 208, he cannot help but note that Marcellus – if one counted the inauguration that had been invalidated in 215 – had entered the consulship for the fifth time.[44] Rightly so. Only Fabius of Romans in living memory had held five consulships, his fifth only the year before; only Gaius Marius in the late second century would ever hold more. Both consuls were assigned to Italy, but a series of pressing religious matters delayed their campaign. The gods again had reportedly sent many signs indicating their displeasure. It was the duty of the consuls, as the chief magistrates of the Republic, to oversee the rituals necessary to restore the proper relationship with the gods. This took several days, however, for the initial sacrifices of animals to the gods did not produce favourable omens and needed to be repeated until it was clear that the gods had accepted the offerings of the Republic.[45]

Once the sacrifices were deemed favourable, Crispinus travelled with new recruits to the army in Lucania. Marcellus, however, still had more business to settle. The college of Roman priests, the *pontifices*, was blocking the formal dedication of the temple to Honos and Virtus that Marcellus had vowed back at Clastidium, nearly fifteen years ago. The priests declared that one temple could not be dedicated to two gods. To do so would confuse the signs the gods sent. For example, the priests argued, if lightning struck the temple to Honos and Virtus, it would not be clear which god was offended and, thus, which god needed to be placated through sacrifices. Why this objection was noted at this particular point is hard to determine. Surely, if this were a well-established concern, it could have been raised years ago. Why now?

When pondering this question, one cannot help but note that Fabius was not only an augur but a *pontifex*, one of that college of priests that objected to

Marcellus' dedication. That may help with establishing the motive; Fabius can hardly have wanted the rival temple to be built. It does nothing to explain the timing. Surely, Fabius should, could, and would have raised this objection years earlier, perhaps when plans for the temple were initially made? Perhaps the decisive factor was that construction of the temple had not, it seems, actually begun until after Marcellus had taken Syracuse. If Fabius was the primary opponent, perhaps he saw no reason to obstruct the temple so long as it was not actually under construction. Now that it was nearing completion and ready to be dedicated, it was the opportune time for Fabius or some others among the *pontifices* to object. However this may have come about, the only practical solution for the consul, no doubt eager to continue his stalking of Hannibal, was to order the swift construction of a temple of Virtus alongside the temple of Honos.[46] But the delay was enough to insure that he would not live to see the dedication of his memorial to Clastidium and Syracuse.

Finished satisfying the religious obligations that were no doubt very important to his public image – possibly to his private scruples too, though we shall never know – Marcellus gathered his new recruits at Rome and returned to his army at Venusia.[47] Crispinus, meanwhile, had initiated large-scale operations against the city of Locri in Bruttium, on the southern coast near the toe of the Italian peninsula. Hannibal's occupation of Lacinium, however, a promontory east along the coast from Locri, caused Crispinus to abandon his plans. It is difficult to see why that would have been. One might argue that Hannibal's movement threatened Crispinus' lines to Rome, but clearly the Romans had been communicating with and supplying armies in nearby Sicily successfully for years by ship. Even more puzzling, Crispinus abandoned Locri and marched his army to join Marcellus in Apulia, marching past, in other words, Hannibal's position in Lacinium. Perhaps the change of plan, therefore, came not because Crispinus had been outmaneuvered, but because Marcellus had finally reached Venusia, and there was an opportunity for the two consular armies to defeat Hannibal decisively.[48]

Certainly, that seems to have been the plan. The consular armies met between the towns of Venusia and Bantia, maintaining separate camps but combining operations. Once the camps were established, the consuls began what was now practically a ritual: leading the armies out in battle formation daily to tempt Hannibal to fight. Hannibal, for his part, had no desire to face such a large force. And so the cat-and-mouse game began for another season. Hannibal kept his eyes open to opportunities for ambushes, skirmishers engaged here and there, and the main armies kept their distance. The Apulian theatre looked likely to be locked down for the year. Seeing this, the consuls sent instructions to the Sicilian fleet commander, Lucius Cincius, to take advantage of Hannibal's immobility and carry on the siege of Locri by sea. Meanwhile, Roman garrison troops from Tarentum would attack the landward side. Hannibal received reports of these movements, however, and sent a force to ambush the Roman detachment. The Roman garrison troops were soundly defeated and the broken remnants returned to Tarentum.[49]

Back at Venusia, the Roman and Carthaginian armies remained in their stalemate. Marcellus and Hannibal had gone through this maneuver for two years straight, the former seeking battle, the latter refusing unless the circumstances appeared to favour him overwhelmingly. One morning, no different at its start from so many others, Marcellus decided to scout a hill near the camp to see if it might serve either as a potential base for a Carthaginian attack or a superior position for the Roman camp. He ordered the officers remaining at camp to ready the troops to move should the hill be suitable for occupying. Then, he and Crispinus, along with some officers, cavalry, and light infantry went to reconnoiter the hill. The expedition followed the road up the hill – right into an ambush. Numidian cavalry were hidden on the hilltop, hoping to catch straggling Roman foragers or other small prey. That day, likely beyond their wildest ambitions, they had caught both consuls. The Roman scouting party was surrounded, blocked from the ridge and prevented from retreating by ambushers from behind. There was nothing to do but cut a way back to the camp or die in the effort. Marcellus died in the fighting. Crispinus was gravely wounded but made it back to camp with the remnants of the expedition, including Marcellus' son, also wounded that day.

We will turn to the controversy his death caused shortly. But even in death, Marcellus' immediate influence on the war in Italy was, strangely enough, not quite over. Hannibal acted quickly to transfer his camp to the hill where the consul had fallen. In the process, the Carthaginian forces came across Marcellus' signet ring. Using this ring, Hannibal sealed a forged letter to Salapia. The letter informed the Salapians that the consul was coming and that they should grant him access to the city. Then, Hannibal marched to Salapia with Roman deserters in the van to hide his army's identity. Late in the night these deserters demanded the Salapians open the gates and allow the consul entrance. As it happened, however, Crispinus had anticipated the trouble Marcellus' lost ring could cause and warned the nearest cities that the consul was dead. The guards of Salapia, sufficiently warned, allowed the Roman deserters into the city, closed the gates, and slaughtered the infiltrators. There was nothing more to be gained at Salapia, and Hannibal marched back to defend Locri.[50]

After the ambush, the consul Crispinus opted to follow Hannibal with his own forces, but ordered the younger Marcellus to lead his father's troops to quarters at Venusia; presumably the son was in need of a task to occupy him, and Crispinus was not willing to risk the dead consul's namesake in battle, especially since he had been wounded in the ambush. Before following Hannibal, Crispinus dispatched a letter to Rome reporting the disaster.[51] All told, the news must have sparked great controversy the moment the letter arrived. One consul had fallen, the other was gravely wounded and incapable of returning to Rome, and Hannibal was engaged in lethal mischief with Marcellus' ring. When the word spread that such horrific losses occurred during a scouting expedition and were, in some sense, avoidable, no doubt the queries and criticisms, founded or not, raced throughout the city among aristocrats and commoners alike.

Somewhere in this all-too-human process of rumour, speculation, and accusation, variant versions of Marcellus' death took shape. It is really not surprising that Marcellus' final moments were subjected to considerable debate and so many variant traditions developed, considering the magnitude of the commander's reputation and the controversy later sparked by his decision to reconnoiter the hill personally. Livy notes:

> I should be very discursive in regard to a single event, if I should aim to rehearse all the statements in which authorities differ concerning the death of Marcellus. Not to mention others, Coelius furnishes successively a threefold relation of what happened: one the traditional account, a second set down in the eulogy pronounced by his son, who was present, Coelius says, when it happened, a third which he himself contributes as investigated and established by him. But the divergent reports fall within this range, that most authorities relate that he left the camp to reconnoiter a position, while all say that he was overwhelmed by an ambush.[52]

Livy's source, Coelius Antipater, who wrote in the late second century, may have been giving himself too much credit here. Granted, tradition was hardly a sure source of valid evidence, and the account the son gave of the great commander at his funeral may well have been embellished. Still, if neither the traditional account nor the eyewitness account of the younger Marcellus held sufficient truth, it is difficult to see how a Roman writing some ninety years later could conduct an independent investigation that would yield superior results.

So what did happen on the day Marcellus died? Clearly, the sources agreed that Marcellus' group was ambushed. Polybius, providing our earliest surviving version of the account simply says that Marcellus and several others were killed at the start – though whether this means in the initial surprise attack or early fighting, it is impossible to say. The rest of the detachment scattered and fled, every man for himself. The whole incident was over almost before it had begun.[53] Livy portrays the ambush as a more prolonged engagement. In his version, a desperate skirmish broke out as the Roman cavalry fought for their lives and the lives of their consuls. The Etruscan component of the cavalry fled the scene, dooming the Roman force. Nevertheless, the cavalry troopers from Fregellae continued to fight bravely. Of the two consuls, Crispinus was gravely wounded by a pair of javelins, while Marcellus, struck by a spear thrust, fell from his horse and died. Somehow a small group managed to return to the safety of the Roman camps along with Crispinus and the younger Marcellus, who was also wounded.[54] Strictly speaking, Livy does not say how long Marcellus lasted, though he does give the impression the general was engaged in fighting.

Plutarch follows this version: the cavalry troopers of Fregellae stood with the consuls until the one was killed and the other gravely wounded.[55] He gives the impression of a fight that lasted more than the instant Polybius suggested. Plutarch's version also suggests that Marcellus died actively fighting, however quickly. Plutarch contrasts the Etruscans among the cavalry who fled with the Fregellans who banded around the consuls and defended them. Crispinus was seriously wounded and forced to flee, but Marcellus was pierced in the side with a spear and died. Seeing the consul slain, a few of the remaining Fregellan cavalry grabbed his son and fled for camp. Perhaps Marcellus did die fighting, but it may also be that his witnesses wanted to make what was a sudden, unexpected and seemingly preventable death, as glorious as possible, a difficult task.

It may seem trivial to puzzle out the details of his death. In the end, the old war-horse Marcellus – he was after all over sixty, respectably old for a Roman who was still commanding armies – was dead. He died in battle, surely a horrible way to die, however glorified by the poets. But the intense debate over the manner of his death offers a fascinating look into the ways that the variant historical traditions at Rome were established, debated, and mutated as Roman writers sought to provide object examples of exemplary and undignified behaviour for their readers. Polybius, a former military commander in his own right and no particular fan of Marcellus, gave a scathing assessment half a century or more later:

> Marcellus, it must be confessed, brought this misfortune on himself by behaving not so much like a general as like a simpleton. Throughout this work I am often compelled to call the attention of my readers to such occurrences, as I observe that generals are more liable to make mistakes in this matter than in any other parts of their duty as commanders, although the error is such an obvious one. For what is the use of a general or commander who does not comprehend that he must keep himself as far away as possible from all partial encounters in which the fate of the whole army is not involved? Of what use is he if he does not know that, if circumstances at times compel commanders to undertake in person such partial encounters, they must sacrifice many of their men before the danger is suffered to approach the supreme commander of the whole? ... And as for saying 'I should never have thought it' or 'Who would have expected it to happen?' that in a general is a most manifest sign of incompetence and dullness.[56]

Though one might suspect that Polybius insults Marcellus too wantonly considering the many successes of the commander, the criticism, nevertheless, stuck in the tradition. Livy, writing at the beginning of the Empire, softened the blow, not willing to excoriate the great commander whose tales of victories he had written about in the past five books. Still, he suggested:

> Marcellus' death was pitiable both for other reasons and also because it was neither consistent with his age – for he was now more than 60 years old – nor with his foresight as a veteran commander, that with such imprudence he had carried himself and his colleague and almost the entire state over the brink.'[57]

Indeed, by Livy's day at the latest the tradition developed that Marcellus had received sufficient warning from the gods that his scouting expedition would end poorly. Where Polybius is silent on the matter, Livy notes that, according to some sources Marcellus had offered sacrifices before setting out. The liver of the first sacrificial victim was flawed, while the second was exceptional. The mixed results displeased the *haruspex*, the priest on duty charged with interpreting the outcome of sacrifices. Marcellus, however, deliberately ignored the sign from the gods and went on to die.[58] A century after Livy, Plutarch, himself fascinated with matters of religion enough to become a priest, essentially gives Livy's telling with just a bit more descriptive detail.[59] By his day, the tradition already included the details from Livy's day, that Marcellus had ignored the signs of the gods and died bravely in battle. The report that Marcellus ignored the divine signs no doubt came from a critic; presumably, the account that he died bravely in battle came from his son or Crispinus. Both statements may well have been true, even though Polybius made no mention of them. After he had ignored the *spolia opima*, it is not surprising that Polybius would also pass on any attempt to glorify Marcellus' death. True or not, however, the version promoted by Livy and Plutarch fits their moralizing tone: Marcellus had behaved foolishly, perhaps, but he also had died bravely, as a Roman aristocrat should.

The variant accounts continued when it came to the matter of his body. Plutarch provides at least two possibilities, the first, that Hannibal appropriately prepared Marcellus' body and burned it. The remains were then placed in a silver urn and sent to the consul's son. According to some ancient sources, however, the urn was fought over by the troops delivering it, and in the struggle Marcellus' ashes were scattered far and wide. Then Plutarch adds, 'Such, then, is the account given by Cornelius Nepos and Valerius Maximus; but Livy and Augustus Caesar state that the urn was brought to his son and buried with splendid rites,'[60] which is odd enough since Livy, so far as we can recover, said no such thing. According to his account, Marcellus was buried by Hannibal's forces on the hill where he was slain.[61]

Whether the body or ashes were lost, clearly Marcellus was given a funeral celebration fitting a Roman aristocrat: Livy's reference to a eulogy by Marcellus' son is sufficient testimony to support what common sense suggests. Polybius provides us with our most detailed description of an aristocratic funeral in the Republic, and it is worth considering his words when visualizing the celebration held for Marcellus' life.

> Whenever any illustrious man dies, he is carried at his funeral into the forum to the so-called rostra, sometimes conspicuous in an upright posture and more rarely reclined. Here with all the people standing round, a grown-up son, if he has left one who happens to be present, or if not some other relative, mounts the rostra and discourses on the virtues and successful achievements of the dead. As a consequence the multitude and not only those who had a part in these achievements, but those also who had none, when the facts are recalled to their minds and brought before their eyes, are moved to such sympathy that the loss seems to be not confined to the mourners, but a public one affecting the whole people. Next after the interment and the performance of the usual ceremonies, they place the image of the departed in the most conspicuous position in the house, enclosed in a wooden shrine. This image is a mask reproducing with remarkable fidelity both the features and complexion of the deceased. On the occasion of public sacrifices they display these images, and decorate them with much care, and when any distinguished member of the family dies they take them to the funeral, putting them on men who seem to them to bear the closest resemblance to the original in stature and carriage. These representatives wear togas, with a purple border if the deceased was a consul or praetor, whole purple if he was a censor, and embroidered with gold if he had celebrated a triumph or achieved anything similar. They all ride in chariots preceded by the *fasces*, axes, and other insignia by which the different magistrates are wont to be accompanied according to the respective dignity of the offices of state held by each during his life; and when they arrive at the rostra they all seat themselves in a row on ivory chairs. There could not easily be a more ennobling spectacle for a young man who aspires to fame and virtue. For who would not be inspired by the sight of the images of men renowned for their excellence, all together and as if alive and breathing? What spectacle could be more glorious than this? Besides, he who makes the oration over the man about to be buried, when he has finished speaking of him recounts the successes and exploits of the rest whose images are present, beginning with the most ancient. By this means, by this constant renewal of the good report of brave men, the celebrity of those who performed noble deeds is rendered immortal, while at the same time the fame of those who did good service to their country becomes known to the people and a heritage for future generations.[62]

Certainly, there were many funerals where the deceased might be eclipsed in deeds by his ancestors. In this case, Marcellus was without question the star of his family. And though his body could not be displayed in the funeral, there is good reason to suspect that the eulogy delivered by his son was rare in the number and magnitude of the deeds it praised – or to put it another way, rare in the legitimate number and magnitude of deeds praised. Five times elected consul; winner of the *spolia opima*; celebrator of a triumph, a second triumph on the Alban Mount, and an ovation; a skilled duelist; the first Roman general to win any sort of victory in pitched battle against Hannibal; the sacker of Syracuse; one who had held *imperium* and commanded armies in the war against Hannibal for more consecutive years than any other living aristocrat.[63] No doubt, there was much for the son, family, and city of Marcellus to celebrate about his life and achievements.

What of the Republic without its sword? By 208, it cannot truly be said that the war against Hannibal was won, but Marcellus had played a crucial role in turning the tide against the Carthaginian invader. The year 208 saw the last major military crisis during the war in Italy. Hannibal's brother, Hasdrubal, marched another army from Spain to northern Italy with the goal of refreshing Hannibal's forces significantly, a move that could have shifted the balance of the war back toward the Carthaginian. Ultimately, however, Hasdrubal's army was shattered at the River Metaurus in northern Italy (207), and Hasdrubal's head was later cast at the feet of a shocked Hannibal in the south. After this defeat, Hannibal's prospects for winning the war in Italy dissipated, at least in his own estimation. He led his troops south to Bruttium, the heel of Italy, and remained there in 206. His army was still far too powerful to be rooted out of the region, but Hannibal never again made serious forays into the rest of Italy.

Meanwhile, the young but soon to be spectacularly famous Publius Cornelius Scipio was honing his command skills in Spain. His father of the same name and his uncle had commanded the Roman operations in Spain since the beginning of the war. Both lost their lives in battle in 211. Though only twenty four and far too young for such an honour, the younger Scipio petitioned to lead reinforcements to Spain and take over command of the forces there. Both because of his already developed reputation as an officer and his family connection, the Roman assemblies willingly put their trust in the young man. Over the next few years, Scipio showed himself to be an outstanding general, and after a number of sieges and smaller battles, the Carthaginian forces in Spain were defeated decisively at Ilipa in 206. With the expulsion of Carthaginian forces from Spain, Scipio returned to Rome to seek the consulship for 205, though he was only thirty-one and had never held the praetorship.

Scipio won election to the consulship for 205 and planned to launch an invasion of Africa. The usual senatorial rivalries disrupted his plan, however, and he was given command over Sicily, already long pacified. Scipio made good use of his time on the island to prepare an invasion force. After his consulship ended he was made proconsul for 204 and at the close of the year landed an invasion force in Africa. It was the threat of this Roman force, which began to carve into Carthaginian territory, and the pleas for assistance from the Carthaginian senate that finally dislodged Hannibal from Italy. He gathered his troops and left Europe late in 203. The next year, the two armies maneuvered until they ultimately decided upon the plains of Zama in North Africa as the ground for their final battle. That day Scipio and the Roman army were the victors; Hannibal and his forces were decisively defeated.

The second war against Carthage was over. This time Carthage had lost its hold in Sicily, and the Roman empire now extended across the western Mediterranean. Over the next fifty years or so, the Romans would come into conflict with most of the remaining great powers of the Mediterranean, eventually dominating each. This process continued into the Empire, at which point the Romans had a new name for the Mediterranean, simply *mare nostrum* ('our sea'). That was some time off. In the short term, Carthage, though its fleets were destroyed and it was required to pay a large war indemnity, was left essentially unscathed. It essentially retained its holdings in Africa and bounced back quickly. It was not until just over fifty years later, in the third and final war against Carthage, really a protracted siege more than a war, that the Romans decided – literally – to remove Carthage from the face of the earth. They razed the city, sowed salt in its fields, and placed a Roman colony nearby. Carthage was no more.

Marcellus, however, did not live even to witness the victory of Scipio over Hannibal. Indeed, it would be very interesting to know, had Marcellus lived – he would have been in his seventies – whether he would have claimed the right to command the invasion of Africa and what opposition that might have inspired. Ultimately, though, Roman tradition and writing preserved his name and glory alongside Scipio's. Most immediately, of course, his story was critical to his descendants. Through his deeds, Marcellus firmly established his family in the highest ranks of the aristocracy. Though there had been significant gaps in the office-holding patterns of the family before our subject – his father, it may be recalled, seems not to have held any major political office – Marcellus' son held the consulship several times, and his son after that. By the mid-first century BC and the very end of the Republic, the Claudius Marcellus family was a very distinguished branch of the Roman aristocracy. Members of the Marcellus family continued to hold consulships until the very end of the Republic: a Marcus Claudius Marcellus was consul in 50 BC and a great rival of the Gaius Julius Caesar who, the next year, would march against Rome and begin the rounds of civil wars that would dismantle the Republic. Despite siding against Caesar, the Marcelli continued to prosper. Indeed, Octavian, the adopted son of Julius Caesar who would come to be the first of the Roman emperors, was tied through his sister's marriage to the Claudius Marcellus family. He had a nephew and son-in-law named Marcus Claudius Marcellus, whom he particularly favoured as a potential heir before the young man's untimely death in 23 BC. When the young man died, the grief-stricken Octavian – Augustus, as he was now titled – delivered a eulogy that drew upon the story of the famous patriarch from the third century.[64]

These descendants, as all aristocrats hoped to do, capitalized on the fame of the great warrior and commander. While the war against Hannibal continued on, Marcellus' son made sure that the temples to Honos and Virtus were dedicated, and he sponsored the playwright Naevius as he completed and staged the play *Clastidium*, which told of the spectacular victory won against the Gauls in 222. These feats were surely commemorated at least once a generation at funerals for members of the Marcellus family. Nor was this the only time. On at least two occasions in the last century of the Republic, relatives of the family who happened to be officers in charge of the mint, issued coins referring to Marcellus' achievements. One issued around 100 referred back to the victory over Syracuse. The other, issued perhaps in the late 40s BC, had the likeness of the general on the obverse and a picture of the *spolia opima* in the temple of Jupiter on the reverse.[65] Coins like this provided easy self-promotion for the latest generation of the Marcellus family.

Then, of course, there was the treatment of his deeds by the historians and poets of the Augustan age and beyond, which we have encountered regularly in these pages. Livy and Augustus, both interested in reviving what they saw as ancient Roman morality, were particularly interested in heroes like Marcellus. He was the last – and possibly the first – to win the *spolia opima*, the one who bought the Romans time after Nola, the virtuous aristocrat without peer, symbol of the grit and fortitude that Augustus, Livy, and so many other Roman writers wished to praise after decades of upheaval and civil war. Although it is far from clear that Marcellus would have recognized himself underneath the layers of celebrity, this portrayal continued in later histories for as long as the Empire lasted. He had, in many ways, the consummately successful career of an aristocrat in the middle Republic.

Conclusion

The man died and the legend lived on. Ultimately, it is the man that concerns this book most. In the end, he had one of the most spectacular military and political careers of all when it came to aristocrats of the middle Republic. It is important to point out, however, that it is not at all clear that Marcellus was categorically a sounder strategist or tactician than other Roman generals of the period. Certainly, his cavalry victory at Clastidium suggested he was, at the very least, competent as a commander; elsewhere, as these chapters have explored, he clearly made some sound strategic and tactical decisions in the field. The same, though, could be said for others. Fabius had managed to conduct a successful war of attrition against Hannibal in 217, shadowing his enemy closely but only engaging at what seemed to be the most opportune of moments. His actions bought the Republic time to rally from the first two catastrophic defeats Hannibal inflicted. Claudius Nero was clearly also a sound strategist. As consul in 207, he kept Hannibal at bay in the south with the bulk of his army while marching with a portion hundreds of miles north to join his colleague Livius Salinator, defeating the invading Hasdrubal, and then returning to face Hannibal in the south. The Scipios in Spain made significant progress in that theatre until their demise, and, of course, Scipio Africanus concluded the war skillfully. These are only the most famous commanders from the period; a number of lesser-known generals executed their commands skillfully.

One can go further. Regardless of his skills, Marcellus arguably had a military record no better than many of his rivals. Triumphing against the Gauls was spectacular, but others had done so, and would continue to do so. Indeed, his assault on Syracuse failed and he was forced to capture the city through treachery. Nothing unusual there; Fabius had to do the same with Tarentum, as did many other Roman commanders. Marcellus was defeated by Hannibal in at least one battle and never won a decisive victory against his army, however critical to morale the victory at Nola in 216 was. Marcellus certainly had a more respectable command record than most, but the evidence does not compel one to believe he was categorically a better general than his rivals.

Indeed, command skill, however desirable, was not essential to political success in the middle Republic. It was noted previously that one of the foundations of aristocratic competition, the great leveler, was the critical assumption that any aristocrat possessed the technical skill necessary to command armies. It is worth considering that this was more than empty rhetoric designed to secure the interests of the aristocracy. There was truth to the claim that it did not require spectacular military skills for an aristocrat to command an army successfully. The best evidence is in the record: Roman armies were regularly commanded by amateurs in the Republic, yet the Romans came to dominate the Mediterranean. How was this possible? What role did a commander's skills have in determining success in battle and war? The answer, of course, is that it depended. One could make poor strategic decisions and issue commands that were counterproductive if not destructive. Conversely, one could be a brilliant commander able to get every last bit of performance out of one's troops and resources.

One of the keys that enabled amateurs to command successfully in the Republic was the way that individuals and groups at several points within the system had input on important elements of strategy and tactics. Some decisions were ultimately left to the individual general, but the general would have many opportunities, if he chose, to gain insight from others. Generally speaking, in any given year, the senate determined the province in which a commander would be active. In the war against Hannibal, this was often tantamount to determining the enemy the general would fight. So the senate as a group played a role in hammering out the bare outlines of a commander's strategy for the year. Sometimes they provided more than that: explicit instructions for cities to capture or garrison, regions to support or suppress, etc. None of this prevented generals from acting very independently in the field, and they often did so. The point is simply that a less-skilled strategist had the structure of the senate's commands to follow as a guide.

When it came to tactics, the great strength of the Roman military system came into play and offered a considerable edge to otherwise less-than-spectacular commanders. There were certainly more and less advantageous battlegrounds one could choose, and Roman commanders who made critical miscalculations assuredly contributed greatly to the death of thousands of Romans. Nevertheless, the manipular army refined over the many decades was a tactically sophisticated and effective system that functioned on a basic level independently of the commander. The division of infantry into *velites*, *hastati*, *principes*, and *triarii* was firmly established by Marcellus' day. The veteran soldiers could coach the new recruits, the experienced centurions and standard bearers kept the maniples in order, and the system perpetuated itself through several centuries. It was the collective wisdom of the veteran soldiers and centurions that must have kept the maniples functioning in their generally highly effective fashion. A consul might not have been in battle for a decade or more; an infantry soldier was liable to serve sixteen years in total,[1] and, consequently, there would have been a great deal of collective experience in the ranks. Though we know far less than we would like to about the standard formations of the Roman infantry and their normal procedures of rotating maniples into and out of combat, these formations and procedures were clearly highly effective against the less articulated and less manoeuvrable phalanxes and war-bands of the Gauls, Greeks, and other Mediterranean powers.

Furthermore, even though consuls might well be complete amateurs when it came to commanding field armies, they were certainly familiar with how the manipular system worked. In the middle Republic, Polybius asserts, anyone seeking political office first had to complete ten years of military service, or rather serve in the army in ten separate campaigns, since soldiers were not professionals who regularly served for continuous years at a stint.[2] These years in military service, cavalry service more specifically, would give most any office holder a firm appreciation of how the army worked. Enough appreciation – and this was all that was required – to order the army into positions and set it into operation. Again, a brilliant strategist or tactician could certainly do great things with such an army. The procedures and experience contained in the system, however, made it possible for the merely adequate consul to succeed if he did not actively work against the system – like Varro, for example, when he packed the Roman legions too closely together at Cannae.

So Marcellus may have been an excellent strategist or tactician – and at the least he was clearly skilled – but there is no reason why he had to be in order to win victories, and there is insufficient evidence to suggest he was qualitatively better than his chief rivals in this respect. He clearly did outshine his fellow aristocrats, however, when it came to his personal skill and daring as a warrior. His record for single combat was largely without parallel and the *spolia opima* was an extraordinary capstone to decades of distinction in this regard. Marcellus knew how to fight. Equally as important, however, he seems to have known how to leverage his personal skill and courage in battle to boost the morale of his soldiers. These were two of his critical skills.

The leverage granted by his personal skill as a warrior laid the foundation for his extraordinary political success. As noted frequently, Marcellus was not unique in that he pursued his own self-interest, sought opportunities to advance his own status and reputation. Rather, he was uncommon in how good he was at the game. Successful aristocrats developed the rhetorical and spectacular displays of *virtus* to a fine point, but few could match Marcellus' claims. His initial honours and commendations won as a single combatant; the *spolia opima* gained through slaying a commander and the subsequent dedication of the temple to Honos and Virtus; his sacking of Syracuse, culminating in a triumph and ovation; all of these actions catapulted him to greater glory.

Certainly, Marcellus seems to have been more assertive than some, advancing claims to prizes that went beyond what might be seen as the normal limits of aristocratic competition. The *spolia opima* was one of these. Bolder still was the maneuver to shift a lynchpin in the Republican system itself and become the second of two plebeian consuls. The celebration of two victory ceremonies for one success was probably the least of the three in terms of innovation, but still one that went beyond the normal rules of competition. Then there was the *coup de grace* – personally receiving the patronage of a foreign city and island and being honoured as a Hellenistic-style god-king by the inhabitants of Syracuse.

With the exception of the last honour, which Marcellus could easily and perhaps honestly note he never actually sought from Syracuse and could not prevent the Syracusans from granting, there is a common thread in these seemingly excessive grabs for honour. In most cases, he could claim to be drawing upon the ancient customs of the Romans, keeping the traditions of the Republic alive. This was certainly the case for the *spolia opima*, the ovation, and the triumph *Monte Albano*. In every case, Marcellus could claim that he was simply acting in the service of the Republic and following the will of the gods. Whether it was claiming victories in battle, serving in offices beyond the norm, even in ransacking an enemy city and bringing the wealth to aggrandize his temple, Marcellus seems to have claimed that he only acted as the servant of the Republic and its people and its gods.

Indeed, who could gainsay him? It may seem to some modern readers that Marcellus must have been disingenuous in his claims to have served the Republic – that these were simply pretexts to clothe his ambition for offices and honours. That misses the point. Service to the Republic was the arena in which these aristocrats competed. It has been argued on more than one occasion that the Republic itself was founded so that aristocrats could gain more glory than they could under a king. As noted before, the danger was always that intense competition between these aristocrats would go too far and one or a few would come to dominate the state, effectively hoarding all the offices, glories, and honour, and turning the Republic back into a monarchy, in fact, if not in title. The means of preventing this was to harness competition to the needs of the Republic, to define the field of competition as the needs of the Republic. That way, aristocrats had their glory and honour but the system persisted. This was not a system scientifically engineered to remain balanced. It was a set of conventions, customs, and practices that developed over time and led to the behaviours seen in the aristocrats of the middle Republic.

On several occasions throughout this biography, we have looked at limits to competition, the ways that the aristocracy as a whole, or individual rivals, put the brakes on their opponents to keep them from getting too powerful. Marcellus' career provides such an exceptional means of examining this behaviour precisely because he was so successful in general and because many of his successes took place during the Roman struggle for existence in the second Punic War. One might suppose that if ever there were a Roman so successful in promoting his reputation that could ignore the attacks of his rivals, it was Marcellus, and if ever there were a time when the demands of the Republic were so great, its need so dire, that the aristocracy would cease infighting and band together, it would be the Second Punic War.

Neither was the case. Marcellus was exceptional in his achievements, yet perfectly regular in the setbacks he suffered from the challenges of rivals and opponents. They invoked the displeasure of the gods, claimed he had violated technical points of law and religious propriety, and even challenged his *virtus*. It is too much, of course, to assert that Roman senators saw themselves as caretakers of a system of competition, that they saw themselves in any way as parts of a whole, as this modern analysis suggests. Rather, they simply behaved as Roman aristocrats of their time when they checked Marcellus, but this behaviour was a critical part of the system. In checking Marcellus, they promoted their own interests, limited his ability to realize his ambitions, and no doubt largely unconsciously, kept the system functioning. In short, as a number of historians have noted, the Roman aristocrats of the middle Republic shared an essentially unconscious consensus that there were rules to competition, limits to the glory one could seek, and legitimate channels by which to seek and block glory. Marcellus' claims to honours illustrate the many ways one could claim glory in the name of service; his rivals' challenges illustrate some of the many ways those claims could be thwarted.

It is notable how flexible the Romans were in the rules and points they produced for their competition. Roman aristocrats tended to produce, as established points of law, points that were anything but established, depending on the particular issue and, more importantly, particular political rivalries at stake. Just as the common threads for Marcellus' claims were service to the Republic and respect for the traditions, mostly, the common thread for opposition to Marcellus was the claim that he had or would violate the established order of things. The pattern is clear: the argument was raised that Marcellus had not satisfied the requirements for a triumph, when there were no such formal requirements; some aristocrats claimed his election as the second plebeian consul offended the gods, though the electoral assembly seems to have had little qualm about casting their votes for him; some complained he had violated the rules for the treatment of enemies in wartime, when such rules were highly fluid; the priests declared that dedicating a temple to two gods would disrupt the normal ability of the Romans to detect the will of their divine benefactors, but only did so more than a decade after the initial vow of the temple.

It will not do, however, to conclude that these arguments were purely superficial, able to be bluntly reduced to: 'I don't like Marcellus/I don't want Marcellus to get more glory, therefore I oppose motions that would do so.' These debates were not simply squabbles over the distribution of honours. The Romans did not seize upon the importance of tradition and custom because they made useful tools for political competition. Rather, it was because Roman culture so valued tradition and custom that these were important measuring sticks for framing debates in the political arena, particularly when it came to the claims of an individual. When senators disapproved of Marcellus, it appears they tended to argue that he had been untraditional, immoderate, un-virtuous, and unlawful. When Marcellus defended himself, he argued in the same framework.

It is worth repeating that a substantial factor in this line of behaviour was the lack of extensive written record keeping in the society – something true of essentially all ancient societies. Whereas the United States, for example, has and refers back to its centuries-old written constitution as a guide to the legality of contemporary actions, the Romans had no such document. To make matters more problematic, many if not most of the written documents that existed in the Republic were not collected together in any sort of easily accessible fashion. Instead, they were scattered among the families of the censors, consuls, and other magistrates who created them with little thought for a system of archiving and retrieval. Cicero's speeches and letters provide excellent testimony to the difficulty of obtaining records for even basic facts, such as the names of those who were on a committee a century before or the exact text of decrees of the senate.[3] In short, Roman society generally had to go on memory when it came to decisions about what was and was not tradition, custom, and law. Thus they fought often and passionately, so many debates affecting the distribution of prestige and honour, and so many hinging upon the relevant standards of propriety, law, and custom.

Ultimately, Marcellus was incredibly successful at crafting a military and political reputation that would span the centuries. He did not, however, pose a threat to the continued existence of the Republic. This would seem to be an unnecessary statement, except that less than a century later individual aristocrats could and did begin to challenge the limits of the Roman political system in ways that would eventually lead to catastrophic infighting in the political class, civil wars, and the disintegration of the Republic. Many things, however, had changed for the Romans in the century after Marcellus' death. They went on to rule the Mediterranean, and as the demands of empire and the rewards increased, opportunities arose for individuals to push the limits on competition past their breaking point. Where Marcellus could receive an extended command in Italy by the will of the people, Pompey some 140 years later received a command against the pirates of the eastern Mediterranean that allowed him to engage in campaigns of conquest in the ancient Near East that were unthinkable to Romans of Marcellus' day. Marcellus was, so far as is known, the first to receive such honours as games and festivals in his honour from a major Greek city; such honours would multiply for generals in the centuries after his death. In short, the Roman world was very different in 50 BC from what it was at the end of the third century. Marcellus was perhaps the most successful aristocrat of his day, but ultimately, his ambitions were well harnessed within the still strong rules of competition.

*   *   *

When Livy began his monumental history he expressed what was a common idea among ancient historians, that the study of history was the study of moral examples:

> In history you have a record of the infinite variety of human experience plainly set out for all to see. In that record you can find for yourself and your country both examples and warnings; fine things to take as models, base things, rotten through and through, to avoid.[4]

By the standards of the Romans themselves, then, Marcellus, the sword of the Republic, had earned a place among the very greatest who had ever led the Republic. His victories were carved in stone on the lists of triumphs; his deeds enshrined in the works of the poets and playwrights; his family itself rose from a modestly successful political family to one of the great noble families of the Republic. The legend of Marcellus would go on far beyond most other Romans. In death, he became the exemplar of the *virtus* that he claimed to display so often in life.

Appendix

Marcellus' Record by Comparison

Since the text so often refers to Marcellus' great success as a politician and commander and the distinction of his record, it is appropriate to set out clearly how his record compared to those of his peers. When it came to the total numbers of honours and offices, Marcellus's record was unrivalled quantitatively. By the year of his death he had the following honours:

- five elections to the consulship (though he was forced to step down in 215, the Roman records marked this as an official consulship);
- two praetorships (that are known);
- four years as proconsul;
- membership in the college of augurs for almost two decades;
- a triumph at Rome, a triumph on the Alban Mount, and an ovation;
- the *spolia opima*;
- the personal patronage over Syracuse.

A number of these honours had never been granted to any Roman in living memory, notably election as the second plebeian to the consulship, the *spolia opima*, and the divine honours bestowed by the Syracusans. Marcellus held *imperium* as praetor in 216, the year of Cannae. From that year on, he held *imperium* as either a consul or proconsul until he died, a total of nine consecutive years. Of the sixteen consulships available from 215 to 208, Marcellus was elected to four.

Consider, in comparison, the records of the other great aristocrats of the time. Fabius Maximus was consul in 233, 228, 215, 214, and 209, censor in 230, and dictator in 217. He earned a triumph over the Ligurians in 233 and a triumph over Tarentum in 209. He had been an augur since 265 and a *pontifex* since 216. He also received the prized honour of *princeps senatus* in 209 and 204.[1] His was certainly an extraordinarily successful career. As far as military commands went, however, he had only held *imperium* for four of the ten years from 218 to 208, when Marcellus died.

Quintus Fulvius Flaccus' career seems to match that of Marcellus better. Flaccus held the consulship in 237, 224, 212, and 209, a censorship in 231, and praetorships in 215 and 214. He was dictator in 210, *magister equitum* in 213, and proconsul in 210 and 208.[2] So he held *imperium* from 215 to 208, a record very close to that of Marcellus. A close look at his commands stops the comparison. He was the urban praetor in 215 and 213, tasked with judging law cases at Rome, and his primary service as *magister equitum* was to hold consular elections.[3] His string of field commands did not compare to those of Marcellus, and Flaccus never triumphed.

The elder Publius Cornelius Scipio did have a run of consecutive commands comparable to those of Marcellus. After serving as consul in 218, Scipio had his command in Spain renewed regularly from 217 until his death in 211.[4] Yet he only won election to the consulship once, and while his task in Spain was critical to the Roman war effort, it effectively removed him from Italian affairs and elections. Scipio simply could not compete with the number of elected offices and victory celebrations Marcellus had.

Other figures were clearly not as successful. Gaius Terentius Varro, the consul in command at Cannae, wielded *imperium* for a number of years after that battle. He served as proconsul in Picenum from 215 to 213 and as propraetor in Etruria for 208 and 207. Clearly, Varro was able to obtain commands, but not of the number and type that Marcellus did.[5] T Manlius Torquatus, was far more distinguished than Varro and held consulates in 235 and 224, was elected censor in 231, served as propraetor in Sardinia for 215, and was dictator in 208.[6] He had even won a triumph over the Sardinians in 235.[13] From the beginning of the war with Hannibal to the death of Marcellus, however, he held *imperium* once.

Only Scipio Africanus held more successive commands than Marcellus. From 210 to 201, Scipio was a pronconsul.[7] Even the great Africanus would only hold the consulship twice, however, and he had not even held his first by the time Marcellus died. He was simply too young to be a rival to Marcellus during the latter's life.

Notes and References

Introduction

1. Plut. *Marc.* 9.
2. Plut. *Marc.* 1 (Scott-Kilvert trans.).
3. On Fabius Pictor: Michael von Albrecht (revised by Gareth Schmeling), *A History of Roman Literature from Livius Andronicus to Boethius: with Special Regard to its Influence on World Literature*, Volume 1 (Leiden, 1997); *Mnemosyne; Supplementum*, Vol. 165.1, pp. 371–372.
4. On Cato: Albrecht, *A History of Roman Literature*, pp. 390–396.
5. The seminal study of Polybius is FW Walbank, *A Historical Commentary on Polybius*, 3 Vols. (Oxford, 1979); See also the more general FW Walbank, *Polybius* (Berkeley, 1990).
6. Cic. *de Div.* 2.3.
7. The critical English studies of Livy include PG Walsh, *Livy: His Historical Aims and Methods* (Cambridge, 1961); TJ Luce, *Livy: the Composition of His History* (Princeton, 1978); More recently, see DS Levene, *Livy on the Hannibalic War* (Oxford, 2010). See also Robert Ogilvie's preface to Aubrey De Selincourt (trans.), *The Early History of Livy* (London, 2002).
8. Liv. *Preface* 9–11. (De Selincourt trans.).
9. Liv. *Preface* 11–12. (De Selincourt trans.).
10. On Roman historians between Cato and Livy: Albrecht, *A History of Roman Literature*, pp. 374–386.
11. Cic. *Brut.* 62. Translated by Michael Crawford in *Roman Republic* (Cambridge, Ma., 1993), p. 9.
12. Liv. 8.40. *cf.* 7.9.3–6. (Radice trans.).
13. PG Walsh, 'The Negligent Historian: 'Howlers' in Livy', in *Greece & Rome, Second Series*, 5 (1958), pp. 83–88. The translation of Polybius is his; the translation of Livy is mine.
14. EM Carr, 'The Tragic History of Marcellus and Livy's Characterization', in *The Classical Journal*, 80 (1985), pp. 131–141, gives an excellent comparison of aspects of Livy and Plutarch's accounts of Marcellus; the differences he attributes in part to Livy's greater use of Coelius Antipater as a source.

Chapter 1

1. Plut. *Marc.* 2.1–2. (Perrin trans.).
2. SP Oakley, 'Single Combat in the Roman Republic', in *Classical Quarterly*, 35 (1985), pp. 409–410.
3. Helpful surveys of aristocratic politics include N Rosenstein, 'Aristocratic Values', in N Rosenstein and R Morstein-Marx (eds.), *A Companion to the Roman Republic* (West Sussex, 2006), pp. 365–382; See also TC Brennan, 'Power and Progress under the Republican Constitution', in H Flower (ed.), *Cambridge Companion to the Roman Republic* (Cambridge, 2004), pp. 31–65.
4. A Lintott, *The Constitution of the Roman Republic* (Oxford, 1999), pp. 129–131.
5. TC Brennan, *The Praetorship of the Roman Republic*, Vol. 2 (Oxford, 2000), pp. 85–95,

discusses the introduction of the second, third and fourth praetors. See also Lintott, *Constitution of the Roman Republic.*

6. The classic study of assemblies comes from LR Taylor, *Party Politics in the Age of Caesar* (Berkeley, 1961), pp. 50–75. See more recently, Lintott, *Constitution of the Roman Republic*, pp. 40–63.

7. Fergus Millar has done much to remind historians that the Republic was more than an oligarchy. See 'The Political Character of the Classical Roman Republic, 200–151 BC', in *Journal of Roman Studies*, 74 (1984), pp. 1–19; 'Politics, Persuasion and the People before the Social War (150–90 BC)', in *Journal of Roman Studies*, 76 (1986), pp. 1–11; and, most recently, his chapter on approaches to the subject in his *The Crowd in Rome in the Late Republic* (Ann Arbor, 2002), pp. 1–12.

8. FX Ryan, *Rank and Participation in the Republican Senate* (Stuttgart, 1998), pp. 96–136, provides an outstanding analysis of the scholarship and evidence on these thorny issues.

9. See AE Astin, 'The Lex Annalis before Sulla', in *Latomus*, 16 (1957), pp. 588–613, and 17 (1958), pp. 49–64; RJ Evans and M Kleijwegt, 'Did the Romans like Young Men? A Study of the Lex Villia Annalis: Causes and Effects', in *Zeitschrift für Papyrologie und Epigraphik*, 92 (1992), pp. 181–195.

10. Plut. *Marc.* 2.3; on the age range covered by the description, see KJ Dover, *Greek Homosexuality* (Cambridge, Ma., 1978), p. 16, p. 86.

11. R Develin, *Patterns in Office-holding* (Brussels, 1979), pp. 71–80. The ages of magistrates in office is a complex subject and very little hard data is available. Develin's minimum ages for 11 of the 20 plebeian consuls from 199 to 180 are relatively secure, however, and there is no compelling reason in this instance to doubt his figures. The average age given is my own, calculated from Develin's table on page 79. Develin notes, however, that he would augment the ages of the plebeian consuls in a number of cases.

12. M Claudius Marcellus' offices: military tribune (208), tribune of the plebs (204), curule aedile (200), praetor (198), consul (196), censor (189). TS Broughton, *Magistrates of the Roman Republic*, Vol. 2 (New York, 1951), p. 546.

13. Develin, *Patterns in Office-holding*, pp. 63–71, for the period from 286–201.

14. Develin, *Patterns in Office-holding*, pp. 63–71. Averaging Develin's estimates for the ages of plebeian consuls provides an age of 36. Develin's estimates are often minimums, however, and he urges that several years be added in a majority of instances, giving the top end of 39.

15. Plutarch *Marc.* 3 notes the Romans feared the Gauls more than any others.

16. RF Vishnia, 'Cicero 'De Senectute' 11, and the Date of C Flaminius' Tribunate', in *Phoenix*, 50 (1996), pp. 138–145.

17. Polyb. 2.21.7–9.

18. Polyb. 2.22.1; Plut. *Marc.* 3.1.

19. Polyb. 2.23.4.

20. Polyb. 2.25.1.

21. Polyb. 2.23.

22. Polyb. 2.25.1–11.

23. Polyb. 2.26.1–8.

24. Polyb. 2.27.1–3.

25. Polyb. 2.27.4.

26. The scholarship on the Roman army in the Republic is extensive. For some of the more detailed recent studies, see J Rich and G Shipley, *War and Society in the Roman World* (London, 1993); A Goldsworthy, *The Roman Army at War, 100 BC–AD 200* (Oxford, 1996); Adrian Goldsworthy, *The Roman Army at War* (Oxford, 2000); J McCall, *The Cavalry of the Roman Republic* (London, 2001); A Goldsworthy, *The Complete Roman Army* (New York, 2003). Helpful recent articles include P Sabin, 'The Face of Roman Battle', in *Journal of Roman Studies*, 90 (2000), pp. 1–17; A Zhmodikov, 'Roman Republican Heavy Infantrymen in Battle (IV – II Centuries BC)' in *Historia: Zeitschrift für Alte Geschichte*, 49 (2000), pp. 67–78.

27. Polyb. 6.19–26 is the main source for this book's account of the Roman army.
28. Polyb. 6.26.1–7.
29. Polyb. 6.25; see also McCall, *Cavalry of the Roman Republic*, pp. 36–52.
30. See for example, Polybius' descriptions of deployments at Trebia (3.72.10–73.1) and Cannae (3.113).
31. CJJJ Ardant du Picq (Colonel JN Greely and Major RC Cotton trans.), *Battle Studies*, 1921; Electronic version available at Project Gutenberg http://www.gutenberg.org/cache/epub/7294/pg7294.html.
32. Polyb. 2.27.1–28.1.
33. Polyb. 2.30.6–9 (Paton trans.).
34. Polyb. 2.30.1–9.
35. Polyb. 2.31.1–6.
36. Polyb. 2.31.8–11.
37. Polyb. 2.32.1–33.9; Liv. *Per.* 20.8.
38. Polyb. 2.34.1.
39. Plut. *Marc.* 6.1.
40. WV Harris, *War and Imperialism in Republican Rome* (Oxford, 1979), pp. 10–40, offers a seminal survey of the aristocracy's attitudes to war. JA North's review article, 'The Development of Roman Imperialism', in *Journal of Roman Studies* 71 (1981), pp. 1–9, provides an excellent reflection on Harris and on the motivations for aristocrats to go to war.
41. Polyb 2.34.3–4; Plut. *Marc.* 6.2.
42. Polyb. 2.34.5; Plut. *Marc.* 6.3 – though Plutarch has it that the Gauls and Marcellus just happened to meet at Clastidium.
43. Polyb. 2.34.6.
44. Plut. *Marc.* 6.3.
45. Liv. 27.25.7–10.
46. M McDonnell, *Roman Manliness* (Cambridge, 2006), p. 188, pp. 216–224, provides a detailed consideration of the issues involving Fabius, Marcellus, and the temple to Honos, including raising the question of Fabius' potential rivalry with Marcellus. The discussion over the next few pages is indebted to him.
47. McDonnell, *Roman Manliness*, pp. 188.
48. Plut. *Marc.* 6.6–7.4.
49. Liv. *Per.* 20.11; Verg. *Aen.* 6.855–859; Plut. *Marc.* 7.1–3; Val. *Max* 3.2.5. Prop 4.10.
50. Polyb. 2.34.8–9; Plut. *Marc.* 7.4.
51. Plut. *Marc.* 6. (Scott-Kilvert trans.).
52. Again, Polybius refers to such at the Telamon: 2.27.6.
53. Polyb. 2.27.7; 2.30.3.
54. Polyb. 2.30.8.
55. Polyb. 2.28.9–11, 2.30.9.
56. Polyb. 2.34.8. (Moore trans.).
57. Polyb. 2.34.8 (Moore trans.); See also McCall, *The Cavalry of the Roman Republic*, p. 57.
58. Polyb. 2.34.10–14.
59. For a recent analysis of the triumph, see Mary Beard, *The Roman Triumph* (Cambridge, Ma., 2009).
60. This discussion of the *spolia opima* is based on Harriet I Flowers, 'The Tradition of the Spolia Opima: M Claudius Marcellus and Augustus', in *Classical Antiquity*, 19 (2000), pp. 34–64.
61. Harriet I Flowers, 'Fabulae Praetextae in Context: When Were Plays on Contemporary Subjects Performed in Republican Rome?', in *The Classical Quarterly, New Series*, 45 (1995), p. 183.
62. Virg. *Aen.* 6.855–859.
63. Plut. *Marc.* 8.1 (Paton trans.).
64. Plut. Marc. 8.1–3. (Paton trans.).
65. Flower, 'The Tradition of the Spolia Opima', in *Classical Antiquity*, 19 (2000), pp. 34–64.

66. For a review of this model of Roman politics, see KJ Hölkeskamp, 'Fact(ions) or Fiction? Friedrich Münzer and the Aristocracy of the Roman Republic: Then and Now', in *International Journal of the Classical Tradition*, 8 (2001), pp. 92–105.

Chapter 2
 1. A Goldsworthy, *The Punic Wars* (London, 2001), pp. 27–28.
 2. Goldsworthy, *Punic Wars*, pp. 65–128, especially pp. 66–69, pp. 74–5, pp. 84–95.
 3. Goldsworthy, *Punic Wars*, pp. 128.
 4. Goldsworthy, *Punic Wars*, pp. 129–130.
 5. Liv. 21.1.4.
 6. J Briscoe, 'The Second Punic War', in *The Cambridge Ancient History* (Cambridge, 1989), pp. 45–46.
 7. Briscoe, 'The Second Punic War', pp. 44–46.
 8. Briscoe, 'The Second Punic War', p. 47; JF Lazenby, *Hannibal's War: A Military History of the Second Punic War*, (Warminster, 1998), pp. 35–37, p. 50 ; Goldsworthy, *Punic Wars*, pp. 158–163.
 9. Lazenby, *Hannibal's War*, pp. 29–30, but see Briscoe, 'The Second Punic War', p. 46 for the argument that Hannibal probably did not have a good understanding of Italian geography and thus the Roman alliance system.
10. K Lomas, 'Italy During the Roman Republic', in HI Flower (ed.), *The Cambridge Companion to the Roman Republic* (Cambridge, 2004), pp. 204–206.
11. Dion. Hal. 6.95 as translated by CJ Smith, *Early Rome and Latium: Economy and Society C. 1000 to 500 BC* (Oxford, 1996), p. 212.
12. Lomas, 'Italy During the Roman Republic', p. 206.
13. Lazenby, *Hannibal's War*, p. 48, pp. 52–53; Goldsworthy, *Punic Wars*, pp. 169–173.
14. McCall, *Cavalry of the Roman Republic*, pp. 73–75.
15. McCall, *Cavalry of the Roman Republic*, pp. 34–37.
16. Goldsworthy, *Punic Wars*, pp. 173–174.
17. Goldsworthy, *Punic Wars*, pp. 174–175.
18. McCall, *Cavalry of the Roman Republic*, pp. 35–36.
19. Goldsworthy, *Punic Wars*, pp. 175–181.
20. Goldsworthy, *Punic Wars*, pp. 181–196.
21. Liv. 22.35.
22. McCall, *Cavalry of the Roman Republic*, pp. 36–37.
23. Polyb. 3.113.2.
24. McCall, *Cavalry of the Roman Republic*, pp. 37–38.
25. McCall, *Cavalry of the Roman Republic*, pp. 37–38.
26. Goldsworthy, *Punic Wars*, pp. 213–214.
27. Liv. 22.49. (Roberts trans.).
28. Liv. 22.54, 22.56.
29. Liv. 22.57; Plut. *Marc.* 9.
30. Liv. 23.7.
31. Liv. 23.14.5.
32. Liv. 23.14.7.
33. On the position of Casilinum see Lazenby, *Hannibal's War*, p. 93.
34. Liv. 23.14.5.
35. Liv. 23.14.
36. Liv. 23.15.
37. Liv. 23.15.7–16.1; Plut. *Marc.* 10–11.1.
38. Liv. 23.15.7–16.8–9; Plut. *Marc.* 10.2–3.
39. Liv. 23.15.15; Plut. *Marc.* 10.5.
40. Liv. 23.16.2.

41. Liv. 23.16.6.
42. Plutarch makes a similar inference, that Marcellus brought psychological support to the Neapolitians. Plut. *Marc.* 10.1.
43. Liv. 23.16.8.
44. Liv. 23.16.8–9; Plut. *Marc.* 11.1–4.
45. Liv. 23.16.8–9.
46. Liv. 23.16.11–12; Plut. *Marc.* 11.2.
47. Liv. 23.16.11–12; Plut. *Marc.* 11.2.
48. Liv. 23.16.16.
49. Liv. 23.16.16; Plut. *Marc.* 11.4.
50. Cic. *Brut.* 12.
51. Liv. 23.16.16; Cic. *Brut.* 12; Val. *Max.* 4.1.7; Plut. *Marc.* 11.4.
52. Liv. 22.17.1.
53. Liv. 23.17.5–8.
54. Liv. 23.17.2–3.
55. Liv. 23.31.3–4.
56. Liv. 23.17.8–9.
57. Liv. 23.17.8, 11.
58. Liv. 23.18.1–5.
59. Liv. 23.17.5–9.
60. Liv. 23.15.2–4.
61. Liv. 23.24.3.
62. Liv. 23.19.3.
63. Liv. 23.22.1–3.
64. Liv. 23.22.1–23.9.
65. Liv. 23.23.5–7.
66. Liv. 23.24.1–3.
67. Liv. 23.24.3–5.
68. On these points, see N Rosenstein, *Imperatores Victi* (Berkeley, 1990).
69. Liv. 23.24.6–14.
70. Liv. 23. 25.6–10.
71. Again, Ryan, *Rank and Participation in the Republican Senate*, esp. pp. 96–136, tackles these difficult problems very well.
72. Liv. 23.25.2.
73. W Jashemski, *Origins and History of the Proconsular and the Propraeotian Imperium to 27 BC* (Chicago, 1950), p. 14.
74. Liv. 23.30.19.
75. Liv. 23.31.1–6.
76. Liv. 23.31.7–8.
77. Liv. 23.8–9.
78. Liv. 23.31.7–10 (Moore trans.).
79. R Billows, 'Legal Fiction and Political Reform at Rome in Early Second Century BC', in *Phoenix*, 43 (1989), pp. 112–133.
80. Liv. 23.31.13–14.
81. Liv. 23.31.13–14.
82. An excellent discussion of these issues of early Roman history can be found in T Cornell, *The Beginnings of Rome* (London, 1995), pp. 242–340.
83. On the coalescing of an aristocracy, see KJ Holkeskamp, 'Conquest, Competition, and Consensus: Roman Expansion in Italy and the Rise of the Nobilitas', in *Historia*, 42 (1993), pp. 12–39.
84. Cic. *De Div.* 2.73 (Falconer trans.).
85. See Rosentein, *Imperatores Victi*, pp. 80–81.

86. Liv. 23.31.14.
87. Liv. 30.26.7–10.
88. J Linderski, 'The Augural Law,' in *Aufstieg und Niedergang der Römischen Welt*, 2.16.3 (1986), 2168–2172.
89. Liv. 23.32.2–3.
90. Liv. 23.33.41.13–14.
91. Liv. 23.41.13–42.13.
92. Liv. 23.48.2.
93. Liv. 24.7.10–9.3.
94. Liv. 24.9.9.
95. Liv. 24.8–10.
96. Liv. 24.19.4–8.
97. Liv. 24.19.8–9 (Moore trans.).
98. Liv. 24.18.8–11.

Chapter 3
1. Liv. 24.4.1; Livy's chronology for the revolt of Syracuse and Marcellus' campaign is notorious for its confusion. In this work, I have followed the chronology worked out by A Eckstein, *Senate and General* (Berkeley, 1987), pp. 345–349.
2. Polyb. 7.3–4; Liv. 24.6.1–8.
3. Polyb. 7.5.
4. Polyb. 7.7.3
5. Eckstein, *Senate and General*, p. 348.
6. Liv. 24.21.1–23.4.
7. Liv. 24.24.1–3.
8. Liv. 24.24.1–4.
9. Liv. 24.27.1–5.
10. Eckstein, *Senate and General*, p. 348.
11. Liv. 24.20.3, 7.
12. Liv. 24.21.1–2
13. Liv. 24.27.6–7.
14. Liv. 24.27.7–28.9.
15. Liv. 24.29.1–6.
16. Liv. 24.29.12.
17. Liv. 24.30.
18. Liv. 24.32.
19. Liv. 24.33.2–8; On the chronology, Eckstein, *Senate and General*, pp. 345–349.
20. Polyb. 8.3.4 (Paton trans.).
21. Liv. 25.24.10–11; J Peddie, *Hannibal's War* (Thrupp, Gloucestershire, 1997), p. 157.
22. Polyb. 8.3.5.
23. Polyb. 8.3.3. Liv. 24.33.41–6.
24. Polyb. 8.3.1.
25. Liv. 23.25.8, 24.18.9–10, 25.5.10, 26.1.7–9, 26.1.14, 26.2.14; Front. *Strat.* 4.44; Plut. *Marc.* 13.
26. Liv. 25.6.10.
27. Liv. 25.6.22 (Moore trans.).
28. Liv. 25.7.3–4.
29. See Eckstein, *Senate and General*, pp. 345–9, and FW Walbank, *A Historical Commentary on Polybius* (Oxford, 1967), p. 2, p. 3, p. 69.
30. Plut. *Marc.* 13 (Perrin trans.).
31. PA Brunt, *Italian Manpower* (London, 1971), pp. 648–654, worked this out years ago; I have sifted through the available evidence several times over the past 15 years and failed to find a better solution.

32. Brunt, *Italian Manpower*, pp. 648–654.
33. Brunt, *Italian Manpower*, p. 654.
34. Liv. 23.25.8, 24.18.9–10, 25.5.10, 26.1.7–9, 26.1.14, 26.2.14; Front. *Strat.* 4.44; Plut, *Marc.* 13.
35. Liv. 25.6.2–23 (Roberts trans.).
36. Polyb. 8.3.5–4.2.
37. Polyb. 8.4.1–11.
38. Polyb. 8.4.1.
39. Polyb. 8.3.5.
40. Polyb. 8.5.6
41. Polyb. 8.5.8–11; See also Diod. 26.8 and Zonaras 9.4 for the addition of defences consisting of lenses that focused the sun into a heat ray to burn ships – presumably a legend.
42. Polyb. 8.6.5.
43. Polyb. 8.7.6–12; Liv. 24.34.13–16.
44. Polyb. 8.7.12; Liv. 24.35.1–3.
45. Liv. 24.35.3–4.
46. Liv. 24.35.9–10.
47. Liv. 24.35.9–36.1.
48. Liv. 24.36.2–3, 8–10.
49. Liv. 24.36.3–7; Lazenby, *Hannibal's War*, pp. 107–108.
50. Liv. 24.36.9–10.
51. Liv. 24.37.1–39.9.
52. Liv. 24.39.12–13; Old camp: Liv. 24.33.3.
53. Liv. 24.43.5; 24.44.4–5.
54. Liv. 25.23.1–7.
55. Liv. 25.23.8–14.
56. Front. *Strat.* 3.3.2.
57. Liv. 25.23.13–24.4; Polyb. 8.37.2–12.
58. Liv. 25.24.11–12.
59. Liv. 25.25.2–3
60. Liv. 25.25.10.
61. Though we should avoid assuming that generals had complete control over the behaviour of their soldiers in such heated and chaotic situations as the capture of a city. See A Ziolkowlski, 'Urbs direpta or how the Romans sacked cities', in G Rich and J Shipley (eds.), *War and Society in the Roman World* (London, 1993), pp. 69–91.
62. Liv. 25.25.7–11.
63. Liv. 25.25.3–6.
64. Liv. 25.26.7–15.
65. Liv. 25.27.1–13.
66. Liv. 25.28.1–29.
67. Liv. 25.29.8–10.
68. Liv. 25.30.1–5.
69. Liv. 25.30.5–12.
70. Liv. 25.30.12.
71. Liv. 25.31.1– 7.
72. Liv. 25.31.8–9; Plut. *Marc.* 21.
73. Liv. 25.31.9.
74. Liv. 25.31.9–10; Plut. *Marc.* 19.4–5.
75. Cic. *2 Verr.* 1.55; 4.121; Liv. 25.31.11.
76. Cic. *De Rep.* 1.21.
77. Liv. 25.40.1–5.
78. Liv. 25.40.5–6.
79. Liv. 25.40.11–12.

80. Liv. 25.40.8–12.
81. Liv. 25.40.12–13
82. Liv. 25.41.6.
83. Liv. 25.41.4–5.
84. Liv. 25.41.5–7.
85. Liv. 25.41.7.

Chapter 4
1. Liv. 26.21.2.
2. Although as M Beard, *The Roman Triumph* (Cambridge, Ma., 2007), pp. 202–205 shows it is not at all clear what exactly the rules were for *imperium* lapsing, which should be of little surprise to readers at this point.
3. Liv. 26.21.1.
4. Liv. 45.35–39.
5. Liv. 26.21.1–2.
6. Liv. 26.21.3–4.
7. 24.44.4–5 (Moore trans.).
8. Liv. 25.3.6 (Moore trans.).
9. Liv. 26.1.6–7 (Moore trans.).
10. Polyb. 8.7.6.
11. Liv. 25.26.7.
12. Liv. 25.41.7.
13. Liv. 26.21.10–17.
14. Liv. 26.21.4.
15. Liv. 26.21.4.
16. For 295 to 293 see A Degrassi, *Inscriptiones Italiae* (Rome, 1937), 13.73; for the triumphs in 291 and 290 see Broughton, *Magistrates of the Roman Republic*, 1.182–3.
17. Liv. 10.31.
18. For 294 the Consuls were M Atilius Regulus and L Postumius Megellus. See Degrassi, *Inscriptiones Italiae*, 13.73.
19. Broughton, *Magistrates of the Roman Republic*, 1.203, 206, 207, 212, 213.
20. Degrassi, *Inscriptiones Italiae*, 13.75.
21. Polyb. 1.17.1–13; Polyb. 1.62.1–2.
22. Polyb. 2.31.
23. Degrassi, *Inscriptiones Italiae*, 13.79.
24. Polyb. 2.34.1–3.
25. Degrassi, *Inscriptiones Italiae*, 13.79.
26. Plut. *Marc*. 22.1
27. Liv. 26.21.5–6; Plut. *Marc*. 22.1.
28. Plut. *Marc*. 22.1–2.
29. Concerning all these points, see JS Richardson, 'The Triumph, The Praetors and the Senate', in *Journal of Roman Studies*, 65 (1975), pp. 55–56.
30. Liv. 26.21.6; Plut. *Marc*. 22.1; *De Vir. Ill*. 45.7.
31. Richardson, 'The Triumph, The Praetors and the Senate', pp. 55–8.
32. Richardson, 'The Triumph, The Praetors and the Senate', p. 55.
33. Richardson, 'The Triumph, The Praetors and the Senate', p. 55.
34. Liv. 26.21.6–9. (Roberts trans.).
35. Plut. *Marc*. 28; See McDonnell, *Roman Manliness*, pp. 219–220.
36. Polyb. 9.10–12.
37. Liv. 25.40.2–4.
38. Plut. *Marc*. 21 (Perrin trans.).
39. Liv. 26.22.1–10.
40. Liv. 26.22.15 (Moore trans.).

41. Liv. 26.26.6–9 (Moore trans.).
42. DF Epstein, *Personal Enmity in Roman Politics 218–43 BC* (London, 1987), p. 21.
43. Liv. 26.29.5.
44. Liv. 26.29.6–8.
45. Liv. 26.30.1–11; Plut. *Marc.* 23.3–5.
46. Liv. 26.31.9–11. (Moore trans.); Cf. Plut. *Marc.* 23.4–5.
47. Plut. *Marc.* 23.4–5.
48. Liv. 26.32.4–5 (Roberts trans.).
49. Liv. 26.33.1–34.13.
50. Liv. 26.33.1–34.13.
51. Liv. 26.31.1.
52. Liv. 26.33.4.
53. Liv. 25.40.2.
54. Plut. *Marc.* 21.3–5.
55. Liv. 22.60.3–61.1; 23.22.4–8 (Roberts trans.); 26.32.1–2.
56. The Syracusans offered to surrender themselves and become Marcellus' clients in 211 but were prevented from doing so by the Roman deserters and mercenaries who were defending Achradina. This may have been part of the Sicilian argument when accusing Marcellus of refusing to accept their initial surrender, either in the senate house or when travelling among the houses of senators, rousing opposition to Marcellus.
57. Liv. 26.32.5–8; Plut. *Marc.* 23.6–7.
58. Plut. *Marc.* 23.7.
59. JB Rives, 'Marcellus and the Syracusans', *Classical Philology,* 88 (1993), pp. 32–35.

Chapter 5

 1. Liv. 26.35.1–36.12.
 2. Liv. 26.38.1–6.
 3. Liv. 26.38.6.
 4. Liv. 26.37.6–14.
 5. Liv. 27.1.1–3.
 6. Liv. 27.1.4–14.
 7. Liv. 27.1.14–15.
 8. Liv. 27.2.1–6.
 9. For this point about Roman battles in general see P Sabin, 'The Face of Roman Battle', in *Journal of Roman Studies,* 90 (2000), pp. 1–17.
10. Liv. 27.2.10–11.
11. Liv. 27.2.11–12.
12. Liv. 27.4.1–4.
13. Liv. 27.7.11–13; 27.8.13.
14. Liv. 27.9.7–10.11.
15. Liv. 27.11.2–6 (Moore trans.).
16. Liv. 27.11.9–12.
17. Liv. 27.11.12–16.
18. Liv. 27.12.1–8 (Moore trans.).
19. Liv. 27.12.7–9.
20. Liv. 27.12.9–13.
21. Liv. 27.12.15.
22. Plut. *Marc.* 25.4.
23. P Culham, 'Chance, Command, and Chao in Ancient Military Engagements', in *World Futures,* 27 (1989), pp. 191–205 is an outstanding analysis of how entropy worked its way into ancient infantry formations.
24. Liv. 27.12.14–17.

25. Liv. 27.14.4.
26. Plut. *Marc.* 26.3.
27. Liv. 27.14.7–13.
28. Liv. 27.14.13–14.
29. Liv. 27.15.1.
30. Liv. 27.20.10.
31. Liv. 27.21.3.
32. Liv. 27.15.9–16.7.
33. Liv. 27.16.7–8 (Moore trans.).
34. Plut. *Marc.* 21.3–4.
35. Plut. *Fab.* 22.5–6.
36. Plin. *NH* 34.40.
37. Liv. 27.20.9–13.
38. Liv. 27.20.11–13.
39. Liv. 27.20.12–13.
40. McCall, *Cavalry of the Roman Republic*, pp. 91–5.
41. Rosenstein, *Imperatores Victi*, pp. 114–52.
42. Liv. 27.21.4–5.
43. Liv. 27.21.6–8.
44. Liv. 27.22.1.
45. Liv. 27.23.4.
46. Liv. 27.25.9.
47. Liv. 27.25.
48. Liv. 27.25.11.4.
49. Liv. 27.26.4–6.
50. Liv. 27.28.1–13.
51. Liv. 27.29.2.
52. Liv. 27.27.12–14 (Moore trans.).
53. Polyb. 10.32.5–6.
54. Liv. 27.27.3–7.
55. Plut. *Marc.* 29.7–9.
56. Polyb. 10.32.7–12 (Paton trans).
57. Liv. 27.27.11 (Moore trans).
58. Liv. 27.26.13–27.2.
59. Plut. *Marc.* 29.4–5.
60. Plut. *Marc.* 30.1–4 (Perrin trans.).
61. Liv. 27.28.1–2.
62. Polyb. 6.53–54 (Paton trans.).
63. See Appendix A.
64. H Flower, 'The Tradition of the Spolia Opima: M Claudius Marcellus and Augustus', in *Classical Antiquity*, 19 (2000), p. 54.
65. Flower, 'The Tradition of the Spolia Opima', p. 47.

Conclusion
1. Polyb. 6.19.2.
2. Polyb. 6.19.2; McCall, *Cavalry of the Roman Republic*, p. 116.
3. P Culham, 'Archives and Alternatives in Ancient Rome', in *Classical Philology*, 84 (1989), pp. 100–115, provides an illuminating, almost troubling, account of the state of record keeping in the Republic.
4. Liv. *Preface* 10 (De Selincourt trans.).

Appendix A

1. Broughton, *Magistrates of the Roman Republic*, 2.563, 567; Degrassi, *Inscriptiones Italiae*, 13.77.
2. Broughton, *Magistrates of the Roman Republic*, 2.567.
3. Liv. 23.30.18, 24.9.5–6, 25.2.3–5.
4. Broughton, *Magistrates of the Roman Republic*, 2.551.
5. Broughton, *Magistrates of the Roman Republic*, 2.625.
6. Broughton, *Magistrates of the Roman Republic*, 2.587.
7. Degrassi, *Inscriptiones Italiae*, 13.77.

Bibliography

Albrecht, Michael von, *A History of Roman Literature from Livius Andronicus to Boethius: with Special Regard to its Influence on World Literature*, Vol. 1 (Leiden, 1997).

Ardant du Picq, Charles Jean JJ (Colonel JN Greely and Major RC Cotton trans.), *Battle Studies*, 1921; Project Gutenberg: http://www.gutenberg.org/cache/epub/7294/pg7294.html. Accessed 6/28/2011.

Astin, AE, 'The Lex Annalis before Sulla', *Latomus*, 16 (1957), pp. 588–613, and 17 (1958), pp. 49–64.

Beard, Mary, *The Roman Triumph* (Cambridge, Ma., 2009).

Billows, Richard, 'Legal Fiction and Political Reform at Rome in the Early Second Century BC', *Phoenix*, 43 (1989), pp. 112–133.

Brennan, T Corey, 'Power and Progress under the Republican Constitution', in Harriet Flower (ed.), *Cambridge Companion to the Roman Republic* (Cambridge, 2004), pp. 31–65.

Brennan, T Corey, *The Praetorship of the Roman Republic*, Vol 2. (Oxford, 2000).

Briscoe, John, 'The Second Punic War', in AE Astin, FW Walbank, and MW Frederiksen (eds.), *The Cambridge Ancient History*, Vol. 8 (Cambridge, 1989), pp. 44–63.

Broughton, Thomas RS, *Magistrates of the Roman Republic*, Vol. 2 (New York, 1951).

Brunt, Philip, *Italian Manpower* (London, 1971).

Carr, Edwin M, 'The Tragic History of Marcellus and Livy's Characterization', in *The Classical Journal*, 80 (1985), pp. 131–141.

Cornell, Timothy, *The Beginnings of Rome* (London, 1995).

Crawford, Michael, *The Roman Republic* (Cambridge, Ma., 1993).

Culham, Phyllis, 'Chance, Command, and Chao in Ancient Military Engagements', in *World Futures*, 27 (1989), pp. 191–205.

——, 'Archives and Alternatives in Ancient Rome', in *Classical Philology*, 84 (1989), pp. 100–115.

Degrassi, Attilio, *Inscriptiones Italiae*, Vol. 13 (Rome, 1937).

De Selincourt, Aubrey (trans.), *The Early History of Livy* (London, 2002).

Develin, Robert, *Patterns in Office-holding* (Brussels, 1979), pp. 71–80.

Dover, Kenneth J, *Greek Homosexuality* (Cambridge, Ma, 1978).

Eckstein, Arthur, *Senate and General* (Berkeley, 1987).

Epstein, David F, *Personal Enmity in Roman Politics 218–43 BC* (London, 1987).

Evans, Richard J and Marc Kleijwegt, 'Did the Romans like Young Men? A Study of the Lex Villia Annalis: Causes and Effects', in *Zeitschrift für Papyrologie und Epigraphik*, 92 (1992), pp. 181–195.

Flower, Harriet I, 'Fabulae Praetextae in Context: When Were Plays on Contemporary Subjects Performed in Republican Rome?', in *The Classical Quarterly, New Series*, 45 (1995), pp. 170–190.

——, 'The Tradition of the Spolia Opima: M Claudius Marcellus and Augustus', in *Classical Antiquity*, 19 (2000), pp. 34–64.

Goldsworthy, Adrian, *The Roman Army at War, 100 BC–AD 200* (Oxford, 1996).

——, *The Punic Wars* (London, 2001).

——, *The Complete Roman Army* (New York, 2003).

Harris, William V, *War and Imperialism in Republican Rome* (Oxford, 1979).

Hölkeskamp, Karl J, 'Fact(ions) or Fiction? Friedrich Münzer and the Aristocracy of the Roman Republic: Then and Now', in *International Journal of the Classical Tradition*, 8 (2001), pp. 92–105.

Jashemski, Wilhelmina, *Origins and History of the Proconsular and the Propraeotian Imperium to 27 BC* (Chicago, 1950).

Lazenby, John F, *Hannibal's War: A Military History of the Second Punic War*, (Warminster, 1998).

Levene, David, *Livy on the Hannibalic War* (Oxford, 2010).

Linderski, Jerzy, 'The Augural Law,' in *Aufstieg und Niedergang der Römischen Welt*, 2.16.3 (1986), 2146–2312.

Lintott, Andrew, *The Constitution of the Roman Republic* (Oxford, 1999), pp. 129–131.

Lomas, Kathryn 'Italy During the Roman Republic', in Harriet I Flower (ed.), *The Cambridge Companion to the Roman Republic* (Cambridge, 2004), pp. 199–224.

Luce, Torrey, *Livy: the Composition of His History* (Princeton, 1978).

McCall, Jeremiah, *The Cavalry of the Roman Republic* (London, 2001).

McDonnell, Myles, *Roman Manliness* (Cambridge, 2006).

Millar, Fergus, 'The Political Character of the Classical Roman Republic, 200–151 BC', in *Journal of Roman Studies*, 74 (1984), pp. 1–19.

——, 'Politics, Persuasion and the People before the Social War (150–90 BC)', in *Journal of Roman Studies*, 76 (1986), pp. 1–11.

——, *The Crowd in Rome in the Late Republic* (Ann Arbor, 2002).

North, John A, 'The Development of Roman Imperialism', in *Journal of Roman Studies*, 71 (1981), pp. 1–9.

Oakley, Stephen, 'Single Combat in the Roman Republic', in *Classical Quarterly*, 35 (1985), pp. 409–410.

Peddie, John, *Hannibal's War* (Thrupp, Gloucestershire, 1997).

Rich, John and Graham Shipley, *War and Society in the Roman World* (London, 1993).

Richardson, John, 'The Triumph, The Praetors and the Senate', in *Journal of Roman Studies*, 65 (1975), pp. 50–63.

Rives, James, 'Marcellus and the Syracusans', in *Classical Philology*, 88 (1993), pp. 32–35.

Rosenstein, Nathan, *Imperatores Victi* (Berkeley, 1991).

——, 'Aristocratic Values', in Nathan Rosenstein and Robert Morstein-Marx (eds.), *A Companion to the Roman Republic* (West Sussex, 2006), pp. 365–382.

Ryan, Francis, *Rank and Participation in the Republican Senate* (Stuttgart, 1998).

Sabin, Philip, 'The Face of Roman Battle', in *Journal of Roman Studies*, 90 (2000), pp. 1–17.

Smith, Christopher, *Early Rome and Latium: Economy and Society C. 1000 to 500 BC* (Oxford, 1996).

Taylor, Lily, *Party Politics in the Age of Caesar* (Berkeley, 1961).

Vishnia, Rachel F, 'Cicero 'De Senectute' 11, and the Date of C. Flaminius' Tribunate', in *Phoenix*, 50 (1996).

Walbank, Frank, *A Historical Commentary on Polybius*, 3 Vols. (Oxford, 1979).

——, *Polybius* (Berkeley, 1990).

Walsh, Patrick, 'The Negligent Historian: 'Howlers' in Livy', in *Greece & Rome, Second Series*, 5 (1958), pp. 83–88.

——, *Livy: His Historical Aims and Methods* (Cambridge, 1961).

Zhmodikov, Alexander, 'Roman Republican Heavy Infantrymen in Battle (IV–II Centuries BC)', in *Historia: Zeitschrift für Alte Geschichte*, 49 (2000), pp. 67–78.

Ziolkowlski, Adam, 'Urbs direpta or how the Romans sacked cities', in G Rich and J Shipley (eds.) *War and Society in the Roman World* (London, 1993), pp. 69–91.

Index